THE IMMANENT DIVINE

"Whereas the problematics of Western thought have usually set the agenda for comparative philosophy and theology, John Thatamanil employs the South Asian problematic of non-dualism to forge a sophisticated comparison of Sankara and Tillich. . . . The result is a set of startling comparative observations about creation and selfhood. Because of his exploration, we know much more than we did before about both figures and the traditions they represent. His comparison elicits new answers to new questions. Thatamanil's comparative method is an original advance and brilliantly deployed."

—Robert Cummings Neville
Professor of Philosophy, Religion, and Theology, Boston University
Author of *Religion in Late Modernity* and *Behind the Masks of God*

THE IMMANENT DIVINE

God, Creation, and the Human Predicament

John J. Thatamanil

FORTRESS PRESS
Minneapolis

q|ii THE IMMANENT DIVINE
God, Creation, and the Human Predicament

The author and Fortress Press gratefully acknowledge the University of Chicago Press, publishers of Paul Tillich, *Systematic Theology*, vols. 1–3 (1951–1963); and Advaita Ashrama, Calcutta, publishers of *Eight Upanisads with the Commentary of Sankaracarya*, vol. 1, trans. Swami Gambhirananda (1991), *Brahma Sutra Bhasya of Sri Sankaracarya*, trans. Swami Gambhirananda (1993), and *Bhagavad Gita with the Commentary of Sankaracarya*, trans. Swami Gambhirananda (1991).

Cover image: Boater in Fog, India © Royalty-Free/Corbis
Cover design: Diana Running
Book design: Beth Wright, Trio Bookworks

Library of Congress Cataloging-in-Publication Data
Thatamanil, John J.
  The immanent divine : God, creation, and the human predicament / John J. Thatamanil.
     p.   cm.
  Includes bibliographical references and index.
  ISBN-13: 978-0-8006-3793-4 (alk. paper)
  ISBN-10: 0-8006-3793-3
  1. Immanence of God—History of doctrines—20th century. 2. Theological anthropology. 3. Theology, Doctrinal. 4. Sankaracarya. 5. Tillich, Paul, 1886–1965. I. Title.
  BT124.T43 2006
  231—dc22

                                        2006009379

Manufactured in the U.S.A.
10   09   08   07   2   3   4   5   6   7   8   9   10

To Harold Oliver

world philosopher, mentor, friend

Contents

ⸯⸯⸯ

6. Reimagining Immanence:
Toward a Christian Nondualism / 169

Preface

◡◠◡

This book is an exercise in comparative theology, one that engages in conversation with the Hindu tradition of Advaita Vedanta and, in particular, with its eighth-century master teacher, Sankara. Sankara's thought is treated herein not merely as an object of historical curiosity; rather, he is engaged as a vital resource and conversation partner, one who has much to offer to contemporary Christian theology.

But why should Christian theology engage other theological traditions in conversation? Is it not, after all, the confessional work of a particular faith family? As such, it hardly seems obvious to suppose that Christian theologians ought to engage theologians from other religious traditions. Moreover, the practical demands of comparative theology seem daunting, even forbidding. The burden of bringing scripture and tradition to bear on the problems and challenges of our time seems vast enough without committing oneself also to the work of learning the languages, insights, and commitments of other religious traditions.

Without launching into an extended methodological discussion about the relationship between Christian theology in general and comparative theology in particular, let me suggest that comparative theology can be understood as motivated by two ancient biblical imperatives: the injunction prohibiting false witness against our neighbors and the deeper injunction actually to love our neighbors.

In our time, no theological claim can be regarded as the private speech of the Christian community alone. Even when we speak among ourselves, we speak in the hearing of others. When we speak about God, we are heard and overheard by a great cloud of witnesses, a cloud that includes persons of faith who are not part of the Christian community. The content of our speech follows a trajectory and takes on meanings that we cannot control. Every theological claim, every statement that has a thematic content that goes beyond the jubilant shout of praise or yearning whisper of prayer, becomes a part of public conversation. Each affirmation we advance intersects in complex ways with the creeds and convictions of persons from other religious communities.

The publicity of such entangling theological speech brings with it the risk of "bearing false witness." Insofar as our affirmations either implicitly or explicitly challenge or even negate the convictions of others, we run the risk of misunderstanding and mischaracterizing them. These risks are not incurred by theologians alone; even (or perhaps especially) editorial cartoonists know well how deeply public and global all our speech acts are.

Feeling the gravity of our fraught communicative situation should not lead us to silence, nor does it mean that we cannot disagree with our religious neighbors. Indeed, to contextualize and historicize our neighbors, to understand the content of their speech but to fail to engage the truth-value of that speech, risks condescension. Even vigorous disagreement is more respectful than intellectual inquiry that treats other people and their religious ideas always and only as objects of our study but never as subjects who can talk back.

Comparative theology is conversational theology. Such theology goes beyond taking an inventory of other people's convictions for the sake of specifically Western intellectual projects like comparative religion and ethnography. Comparative theology takes the content of other people's ideas seriously, seriously enough to challenge those ideas and seriously enough to be changed by those ideas. Comparative theology, as a work of Christian faith, strives mightily to avoid bearing false witness against our neighbors. We do this by entering into dialogue with them in a common inquiry about ultimate matters.

In the course of such conversation, our initial and somewhat minimal motivation to avoid misrepresenting our religious neighbors is caught up in a deeper movement of the Spirit. In the space between my neighbor and me, something like affection, respect, and admiration begins to grow. If by grace what transpires amounts genuinely to love, we will soon find that we cannot authentically claim to love our neighbors *despite* their deepest convictions. We will find it difficult to bypass the central experiences, practices, and insights that animate and sustain persons of other faiths. Should we embrace the calling to love our neighbors, we will find ourselves vulnerable to what is healing and life-giving in their religious traditions.

Comparative theology emerges out of such vulnerability. It seeks to think through what we have learned from other religious traditions even as we strive to keep faith with our prior convictions. It is risky work, a labor of mind and heart that will require us to rethink our own convictions. Finally, comparative theology is an ethical enterprise. It is a project that is undertaken *with* people of other faith even when that engagement occurs primarily by way of a close and patient reading of their religious texts. Comparative theology undertaken in this spirit might lead theologians into the relatively uncharted waters of multiple religious participation. Comparative theologians run the risk of becoming hyphenated, of becoming Hindu-Christians or Buddhist-Christians.

Given the enormous demands of comparative theology, I have tried to make this book as user-friendly as possible. I have deliberately kept scholarly apparatus at a minimum, and I have largely omitted reference to contemporary movements in philosophy and theology with which I am in conversation. I have also eliminated diacritical marks for Sanskrit terms; specialists will not need them and generalists do not want them. The focus remains resolutely on reading Sankara and Paul Tillich together and exploring the promise of that conversation for the future of theology.

I use the notion of the human predicament as my central comparative category. Over the years, I have had the pleasure of teaching a course entitled, "The Human Predicament: What's Wrong with Us and How to Fix It." (I confess that I stole the subtitle for my course from John Silber's book *Straight Shooting: What's Wrong with America and How to Fix It*. Silber was chancellor of Boston University during my student days there.)

The thesis of that course is that a number of the world's religious traditions can be analyzed by appeal to a medical model. I argue that many of the world's religious traditions offer a diagnosis for the human predicament, provide an etiology for that predicament, propose a prognosis, and then prescribe a course of treatment. I urged my undergraduates to employ this medical model to read sacred texts like the *Bhagavad Gita* and the *Tao Te Ching*. My students and I discovered that we could ask the most precise and intriguing questions about how traditions, texts, and thinkers might be compared. We could ask if two religious texts (within or without a given religious tradition) agreed in their diagnoses of the human predicament but disagreed on the question of etiology. We could then ask whether their differing etiological analyses meant that each would offer a different prognosis for the human predicament and hence different therapies. The range of permutations and the precision allowed by these questions far exceeded somewhat standard queries about whether the world's religions were really paths up the same mountain or whether they were planets orbiting around the same sun and the like. There was also an added pedagogical bonus: My students intuitively understood and grasped the significance of these questions and enjoyed the process. Best of all, I did not have to labor to demonstrate that the comparative work we were doing was important.

This book employs the medical model for East-West conversation. More specifically, I use the medical model to understand better the similarities and differences between Christian ecstasy and Hindu nonduality. Conventional wisdom among both theologians and interested nontheologians affirms that the Christian West is enamored of transcendence while the Hindu East is entranced by immanence. I argue instead that this stereotype misses the mark. At stake instead are rival conceptions of immanence. In the Christian West, and in particular in the theology of Paul Tillich, immanence takes the form of ecstasy. The presence of God is felt most intimately when we are grasped by the Holy Spirit and when that Spirit prays in us even when we know not how to pray. In ecstasy, we are taken into the divine life and reunited with divinity. In the Hindu East, and more specifically within the Advaita Vedanta tradition, the ultimate truth is that the human being just *is* Brahman. There is no question of being *reunited with* Brahman because human beings are *never separated from* Brahman. In this book, I seek to determine whether we might critically appropriate insights from both of these ways of imagining the immanent divine and then come to understand how these insights bear upon the human predicament. To that conversation, I invite my readers.

Acknowledgments

~~~

Any book as long in gestation as this one owes its existence to many. In retrospect, I see clearly that my labor as author was a necessary condition for its emergence but by no means sufficient. I am grateful to a great many mentors, colleagues, students, and family members who supported my writing so that this book would come to birth. I think of the assembled host as a birth-team, labor coaches, nurses, obstetricians, and others who worked valiantly by my side as I pushed this baby out. I shall not belabor the metaphor overmuch by assigning specific roles to particular persons.

My thanks to my editors at Fortress Press, most especially Michael West and Josh Messner. My thanks also to my copy editor, David Lott, who wisely suggested I add a glossary.

I am enormously indebted to Francis X. Clooney, David Eckel, and Robert Neville. Bob introduced me to the pleasures and demands of comparative theology. David and Frank worked hard to teach me Sanskrit, Hindu theology, and Indian modes of thought more generally. Leroy Rouner was a constant source of inspiration who encouraged me to set out in my quest for an East-West synthesis. Leroy was also my first Tillich teacher. I am in his debt for introducing me to someone who has become and will likely remain a lifelong conversation partner. It is a source of deep sadness that Leroy did not live to see this book emerge in final form. My thanks also to Ray Hart for introducing me to Meister Eckhart and Nicholas of Cusa.

I owe special thanks to Swami Paramarthananda of Chennai for many hours spent reading Sankara's theology in Sanskrit. My nonmystical reading of Sankara can be traced, in considerable measure, to Swamiji's approach, although he would surely take issue with features of my reconstructed dynamic nondualism. Anant Rambachan also offered encouraging feedback on the Sankara chapters.

Several colleagues have read this manuscript in whole or part and offered feedback. Steven G. Smith was my department chair at Millsaps College, my tennis partner, and also a serious but friendly critic. Readers should be particularly grateful to Smith as this book would have been much longer without his interventions. Other crucial conversation partners include Kristen Brown and Darby Ray.

My thanks go to colleagues at Millsaps and now at Vanderbilt Divinity School who gave me jobs so that I might teach and attend to the craft of writing. I owe special thanks to the Wabash Center for Teaching and Learning in Theology and Religion. A grant from the Wabash Center for pretenure religion scholars at church-related colleges and universities provided me not only an invaluable opportunity to think about teaching but also with some much needed uninterrupted writing time.

Travis Ables, my research assistant, has proofread and formatted nearly every line of this book, and saved me from any number of errors large and small. Every author should be graced with so shrewd and careful a reader! I am grateful for students in my Hindu-Christian Dialogue course who read the chapters on Sankara. I am especially grateful to Glenn Willis and Rick Bryant for their careful reading and frank feedback.

There are a number of friends and supporters without whom I would have never completed this book. They include most especially Loye Ashton, Richard Freis, and John Starkey. My thanks also to Gordon Peerman for his close reading of the whole of this book in its penultimate version. Special thanks to St. Augustine's Episcopal Chapel for welcoming my family and me with such warmth and affection when we moved to Nashville. To be a part of this extraordinary Christian community has been a profound blessing.

I thank my family, especially my father and mother, John T. John, Leelamma John, and my sister Rachel Cherian. I owe a special debt of gratitude to my uncle, Dr. T. M. Thomas, who was my first academic role model. My daughter, Kate, has never known a time when her Dad was not working on a book (and likely never will)! The sound of Katie's laughter floating upstairs into my study has sustained me during many a long day of writing. I am in great debt to my wife, Lyn Fulton-John. Without her, this book might never have been started and surely would never have been finished.

I feel most keenly indebted to Harold H. Oliver, who not only introduced me to Alfred North Whitehead, process philosophy, and Eastern Orthodox theology but also to many other thinkers and traditions that have shaped me in ways that I cannot now name. He has been a mentor and steady conversation partner who has read nearly the entirety of this book and saved me from numerous errors. In our ongoing late-night IM conversations, Harry continues to guide me into philosophical wisdom. I dedicate this book to him with deepest gratitude.

Abbreviations

~~~

AUBh   Sankara. Aitareya Upanishad Bhasya. *Eight Upanisads with the Commentary of Sankaracarya.* vol. 2. Trans. Swami Gambhirananda. Calcutta: Advaita Ashrama, 1992.

BG   *The Bhagavad Gita*: *Krishna's Counsel in Time of War.* Trans. Barbara Stoler Miller. New York: Bantam Books, 1986.

BGBh   Sankara. *Bhagavad Gita with the Commentary of Sankaracarya.* Trans. Swami Gambhirananda. Calcutta: Advaita Ashrama, 1991.

Bh   Bhasya (Sanskrit for "commentary"). All save one of Sankara's authentic works are commentaries. The abbreviation "Bh" will in all cases refer to Sankara's commentary on a given text. Thus, for instance, BGBh refers to Sankara's commentary on the *Bhagavad Gita*.

BSBh   Sankara. *Brahma Sutra Bhasya of Sri Sankaracarcya.* Trans. Swami Gambhirananda. Calcutta: Advaita Ashrama, 1993.

BUBh   Sankara. *The Brhadaranyaka Upanishad with the Commentary of Sankaracarya.* Trans. Swami Madhavananda. Calcutta: Advaita Ashrama, 1988.

CTB   Paul Tillich. *The Courage to Be.* New Haven: Yale University Press, 1952.

CUBh   Sankara. *Chandogya Upanishad with the Commentary of Sankara-carya.* Trans. Swami Gambhirananda. Calcutta: Advaita Ashrama, 1983.

DOF   Paul Tillich. *Dynamics of Faith.* New York: Harper & Row, 1957.

IU   Isa Upanishad. *Eight Upanisads with the Commentary of Sanka-racarya.* vol. 1. Trans. Swami Gambhirananda. Calcutta: Advaita Ashrama, 1991.

IUBh   Sankara. Isa Upanishad Bhasya. *Eight Upanisads with the Com-mentary of Sankaracarya.* vol. 1. Trans. Swami Gambhirananda. Calcutta: Advaita Ashrama, 1991.

KaUBh   Sankara. Katha Upanishad Bhasya. *Eight Upanisads with the Com-mentary of Sankaracarya.* vol. 1. Trans. Swami Gambhirananda. Calcutta: Advaita Ashrama, 1991.

KeU   Kena Upanishad. *Eight Upanisads with the Commentary of Sanka-racarya.* vol. 1. Trans. Swami Gambhirananda. Calcutta: Advaita Ashrama, 1991.

KeUBh   Sankara. Kena Upanishad Bhasya. *Eight Upanisads with the Com-mentary of Sankaracarya.* vol. 1. Trans. Swami Gambhirananda. Calcutta: Advaita Ashrama, 1991.

SOF   Paul Tillich. *The Shaking of the Foundations.* New York: Charles Scribner's Sons, 1948.

ST 1   Paul Tillich. *Systematic Theology*, vol. 1. Chicago: University of Chicago Press, 1951.

ST 2   Paul Tillich. *Systematic Theology*, vol. 2. Chicago: University of Chicago Press, 1957.

ST 3   Paul Tillich. *Systematic Theology*, vol. 3. Chicago: University of Chicago Press, 1963.

TOC   Paul Tillich. *Theology of Culture.* New York: Oxford University Press, 1959.

U   *A Thousand Teachings: The Upadesasahasri of Sankara.* Trans. Sengaku Mayeda. Albany: State University of New York Press, 1999.

VSBh 1   *Vedanta-Sutras with the Commentary by Sankaracarya*, pt. 1. Trans. George Thibaut. Delhi: Motilal Banarsidass, 1988.

VSBh 2   *Vedanta-Sutras with the Commentary by Sankaracarya*, pt. 2. Trans. George Thibaut. Delhi: Motilal Banarsidass, 1988.

chapter one

The Immanent Divine and the Human Predicament

～～～

Oh, East is East, and West is West, and never the twain shall meet,
Till Earth and Sky stand presently at God's great Judgment Seat.
—Rudyard Kipling[1]

I, too, have ropes around my neck, I have them to this day, pulling me
this way and that, East and West, the nooses tightening, commanding, *choose, choose*. I buck, I snort, I whinny, I rear, I kick. Ropes, I do
not choose between you. Lassoes, lariats, I choose neither of you, and
both. Do you hear? I refuse to choose.
—Salman Rushdie[2]

How Far Is East from West? A Question for Comparative Theology

Globalization and hybridity—these are among the watchwords of our time.
The first names an omnipolar movement of capital, technology, people, and
ideas that renders obsolete an older story that speaks of a simple unidirec-
tional flow of modernity from West to East. The second term points to the

1. Rudyard Kipling, "The Ballad of East and West," in *Rudyard Kipling's Verse: Definitive Edition* (Garden City, N.Y.: Doubleday, 1946), 233.
2. Salman Rushdie, "The Courter," in *East, West: Stories* (New York: Pantheon, 1994), 211.

1

complex way in which these "global flows" come to be etched onto the bodies and minds of persons who are compelled to fuse together creatively multiple traditions and values. Contrary to Kipling, East and West have met and continue to meet daily. The setting for such meetings now includes not only the marketplace and cross-cultural marriages but also, as Salman Rushdie's fiction has shown, the psyches of multicultural persons. For such persons, choosing between strands of selfhood might simplify life but such choice is neither possible nor desirable. Surgically separating conjoined twins is simpler. The task at hand is the skillful navigation of double belonging so that it might lead to dual citizenship rather than to cultural homelessness.

This fusion of elements from East and West is especially visible in religious life. Laypersons and virtuoso practitioners alike are becoming hyphenated boundary-crossers. Buddhist-Jews, Hindu-Christians, Buddhist-Christians—the permutations are endless, intriguing, and sometimes disturbing.[3] Religious practices and ideas float across religious boundaries and take root in new soil. Christians do Zen, Buddhists engage in social activism, and everyone does Yoga.

What do Christian theologians have to say about these new religious configurations? Can Christian theologians offer critical guidance for such novel forms of religious practice, or are they bound by tradition to adopt a defensive and ineffectual "Just say no" strategy? Change is slower in religion than in culture at large, and only a few, albeit a growing few, speak and write about the mutual transformation of religious traditions or even multiple religious belonging.[4]

Mainstream theologians have long recognized that other religious traditions represent a real challenge for Christian faith. The emergence of theology of religions as a lively and productive area of specialization demonstrates that theologians well appreciate the dramatic cultural shifts now underway.

3. On the disturbing features of contemporary spirituality movements, see Jeremy Carrette and Richard King, *Selling Spirituality: The Silent Takeover of Religion* (New York: Routledge, 2005). Carrette and King persuasively argue that the discourse of spirituality has done much to reduce spiritual practices to commodities subsumed by and made to serve the interests of global capitalism. Put very concisely, "spirituality is big business" (1). In the process, the commitments of religious traditions to justice and to the collective good are often forgotten.

4. The most famous exponent of the idea of "mutual transformation" is John B. Cobb. See his now-classic work, *Beyond Dialogue: Toward a Mutual Transformation of Christianity and Buddhism* (1982; reprint, Eugene, Ore.: Wipf & Stock, 1998). On the idea of multiple religious belonging, see Catherine Cornille, ed., *Many Mansions? Multiple Religious Belonging and Christian Identity* (Maryknoll, N.Y.: Orbis Books, 2002).

Christian theologians have long been thinking about whether persons from other religious traditions can be saved. They have typically turned within to scripture and tradition in search of alternatives to reigning exclusivist habits of mind that relegate most, if not all, non-Christians to perdition.[5]

But very few theologians have engaged in theological reflection that draws on the resources of more than one tradition. Thinking *about* other traditions rather than thinking *with* them—this has been until quite recently Christian theology's standard approach to religious diversity. Also most thinking about other religions has been confined not to a consideration of those traditions in detail but rather to the broad question of what Christians ought to make of the sheer fact of religious diversity. Is religious polyphony God-willed, or is it a fall away from an original religious simplicity, a polyglot Babel bound to pass away?

The emergence of the fledgling discipline of comparative theology marks a new stage in Christian theology's encounter with other religions.[6] Comparative theologians are not content to think generally about the meaning of religious diversity for Christian faith. Instead they wish to engage specific texts, motifs, and claims of particular traditions not only to understand better these traditions but also to determine the truth of theological matters through conversation and collaboration. Francis X. Clooney, S.J., rightly describes comparative theology as constructive theology proper that draws on resources from more

---

5. For an even-handed and masterful summary of the current conversation in theology of religions, see Paul F. Knitter, *Introducing Theologies of Religion* (Maryknoll, N.Y.: Orbis Books, 2002).

6. Among the most important recent works within comparative theology are those of Joseph Bracken, S.J., Francis X. Clooney, S.J., and James L. Fredericks. See Joseph A. Bracken, S.J., *The Divine Matrix: Creativity as Link between East and West* (Maryknoll, N.Y.: Orbis Books, 1995); Francis X. Clooney, S.J., *Divine Mother, Blessed Mother: Hindu Goddesses and the Virgin Mary* (New York: Oxford University Press, 2004); idem, *Hindu God, Christian God: How Reason Helps Break Down the Boundaries between Religions* (New York: Oxford University Press, 2001); idem, "Comparative Theology: A Review of Recent Books (1989–1995)," *Theological Studies* 56, no. 3 (1995): 521–50; idem, *Theology after Vedanta: An Experiment in Comparative Theology* (Albany: State University of New York Press, 1993); James L. Fredericks, *Buddhists and Christians: Through Comparative Theology to Solidarity* (Maryknoll, N.Y.: Orbis Books, 2004); and idem, *Faith among Faiths: Christian Theology and Non-Christian Religions* (Mahwah, N.J.: Paulist Press, 1999). For a recent book that does not claim to be a work in comparative theology but nonetheless demonstrates how Christian theology is enriched when it draws upon resources from another tradition, in this case Tibetan Buddhism, see Wendy Farley, *The Wounding and Healing of Desire: Weaving Heaven and Earth* (Louisville: Westminster John Knox Press, 2005).

than one tradition and is willing to be changed by what it learns from those other traditions.[7]

Why is comparative theology so late born?[8] Surely one reason is the general assumption that vast, fundamental, and irreconcilable differences separate Christianity from other traditions, especially Eastern ones. On this assumption, religious diversity presents a scene of sheer incommensurability and the fusion of elements drawn from several religious traditions everywhere evident in cultural practice is said to be either impossible or confused—syncretism standing in as the technical word for confusion. But how vast are the differences that separate East from West, and just what are those differences? Ironically, the question cannot be answered apart from comparison. The presumption of qualitative and incommensurable difference has delayed comparison, but only comparison can tell us whether such presumption is warranted.

A major reason for supposing that there is an impassable gap separating East from West is the widespread conviction that Eastern traditions are pantheistic whereas Western traditions are dualistic. When such claims are made, theologians usually have in mind Christianity and Hinduism. On standard accounts, Christianity maintains a strong commitment to creation *ex nihilo*, creation out of nothing, whereas Hinduism affirms that the world emerges out of Brahman, the impersonal ultimate reality at the heart of nondualistic Hinduism. *Creatio ex nihilo*, on the contrary, rules out *creatio ex deo*, creation out of God, whereas Hindu sacred scriptures ultimately teach not only that the world emerges out of Brahman, but that the true Self just *is* Brahman. The traditional Christian commitment to positing a radical and relatively impermeable separation between the creator and creature stands in sharp contrast to Hindu commitments to nonduality (*advaita*). The doctrine of creation appears to erect an unbridgeable chasm between God and the world and so

---

7. Clooney's own words are worth citing here. He writes, "*comparative* theology can also be thought of as truly constructive *theology*, distinguished by its sources and ways of proceeding, by its foundation in more than one tradition (although the comparativist remains rooted in one tradition), and by reflection which builds on that foundation, rather than simply on themes or by methods already articulated prior to the comparative practice. Comparative theology . . . is a theology deeply changed by its attention to the details of multiple religious and theological traditions; it is a theology that occurs truly only *after* comparison." Clooney, "Comparative Theology," 522.

8. It is possible to argue that Christian theology has been practiced comparatively from its very inception. Christian theology's conversation with Jewish traditions, Neo-Platonism, Hellenistic philosophical traditions, and later with Aristotleanism and Islam can all be seen as genuine exercises in comparative theology. The turn to comparative theology in our time is perhaps more truly characterized as a rebirth and renewal of ancient practices of engagement.

also between Hinduism and Christianity. Those who live in a postcolonial glo-
balizing world, the world of Rushdie and postcolonial theorist Homi Bhabha,
may speak of multiple religious identities and hybridity, but when it comes to
theology, there can be no blurring of lines, no crossing of boundaries.[9] God's
creative activity keeps asunder what globalization has brought together. The
question of God's immanence to the world appears to function as a decisive
theological stumbling block to any reconciliation between Hinduism and
Christianity, between East and West.

Intimately related to the question of immanence is the matter of theological
anthropology. Christian tradition posits not only a sharp distinction between
God and creatures but also insists upon the fallibility and sinfulness of human
beings. The doctrine of original sin maintains that human beings are radically
broken and diseased and so incapable of realizing the good apart from divine
healing. Such a robust doctrine of sin also appears to be at odds with Hindu
claims that human beings are innately or essentially divine. At first sight, Hindu
doctrines appear utterly incompatible with Christian theological claims, and
conversation between East and West appears, if not impossible, then at least
unpromising. How is productive conversation possible if differences are so
stark? From a broad aerial view of the religious terrain, Hindu and Christian
traditions do appear to be hopelessly at odds. No fusion of elements drawn
from the two seems theoretically possible even if such fusion is now practically
routine.

But matters become more complex as soon as one considers specific thinkers and texts. A view from closer to the ground demonstrates that religious traditions are neither univocal nor static. After all, Hinduism also includes forms
of dualistic theism and Eastern Orthodox Christianity offers to human beings
the possibility of deification, of becoming divine. This is to say nothing of
Western Christian mystics such as Meister Eckhart and Nicholas of Cusa who
offer accounts of divine immanence that rival Hindu nondualism in affirming a deep underlying unity between humanity and divinity. There are many
Christianities and multiple Hinduisms and differences *within* traditions are as
sharp as differences *across* them.

The turn toward particularity reveals not only a multiplicity of voices
within traditions but also that those traditions are constantly changing. Over
the course of the second half of the twentieth century, the Christian doctrine
of creation has undergone important modifications. Under the influence of
process theology, feminist theology, and the growing power of the ecological
movement, many theologians have reconsidered positions that take the world

---

9. On the notion of hybridity, see Homi Bhabha, *The Location of Culture* (New York:
Routledge, 1994), 4.

to be an extrinsic product of divine activity, a work of the divine will wholly external to the divine life. For decades now, feminist and ecological theologians have been calling us to greater reverence for the world by urging us to see creation as "the body of God."[10] Without pretending that there is anything like a consensus within Christian theology, there has been a marked growth in the sheer number of theologians who affirm some variety of panentheism.[11] Broadly defined, a theology is panentheistic to the extent that it affirms that the world is part of God's life even if God's life is in some sense more or greater than the life of the world. Within panentheistic theologies, the created world is not flatly external to the divine life. God's nature is determined by relation to the world, a world that is understood not merely as a product of God's willing or doing but also as part of God's very being.

The remarkable profusion of panentheistic theologies in the twentieth century should transform the received sense of what is possible in any relationship between Christianity and Eastern traditions, most especially Hinduism. The emergence of panentheism as a live possibility for Christian thought should also prompt theologians to recognize and revalorize submerged moments within Christian history, moments in which the relation between God and creation was characterized by far greater intimacy than some now reigning accounts of Christian doctrine suggest. What was once deemed esoteric need no longer seem so as the dynamic flow of a changing tradition casts new light on the Christian past.

The idea that the Christian doctrines of creation and Eastern notions of nonduality are absolutely incompatible becomes far less plausible once appreciation for the vital diversity within Christian tradition grows. This is not to say that difference will vanish and homogeneity reign. More likely is a new and

---

10. The feminist ecological theologian Sallie McFague is the most distinguished thinker of the concept of the world as God's body. See her book *The Body of God: An Ecological Theology* (Minneapolis: Fortress Press, 1993). For a more recent feminist theology of creation, one that rejects *creatio ex nihilo* altogether for a *creatio ex profundis*, a creation out of the chaotic depths, see Catherine Keller, *The Face of the Deep: A Theology of Becoming* (New York: Routledge, 2003).

11. It would be difficult to offer anything like a comprehensive list of important modern and contemporary panentheistic theologians. Michael Brierley provides a list of more than fifty figures who have either explicitly identified themselves as panentheists or have been so identified by others. His list includes Joseph Bracken, Pierre Teilhard de Chardin, John Cobb, David Ray Griffin, Peter Hodgson, Jay McDaniel, Sallie McFague, and Paul Tillich. See Michael Brierley, "Naming a Quiet Revolution: The Panentheistic Turn in Modern Theology," in *In Whom We Live and Move and Have Our Being: Panentheistic Reflections on God's Presence in a Scientific World*, ed. Philip Clayton and Arthur Peacocke (Grand Rapids, Mich.: Wm. B. Eerdmans, 2004), 1–15.

growing appreciation for the importance of subtle differences, differences discovered by way of careful comparison rather than posited before comparison begins.

Such comparative labor is ultimately unavoidable. Only comparative theology can critically evaluate the sometimes profound but often haphazard, solipsistic, and market-driven hybrid spiritualities now so much in vogue. Comparative theology in its constructive dimension seeks to do what theology has done always and everywhere: guide and orient faithful practice, especially when practice assumes forms heretofore unseen.

In other eras, men and women were accounted wise when they had achieved practical mastery of a single tradition's vision of the world. Our pluralistic era calls also for a different sort of wisdom: the double capacity to see the world multifariously and to show others how creatively to reconcile what such visions disclose when juxtaposed. The promise of comparative theology rests precisely in its aspiration for such pluriform wisdom.

Why Sankara, Why Tillich?

If Christian theology is now open as never before to a concrete engagement with other traditions, then the time has come to put aside unwieldy and unsustainable generalizations about East and West or even Hinduism and Christianity taken as a whole. Christian theology must subject conventional assumptions about immutable differences between traditions to critical scrutiny to determine how the very ideas that seem to be the source of outright conflict between traditions actually play out in the work of specific theologians from different traditions.

This book ventures just such an experiment by comparing one Hindu nondualist with one major modern Christian theologian precisely on the contested issues enumerated above, namely the relationship between God, creation, and the human predicament. The Hindu nondualist is Sankara, the eighth-century master teacher of the Advaita Vedanta[12] tradition, and the Christian theologian is Paul Tillich, the twentieth-century existentialist theologian who best understood that the time had come to formulate a Christian theology worked out in conversation with the history of religions. At the close of his life, indeed

---

12. The term *advaita* means nondualism. The root *dva* is related to the English word *dual* and *a* is the negative prefix. The word *Vedanta* can be broken down into *Veda* and *anta*. The Upanishads are regarded as the end, conclusion, or summation (*anta* is a cognate of the English word *end*) of the Vedas. Taken together, Advaita Vedanta names the school that holds that the highest teaching of the Upanishads is nondualism.

in his final lecture delivered a mere ten days before his death, Tillich reportedly suggested that were he to write his systematic theology anew, he would do so precisely by way of engagement with the world's religious traditions.[13] This project picks up on Tillich's unfulfilled intention by bringing his theology into conversation with Sankara's Advaita Vedanta. It does so not merely to catalog similarities and differences but to demonstrate by example that a new kind of theological venture is possible, one in which genuine conversation takes place between traditions for strictly theological reasons. Through such conversations, theologians can compare, sift, and finally make normative proposals about the similarities and differences discovered during comparison.

For good or ill, when Western theologians and philosophers think of Hinduism, the figure who almost always comes first to mind is Sankara. Even though the very large family of Hindu traditions also includes the dualism of Madhva and the qualified nondualism of Ramanuja, received notions of the monistic mystic East inevitably render Sankara's Advaita Vedanta the prototypical form of Hinduism par excellence.[14] Sankara's theology affirms that the true Self is not the impermanent body-mind complex but rather the Atman. Atman is the eternal light of consciousness (*cit*) that illumines the mind but is not itself the mind; rather it is the inner witness of the workings of mind and body. Sankara insists that the Hindu scriptures teach that this Atman is Brahman.[15] Brahman is ultimately ineffable, but it can be characterized provisionally as the unchanging and infinite ground of the world. It is not a being among beings but is

13. What Tillich actually said is as follows: "I must say that my own *Systematic Theology* was written before these seminars [with Mircea Eliade] and had another intention, namely, the apologetic discussion against and with the secular. Its purpose was the discussion or the answering of questions coming from the scientific and philosophical criticism of Christianity. But perhaps we need a longer, more intensive period of interpenetration of systematic theological study and religious historical studies. Under such circumstances the structure of religious thought might develop in connection with another or different fragmentary manifestation of theonomy or of the Religion of the Concrete Spirit. This is my hope for the future of theology." Paul Tillich, *The Future of Religions,* ed. Jerald C. Brauer (New York: Harper & Row, 1966), 91. It is Eliade who interpreted Tillich to be saying that "had he time, he would write a new Systematic *Theology* oriented toward, and in dialogue with, the whole history of religions." See Mircea Eliade, "Paul Tillich and the History of Religions," in Paul Tillich, *The Future of Religions,* 31.

14. On Western interest in "mystic Hinduism," Advaita, and Sankara in particular see Richard King, *Orientalism and Religion: Postcolonial Theory, India and 'The Mystic East'* (New York: Routledge, 1999), 118–42.

15. Scholarly convention dictates that terms drawn from foreign languages must be italicized unless they have become part of the English language and can now be found in standard English dictionaries. Some examples other than Atman and Brahman include karma, dharma, samsara, and nirvana. Other than such terms and proper names and titles of scriptures, all foreign terms will be italicized.

rather being-itself (*sat*). Precisely this affirmation of the identity of Atman and Brahman qualifies Sankara's position as nondualistic. Moreover, Sankara stipulates that only that which is everlasting and unchanging can be called truly real. By definition then, there is only one reality that qualifies as real in this absolute sense, and that is Atman-Brahman. This is yet another reason why Sankara's position qualifies as a strict nondualism. The goal of spiritual discipline in Advaita Vedanta is knowledge (*jnana*) of the identity between one's true Self and Brahman. Only such transformative knowing leads to liberation from samsara, the beginningless round of birth and death. Given Sankara's prominent role in shaping how the West imagines the East and given his commitment to the radical teaching of nonduality, he is an important interlocutor for an inquiry into Eastern approaches to divine immanence.

On the Christian side, Paul Tillich serves as a compelling conversation partner for Sankara because the German-American's theological program is deeply informed by precisely those moments within Christian tradition in which God's immanence to the world was mostly vigorously announced and championed. Tillich's theology amounts to a twentieth-century distillation of the history of Christian mystical theology.[16] To read Tillich is to hear again in modern idiom the voices of Meister Eckhart, Nicholas of Cusa, and the many other Christian thinkers who kept alive a radical sense of divine presence. As a result of Tillich's extended engagement with mystical thought, his theology offers one of the most robust accounts of divine immanence available in twentieth-century Protestant theology.

Tillich's theological vision is also compelling for comparative theology because of its attractiveness to persons from other religious traditions; no major modern Christian theologian has received more sustained attention from Eastern thinkers than Tillich. Thus far, he has been particularly attractive to Buddhist thinkers. Tillich's own interests lay in this direction. But Tillich's theology can also find a promising hearing in encounters with Hindu theology.[17] Although Tillich's own

---

16. Tillich is deeply indebted to mystical theologies even though he doubts that mystical experience can offer an adequate religious solution to the problems of the human predicament.

17. Except for the valuable work of Terence Thomas, almost no attention has been given to the question of the relationship between Tillich's theology and Hinduism. See Terence Thomas, *Paul Tillich and World Religions* (Cardiff: Cardiff Academic Press, 1999), 101–22. He observes that Tillich certainly knew of Sankara but rightly acknowledges that it is difficult to determine just how much he knew. Particularly frustrating, Thomas notes, is the fact that we do not know whether Tillich read Rudolf Otto's book on Sankara, *Mysticism East and West: A Comparative Analysis of the Nature of Mysticism*, trans. Bertha L. Bracey and Richenda C. Payne (1932; reprint, Wheaton, Ill.: The Theosophical Publishing House, 1987). Thomas concludes, "whether he read Otto's work or not he did not seem to know or at least accept certain interpretations of Sankara given by Otto. For instance he seemed to have no awareness of what Otto regards as the theistic side of Sankara" (109).

engagement with Eastern traditions was largely restricted to Zen Buddhism,[18] he was cognizant of similarities between his own thought and Advaita, though these similarities were never the object of sustained scrutiny in his own work. This book picks up on scattered hints of similarity in order to assess them more thoroughly than Tillich was able to do.[19]

One striking point of similarity is that both Sankara and Tillich character-ize divinity not as an infinite being among beings but rather as being-itself, that which gives being to all beings but is not itself one of those beings. Tillich is justly famous for his radical claim that it would be truer to say that God does not exist than to say that God does.[20] Beings exist and are determinate. To say God does not exist is to stipulate that God is not a determinate being but is rather the source of being for all that exists. Given this shared consensus, it is possible to maintain that both thinkers transcend theism. They are neither theists nor atheists in any conventional sense. It would perhaps be more accu-rate to characterize both as "transtheistic" because both believe that conceiving of God as one albeit special being among others is ultimately inadequate and so must be surpassed. Transtheists do not take theism to be flatly erroneous in every sense. Tillich might rightly pass for a theist given his claim that God is not less but more than personal; symbolizing God as personal is a critical and enduring feature of Tillich's theology. Sankara also ultimately takes leave of theism, but he takes for granted that religious life begins with devotion to Brahman understood as personal Lord and only later moves onto nonduality. In sum, both Sankara and Tillich believe that divinity is better understood as being-itself rather than as one, albeit special, personal being.

Within this context of broad agreement, noteworthy differences come to light, differences that raise sharp questions for theological reflection. As comparison will show, Tillich and Sankara disagree about the nature of

---

18. For an important summary and analysis of Tillich's conversations with the Zen thinker Shin'ichi Hisamatsu, see Joan Stambaugh, *The Formless Self* (Albany: State Univer-sity of New York Press, 1999), 55–71.

19. Readers might object that letting Tillich speak for the Christian tradition in its con-versation with the East amounts to cutting corners. By choosing a theologian who is already deeply committed to divine immanence, I might be accused of escaping difficult issues that would arise had I selected a less congenial conversation partner; for instance, Karl Barth. There is some justification to that charge. But I would argue that comparison is most inter-esting, challenging, and productive when differences are not starkly and glaringly evident. Comparison is far more rewarding when similarities and differences have to be discovered through careful scrutiny. The subtle but important differences that divide Sankara and Til-lich are provocative of thought and lead to rich conversation and even the possibility of mutual transformation.

20. Paul Tillich, *Systematic Theology*, 3 vols. (Chicago: University of Chicago Press, 1951–1963), 1:205. Hereafter, ST.

being-itself. Despite shared agreement that divinity is not finally to be understood as one entity among others, Tillich understands being-itself to be a dynamic creative power that gives rise to what it grounds (even though this "giving rise" cannot be understood to be a causal process), whereas Sankara believes that being-itself is an unchanging absolute not to be identified with the unreal but changing subject-object world. Sankara's metaphors encourage readers to imagine Brahman as an unchanging substratum onto which the changing realities of the world are projected like images on a screen or mirages in a desert. Without the desert, there can be no mirage. In that sense, the desert gives being to the mirage but not in the sense that the desert actively creates the mirage. Brahman, like the desert, remains perfectly still. The ramifications of this disagreement are far reaching, especially for each thinker's account of salvation (soteriology) and each thinker's understanding about what it means to be human (theological anthropology).

The roots of this disagreement can be traced back to the primary scriptures to which each theologian is indebted. Sankara's theology can be read as a sustained exegesis of the famous Upanishadic dictum, "I am Brahman (*aham brahmasmi*),"[21] whereas Tillich's theology can be read as an extended creative meditation on St. Paul's famous confession, "Likewise the Spirit helps us in our weakness; for we do know not how to pray as we ought, but that very Spirit intercedes with sighs too deep for words."[22] Comparing Sankara and Tillich amounts to a close, theologically mediated exploration of the vital sense of divine immanence conveyed in these two fundamental scriptural loci. To understand what is at stake in any conversation between Sankara and Tillich and the traditions they represent, one must appreciate the difference between an account of the ever-present Brahman and an alternative account of Spirit as one who brings about a reunion between humanity and divinity that was not already realized.

Because the writings of Sankara and Tillich are theological elaborations of the sense of divine presence disclosed in these foundational scriptures, the resulting comparison is more than just an exercise in comparative metaphysics. At stake here are not merely two conceptions of divinity, but rather the question of how divinity comes to human beings, how human beings encounter divinity. In Tillich's theology of Spirit, God comes to human beings when they are grasped by the power of being-itself and driven beyond themselves into ecstatic union with the divine life. In Sankara's theology Brahman is always present in human beings as the very light by which we see and know. Ecstatic union as described by Tillich is accomplished by divine

---

21. BUBh 1.4.10.
22. Romans 8:26.

activity whereas Sankara's nonduality is an eternal given awaiting discovery. The philosophical work of comparing Sankara's nondualism with Tillich's panentheism rests on and presupposes this prior scriptural and experiential account of two modes in which immanence is encountered.

This juxtaposition of a critical Upanishadic saying with a fundamental biblical verse demonstrates that turning to specific thinkers need not mean losing sight of broader questions regarding the nature of the relationship between Hinduism and Christianity. To extend a much-abused cliché, focusing on these trees does not amount to losing sight of the forests from which they are drawn; rather, close comparison seeks by way of careful scrutiny of particulars to see how the life of these religious forests finds exemplary expression in these two giant theological redwoods.

A Method for Comparison: On the Idea of Comparative Categories

If successful theological comparison requires sensitivity to how human beings from different religious traditions encounter ultimate reality in the pulsating course of religious life, then exploring God concepts taken in abstraction will not do. We must do more than begin comparison by recognizing that both Sankara and Tillich believe that ultimate reality is being-itself, as important as that discovery proves to be. What is required is a clear articulation of the religious problem that encounter with divinity resolves. To understand Tillich's conception of God or Sankara's notion of Brahman, we must discover how divinity, variously conceived, brings healing to the human predicament.

Do Sankara and Tillich believe that human life can be characterized as predicament? Given Advaita Vedanta's strong sense of the innate divinity of the Self, is Sankara in any position to offer an account of human predicament? And why must comparison begin with some such commonality in the first place? Just how does one compare theologians or traditions widely separated by cultures, languages, and histories?

Similarities and differences between traditions do not stand up and announce themselves; rather, they are discovered by careful investigation. To speak of differences or similarities is already to have learned something about the traditions in question, to have found some category that makes it possible to specify just how traditions differ or agree. As Jonathan Z. Smith and Robert C. Neville have shown, comparison is a triadic relation in which similarities or differences between any two items require the specification of some third respect in light of which it is meaningful to speak of similarity and difference.[23] Put simply, successful comparison requires that the things being compared are compared in the same way. To say that oranges are sweet and apples are red is true, but these two true statements do not add up to an instance of successful comparison strictly speaking because the two are not being compared in the same respect, that is to say, with respect to either color or flavor held constant.

In the case of apples and oranges, it is easy to tell when a shared respect has been identified and what the shared respects for comparison might be in the first place. When it comes to comparing abstract realities such as "religions," it is hard to tell whether Hinduism and Christianity possess shared features that make genuine comparison possible. It is not easy to tell whether comparing Hinduism and Christianity is more like comparing apples and elevators than comparing apples with oranges. That Western scholars have been in the habit of referring to both traditions as religions for a few centuries is no guarantee that we are indeed comparing like with like. In the last decade, a great many religionists have argued that the category *religion* tells us as much if not more about those who have created and continue to use the term than about the traditions to which the term supposedly refers.[24] What are the implications of this discovery for comparison?

Above all, it suggests that comparativists risk distorting the traditions they compare if they begin with general notions of what traditions *must* have in common by virtue of the fact that they are all religions. Using the category *religion* may distort or misrepresent the traditions under study, especially if one's ideas about what counts as a religion and what sorts of features religions ought to have are determined largely by acquaintance with Western prototypes. To minimize the risk of imposing ideas on traditions to be compared, comparativists must treat any respect for comparing things as a hypothesis that might require modification or even abandonment. To suppose, for example, that Sankara and Tillich can be compared with respect to what each has to say about the human predicament is to theorize that both thinkers do in fact have something to say about the human predicament. This is a safe move in Tillich's case; the term "human predicament" is drawn from his own vocabulary. In the case of Sankara, comparison begins with the hypothesis that he

---

23. See Jonathan Z. Smith, *Drudgery Divine: On the Comparison of Early Christianities and the Religions of Late Antiquity* (Chicago: University of Chicago Press, 1990), 51–53; Robert Cummings Neville, *Normative Cultures* (Albany: State University of New York Press, 1995), 59–84.

24. For an engaging, substantive, and comprehensive discussion of the problems posed by the category *religion*, see Richard King, *Orientalism and Religion*, 35–61.

too has something to say about life as predicament. Comparativists must be prepared to acknowledge the possibility that they are flat wrong. Careful comparison might show that Sankara has no account of the human situation as marked by predicament. If that should prove to be the case, then comparison would demonstrate not that Sankara and Tillich have different ideas about the human predicament but rather that the two thinkers are incomparable in this particular respect.

In the terms of Robert Neville's theory of comparison, the general notion of the human predicament is a "comparative category." A comparative category is a formal description of the respect in which two or more things are to be compared. Any such shared respect is, Neville argues, an abstract pattern that is further specified within traditional contexts. For example, traditions do not offer general notions of the human predicament but instead propose particular interpretations thereof. To begin comparison, the comparativist attempts carefully to extract an abstract pattern from its context by purifying it of strictly tradition-specific details so that the pattern so purified can serve as the general level of a comparative category. Tillich's notion of the human predicament can be employed for comparison only if his own very detailed ideas about the human predicament are temporarily distilled out from a more general idea of the human predicament. Once a general notion of the human predicament is formulated, the comparativist has in hand what Neville calls a "vague comparative category."

Comparison moves forward when the ideas to be compared, sin in Tillich's case, and imprisonment within samsara in Sankara's case, are reexpressed as "candidate specifications" of that vague category. The comparativist must show how sin and samsara are different ways of specifying the general idea of the human predicament. No comparison is possible unless vague comparative categories can be so specified because ideas expressed in their own terms are incomparable. Sin just is not samsara; samsara is not sin.

In this comparison, the task at hand is to understand the structure of claims about the human predicament across traditions. First, one must ask, Is it fair to use the term to characterize Sankara's thought? What does understanding the problem of reincarnation as one account of the human predicament say about how religious traditions understand the human predicament in general? Is the human predicament a problem to be solved, an illness in need of treatment, or a captivity from which one needs to be set free? These are all different ways of specifying the vague category of the human predicament. Comparativists understand the general conceptual structure of any pattern only by appreciating how that pattern is filled out by various specifications within and across traditions. We learn about the general meaning of the category of human predicament by trying it out in comparison.

A category is vague if it leaves open the ways in which candidate specifications may relate to one another. Such specifications, therefore, may relate to each other as "contraries, contradictories, different but overlapping, different and overlapping, supplementary, complementary . . ." and so on.[25] To acknowledge that both Sankara and Tillich offer accounts of human life as predicament is not to say that they agree about how to characterize that predicament. Only further comparison can determine the extent and degree of similarity or difference. If specific ideas under consideration can be expressed successfully in the language of the vague category, then the vague category is applicable and adequate with respect to those ideas.

It goes without saying that the comparative categories so derived will be applicable to the tradition from which the category is drawn in the first place. The critical test of the comparative category is its applicability and adequacy for other traditions brought into comparison. Failure is apparent when the attempt to translate the specific ideas of a tradition into the language of the vague category distorts or omits much that is important about those ideas as expressed in their home contexts. If, for example, comparison shows that Sankara's thought has to be contorted to fit into the vague category of the human predicament, then either the notion of the human predicament was not rendered suitably abstract or vague so as to include this Hindu variation on the theme, or, in the worst-case scenario, the category of the human predicament may just be inapplicable to Sankara's nondualism. Even to have discovered that the category is inapplicable is to have learned something, but it would mean that Sankara's ideas must then be compared in some other respect, or if no common respect for comparison can be found, his ideas might turn out to be incomparable to Tillich's own.

Neville's theory does more than show comparativists how to compare ideas from across religious traditions. It also suggests that finding and accumulating a list of comparative categories that work across traditions is precisely how theologians from different traditions develop a common vocabulary.[26] As theologians formulate, test, and revise comparative categories during comparison, they generate comparative categories applicable across traditional divides even as they abandon categories that fail to be generalizable. Vague categories that can be specified differently by various traditions are what religious thinkers need to communicate with each other successfully.

25. Neville, *Normative Cultures*, 63.
26. Ibid., 59–84.

The history of comparative conversation has already yielded a number of categories that theologians and religionists use routinely. Terms like ultimate reality (rather than God or emptiness), ultimate transformation (rather than salvation or liberation), and human condition or predicament (rather than sin or samsara) are vague categories developed by earlier generations of theologians and comparativists who labored to discover terms general enough to encompass specific notions from the world's religious traditions without arbitrariness and distortion. Unfortunately, no neutral, prefabricated, ecumenical Esperanto exists for interreligious dialogue. Only comparison can grow the language needed for comparison.

The Human Predicament as Illness: The Medical Model as a Tool for Comparison

Theological reflection is rarely driven by an abstract quest to understand ultimate reality but is instead typically concerned with the existential question of how human life ought to be lived in relation to ultimate reality. That question regularly brings with it a keen awareness of shortcoming; the world's religious traditions recognize that human beings fail to be what they truly are or become what they ought to be. That awareness seems reason enough to suppose that religious traditions will likely offer accounts of the human situation as marked by predicament—explanations for why human beings routinely fail to live as they should.

This proposal regarding a vague comparative category that at least some religious traditions will share appears to be the sort of speculative venture warned against above, a speculation that inserts into traditions what comparativists later wish to find. To resolve this possible contradiction, this line of speculation should be treated as a hypothesis to be tested against available evidence and if necessary overturned. Here, I argue only that the category of the human predicament seems applicable to both Sankara and Tillich and to the traditions that they represent.

Still more specifically, I propose that both thinkers can be read fruitfully and without distortion as subscribing to an understanding of the human predicament as illness. To test the validity of this still more specific comparative category, I propose an examination of each thinker's theology in terms of a standard fourfold medical model or therapeutic paradigm for understanding and treating the course of a disease. If Sankara and Tillich believe that the human predicament can be understood as illness in need of a cure, we can expect that each will offer the following: (1) a diagnosis of the human predicament, (2) an etiology of the human predicament, (3) a prognosis, and finally (4) a therapy for treating and perhaps even wholly curing the disease.

One reason for believing that the medical model is a useful tool for engaging South Asian traditions is the prominence of the medical model first in Buddhist traditions and then subsequently in other traditions such as Advaita Vedanta. It is a well-known feature of Buddhism that the Four Noble Truths can readily be mapped onto a medical model: (1) All is suffering (diagnosis); (2) Suffering has a cause, namely craving (etiology); (3) Suffering can be brought to cessation (prognosis); (4) The eightfold path is way to bring an end to suffering (therapy). Indologists have argued for some time that the Buddha is not likely to have borrowed this fourfold scheme from some then-extant tradition of medical thinking; there simply is no textual evidence to suggest that this fourfold categorization was present in the medical literature of the Buddha's time. The reigning scholarly hypothesis is that other Indic religious traditions and the Indian medical tradition itself might have borrowed what we now call the "medical model" from the Buddha.[27] Regardless of the trajectory of influence, it does no violence to read the Four Noble Truths in the terms of the medical model. That early Buddhist literature regularly referred to the Buddha as a physician suggests that this analogy was not unwittingly foisted onto Buddhist tradition by nonindigenous sources.

The medical model is a promising tool for comparative religion more generally because it allows for discriminating comparison across traditions. With the fourfold categorical scheme in hand, comparativists can ask a wide range of subtle questions. To what extent and in what way do Sankara and Tillich agree in their diagnoses of the human predicament? In what ways do they disagree? Do they agree on matters of diagnosis but disagree on the question of etiology? If they disagree on etiology, will this disagreement lead to sharply differing prognoses for human well-being? And what of therapy? What are the ramifications of differing diagnoses or etiologies for each thinker's understanding of religious therapy? Are they even treating the same spiritual ailment? These questions transcend in precision and sophistication the sorts of questions customarily posed in theology of religions. It is not that the standard queries of theology of religions become obsolete or irrelevant when new ones are posed. It still makes sense to ask whether persons from other religions are saved, or whether there are in fact many salvations, as theologian S. Mark

---

27. Paul Demiéville, *Buddhism and Healing: Demiéville's Article "Byo" from Hobogirin* (Lanham, Md.: University Press of America, 1985), 2.

Heim has argued.[28] Questions derived from the medical model generate data theologians need to answer the sweeping questions posed by theology of religions. Without knowing whether the religions under consideration have identified and diagnosed the same disease, without knowing precisely what each thinker takes to be the root cause of the illness at hand, it is impossible to know whether there are many salvations or just differing etiologies and therapies for the same ailment.

These new interrogations promise rich and highly textured accounts of similarity and difference, provided of course that the categories presupposed by the questions are applicable to Sankara's Advaita and Tillich's Christianity. Comparativists are obligated not to be carried away by their fondness for any particular set of comparative categories, no matter how compelling they seem at first to be. The possibility that the categories driving comparison may require large-scale revision or perhaps even rejection necessarily haunts the work of sober-minded comparativists.

Disputed Theological Questions: What Is at Stake in the Conversation?

The conversation between Sankara and Tillich will prompt a number of religiously exigent questions, including the following: Can human beings find their way to ultimate reality, or are we rather found by it? Do we meet divinity as we might a stranger whom we have never before met, or is meeting divinity always a matter of recognition, or perhaps even a matter of discovering a treasure hidden within? Comparative theology becomes genuinely constructive when it proceeds to assess competing answers that religious traditions provide to questions such as these.

Of the questions posed above, only the second is likely to generate ready and substantive agreement. Both Sankara and Tillich believe that meeting divinity is always a matter of recognition. Divinity is not a stranger met by chance. Advaitins would applaud Tillich's thesis that "man discovers *himself* when he discovers God; he discovers something that is identical with himself although it transcends him infinitely, something from which he is estranged, but from which he never was and never can be separated."[29] Whether Sankara would agree with the statement in toto depends on a precise analysis of what

---

28. S. Mark Heim, *Salvations: Truth and Difference in Religion* (Maryknoll, N.Y.: Orbis Books, 1995).

29. Paul Tillich, "The Two Types of Philosophy of Religion," in *Theology of Culture* (New York: Oxford University Press, 1959), 10. Hereafter, TOC.

Tillich means by estrangement and transcendence. The conversation between Sankara and Tillich hinges not only on questions about the nature of divinity but also on theological anthropology.

To make headway on both these fronts, inquiry must begin with an appreciation for what Tillich calls "the basic intention of my doctrine of God," namely his desire to go beyond naturalism and supranaturalism (ST 2:5).[30] According to Tillich, any conception of divinity that imagines God to be a supranatural being or deity who can and does regularly intervene from without into natural networks of causation is supranaturalistic. Such supranaturalism is problematic for relatively straightforward reasons, most especially because it is not only utterly incompatible with science but also because it puts God in the position of regularly disrupting the "inviolability of the created structures of the finite" (ST 2:6).

What Tillich finds most problematic about supranaturalist theologies is their dependence on dualism. A dualistic conception of God is problematic for subtle but weighty philosophical reasons; conceiving of God as a being who stands over against the world—and that is what makes this position dualistic—is problematic because it "transforms the infinity of God into a finiteness which is merely an extension of the categories of finitude" (ibid.). Gone is a properly infinite God. What remains is a deity subject to the categories of space, time, causality, and substance. The God of dualism is an entity who resides in heaven, acts in time, causally interacts with other beings, and is one substance among others. Such a God is just one item in a universe that proves to be more encompassing than God is. Precisely this desire to avoid so unworthy a conception of God drives Tillich to insist that God is better regarded as the creative ground of being rather than as a supranatural deity. Tillich quite rightly believes that supranaturalistic theologies err by imagining God to be more akin to the many deities of Greek myth than to the God of Christian faith.

Tillich's rigorous and adamant rejection of dualism marks him as a Christian thinker whose doctrine of God will resonate strongly with Hindu nondualism. And yet the antidualistic character of Tillich's theology remains largely underappreciated. Perhaps only comparativists are best able to appreciate the promise of Tillich's antidualism for dialogue with Eastern religious traditions.

If supranaturalistic dualism is one temptation that Tillich seeks to avoid, the other is naturalism. For Tillich, a theological position is naturalistic to

---

30. Tillich uses the terms "supranatural" and its variations rather than the term "supernatural." For the sake of consistency, I have adopted Tillich's usage throughout.

the extent that it simply "identifies God with the universe, with its essence or with special powers within it" (ibid.). Naturalism, for Tillich, may be the lesser of two evils, but it is problematic nevertheless because it "denies the infinite distance between the whole of finite things and their infinite ground, with the consequence that the term 'God' becomes interchangeable with the term 'universe' and therefore semantically superfluous" (ST 2:7).

The presence in Tillich's discourse of the term *distance* brings into sharp relief the central question of divine immanence, the question that above all haunts Hindu-Christian dialogue. In what sense can the God who is the ground of being be "distant" from the creatures that God grounds? Does Tillich reinstate dualism by appealing to the notion of "distance"? Can any theology that steadfastly dismisses dualism, whether Hindu or Christian, cogently maintain that there is a distance between divinity and the world? And if such distance can be posited, does it not undercut the Advaita affirmation that the true self just is Brahman?

For the purposes of inaugurating the conversation between Sankara and Tillich, it suffices to note that distance has two distinct senses in Tillich's theology. First, Tillich feels compelled to posit a distance between God and creatures for phenomenological reasons. In any encounter with the holy, human beings experience the holy as that which exceeds them utterly. Here the word *distance* is a figure for the sheer depth and awe-inspiring power of the God who is encountered as holy (ibid.).

But distance also bears another meaning, a meaning primarily related not to what presents itself from the side of divinity in the human-divine encounter, but rather from the side of humanity. Distance in this second sense bespeaks human estrangement from the divine life. The term functions to name "the mutual freedom" of God and creature. Distance is a figure for freedom, the freedom of the creature to stand over against God and the freedom of God to stand for the creature who stands against God. Distance and freedom are not terms that suggest that God is elsewhere or that creature is ever at an ontic remove from God. To be is to be sustained in being by the God who is being-itself. In that sense, God is always radically present to the creature. But creaturely freedom itself is distance from God, or put otherwise, creaturely freedom requires distance even if that distance cannot be conceived in traditional supranaturalistic terms.

In sum, at the very heart of Tillich's system is the idea that human freedom requires that creatures must be substantially independent over against the creator—independent despite the fact that human beings have no being apart from God. When human beings exercise their freedom in separation from God, the consequences of separation lead ultimately to estrangement, characterized by unbelief, hubris, and concupiscence, three terms that together describe Tillich's understanding of the human predicament. In this process, separated creatures make themselves centers of their own lives and then attempt to draw everything else into that center.

Because Tillich believes that freedom requires creatures to ex-ist, to stand out of the divine ground, his theological vision gives rise to a somber sense of life as marked by deep ambiguity. Because creaturely life is rooted in but also separated from the divine life, it is never secure. The ambiguities that characterize the human predicament are interrupted only by episodic ecstatic manifestations of unambiguous life. Within Tillich's scheme, it is never possible to envision a robust hope for human well-being. Healing is always fleeting, and the prognosis for the human predicament is guarded at best. Although human life is punctuated by healing events of divine-human reunion, life cannot be characterized as a sustained and incremental movement into healing. Despite some emphasis on sanctification, Tillich rejects the possibility of a settled divine-human reunion. Tillich remains in this respect a deeply Lutheran theologian, a theologian of *simul justus et peccator*.

Sankara, on the other hand, presents an understanding of nonduality in which the human being is *never* other than the Absolute, namely Brahman as being-itself. Nevertheless, he also presents an account of human predicament as marked by ignorance, desire, and aversion. Because the true Self is Brahman, however, Sankara affirms the possibility of liberation while living (*jivanmukti*). In terms of the medical model, Sankara offers a far more optimistic prognosis for the human predicament than does Tillich. Because human beings are never really at a remove from divinity, because the true Self is just Brahman, divine immanence occasions radical hope for sanctification.

What makes Sankara's work intriguing—albeit puzzling for Christian theologians—is his ability to generate a sharply negative account of the human predicament within the framework of nondualism. Even though Sankara believes that human beings are ultimately nothing other than Brahman, he recognizes that we suffer acutely and cause others to do so as well. If it is possible to affirm that human beings belong to divinity without denying or minimizing the gravity of the human predicament, then Christian theologians who seek to deepen and extend Tillich's theological legacy may legitimately wonder whether a doctrine of substantial separation is necessary to generate an account of freedom and predicament. Might it be possible to frame a non-dualistic Christian theology in which a stronger account of human possibilities (such as those offered by Sankara) is combined with a realistic assessment of the depth of estrangement? Is it possible to remove the element of distance that Tillich felt compelled to preserve and thereby mitigate the note of inevitable tragedy that hangs over the whole of Tillich's theology?

Is a Christian Nondualism Possible?

Why might a nondualistic Christian theology be desirable? Ultimately, the quest to imagine the greatest possible intimacy between humanity and divinity is driven by soteriological motivations. At the heart of Christian *mythos* and life is the conviction that human beings are brought to healing and wholeness not merely by a juridical proclamation of divine forgiveness *ad extra*; rather, healing takes place when human beings are taken *into* the divine life. Incarnation itself teaches that human wholeness rests radically on divine immanence.

But does not the very narrative of incarnation and the aspiration for *becoming* divine rather than simply *being* divine suggest the primacy of a distance that is only subsequently bridged by divine initiative? Does not God traverse a distance that human beings cannot? A partial response to these probing, even decisive, questions is to be found in Tillich's rejection of supranaturalism. Even though Tillich retains metaphors of distance and ultimately inscribes these into his ontology, his antidualistic rejection of supranaturalism goes a long way toward disrupting naïve accounts that depict God as a supranatural deity who inhabits another world and only subsequently enters into the human world by supranatural means in a singular, exceptional, and once-for-all moment of radical immanence. Whatever distance might mean, it cannot mean the distance that separates heaven from earth. "God is neither alongside things nor even 'above' them; he is nearer to them than they are to themselves. He is their creative ground, here and now, always and everywhere" (ibid.)

But conversation with Hindu nondualism challenges Christian theologians to carry the antidualistic impulses found in Tillich further. Sankara asks Christian readers to consider an absolute divine presence that goes so far as to make possible an affirmation of nonduality between humanity and divinity. But can a Christian imagination affirm the Upanishadic Great Saying, "I am Brahman," or does that affirmation mark an impermissible transgression by birthing an identity between humanity and divinity that ultimately annihilates intimacy by removing the distance that makes intimacy possible? Are Christians—even those holding to a Tillichian account of God as being-itself—compelled to posit a distance that can be bridged in ecstatic union but never erased or annulled?

These are among the most demanding questions that Christian interlocutors will face when in dialogue with Sankara's nondualism.

What about Hindu nondualists of Sankara's sort? How might they be challenged by conversation with a Tillichian form of Christianity? Ultimately that is a question for Hindu conversation partners. Nonetheless, I suggest that conversation with a Tillichian expression of Christian faith can raise pertinent questions for nondualist Hindu theologians. An element that might need reconsideration in Sankara's theological vision is his fundamental axiom that ultimate reality, Brahman, is unchanging and that only that which is beyond change is ultimately real. The result of maintaining this axiom is the corollary that the experienced world of change must be characterized as unreal, resulting in what Lance Nelson has called the "dualism of nondualism." Sankara cannot avoid positing a sharp duality between an unreal but experienced world flux and a real and unchanging Brahman.[31] Dualism is avoided technically—because only Brahman is really real—but remains practically. Here, Tillich's dynamic vision, which denies that ultimate reality is an unchanging Absolute that stands behind and apart from the realm of change, suggests the possibility of a different kind of immanence than that offered by Sankara, an immanence that also might be called nondual.

Tillich believed that he had to back off from a thoroughgoing nondualism for a host of reasons but most especially because he believed that the very possibility of human freedom requires substantial creaturely independence. But is Tillich right? Does freedom require substantial separation from the divine life? Or does the notion that freedom requires separation depend on a lingering substantialism in Tillich's thought? Can we imagine freedom without separation? Can we imagine that creaturely freedom does not require ontological independence, a move away from the primordial father? If so, then it might indeed be possible to imagine that Tillich's transitory dualism will give way to a full-fledged Christian nondualism.

Comparative Theology as Interfaith Dialogue in Search of Mutual Transformation

Such searching questions suggest that genuine conversation between traditions will go beyond taking note of similarities and differences. Ultimately, if dialogue is marked by vulnerability to truth, it will lead to what John B. Cobb

---

31. Lance E. Nelson, "The Dualism of Nondualism: Advaita Vedanta and the Irrelevance of Nature," in *Purifying the Earthly Body of God: Religion and Ecology in Hindu India*, ed. Lance E. Nelson, 61–88 (Albany: State University of New York Press, 1998).

has called "mutual transformation." In the course of dialogue between traditions, Cobb—speaking from extensive experience—testifies that conversation partners will encounter ideas in the other tradition that seem plausible, compelling, and even true and yet unavailable within one's home tradition. The notion of nonduality is a case in point. When faced with such an eventuality, Cobb argues that theologians will rarely find that such new knowledge can simply be added into a storehouse of past convictions. Instead, dialogue will demand substantive reformulation of past convictions so that new knowledge can be meaningfully integrated with what one had heretofore believed. Cobb is convinced that this movement of "creative transformation" will make an impact on all traditions involved; reformulation must take place on every side if richer and more comprehensive visions of reality are to emerge. As Cobb puts it, "The task is to refine and hone what one has taken to be important to one's own faith and similarly to refine and hone the insight one is learning from others. The goal is to find how the truth in both coheres."[32] The quest for such coherence generates mutual transformation.

Comparative theology, so envisioned, is explicitly interreligious and dialogical.[33] Even if the comparative theologian does her work isolated in the study, the fruits of such research presuppose and are tested by conversation in which theologians from more than one tradition engage in collaboration and mutual criticism. Metaphors of conversation are especially valuable because they serve to alert all involved that the results of comparative theology cannot be anticipated in advance. The unfolding and processive nature of comparative theology is well captured in Gordon Kaufman's argument for a dialogical model of truth. Kaufman maintains that truth should be "perceived as a process of becoming, a reality that emerges (quite unexpectedly) in the course of conversation.... [I]nstead of taking truth to be a property of particular words or propositions or texts ... it is identified as a living reality that emerges within and is a function of ongoing, living conversation among a number of different voices."[34]

Kaufman's conception of truth is appealing for comparative theology because it gives to truth an event-like character. It shows just how and why comparative theology does more than rehabilitate the wisdom of the past; it

32. John B. Cobb, "Dialogue," in *Death or Dialogue? From the Age of Monologue to the Age of Dialogue*, ed. Leonard Swidler, John B. Cobb, Paul F. Knitter, and Monika Helwig (Philadelphia: Trinity Press International, 1990), 7.

33. Francis Clooney also advocates a conception of theology as interreligious, comparative, dialogical, and confessional. See *Hindu God, Christian God*, 7–12.

34. Gordon D. Kaufman, *God, Mystery, Diversity: Christian Theology in a Pluralistic World* (Minneapolis: Fortress Press, 1996), 199–200.

must perforce remain open to transforming insights that can emerge only in and through "a process of free and open conversation on the most profound religious issues—a conversation intended to continue for years, even generations."[35] Kaufman, like Cobb, quite rightly hopes that "deeper religious truth than that presently known in any of our traditions will in due course emerge."[36] This conversation between Sankara and Tillich is inaugurated with the hope of discovering such deeper truth.

A Concluding Note on the Term *Immanence*

As the title of this book indicates, the idea of immanence stands at the heart of this project. This term is a commonplace in Christian theology. But readers must bear in mind that the meaning of the received vocabulary is likely to undergo significant shifts when terms are inscribed within a nondualistic or antidualistic framework. Tillich is rather clear that the meaning of transcendence must be reconceived if one rejects the notion that God is a being who inhabits a special spatio-temporal realm removed from our own. The God in whom all beings always already participate and from whom we are never separated is not transcendent if, by transcendence, one means to refer to the distance that separates two beings one from another. Nonetheless, Tillich does not mean to give up on transcendence altogether and opts instead to redefine the term so that the term's supranaturalistic meanings are purged.

The matter becomes still more intricate in the case of Sankara's nondualism. If the true Self just is Brahman, what might it mean to speak of either immanence or transcendence? In what sense, if any, is Brahman transcendent? What would Brahman transcend? The term *immanence* might well be equally problematic. If the term is meant to refer to how one reality, namely divinity, draws near to another—the world or humanity for example—then it hardly seems useable within a nondualistic theology. Identity seems to trump immanence and render the question of transcendence moot. Only further comparison can determine whether traditional Christian vocabulary for thinking divinity's relationship to the world might be viable in antidualistic theological traditions.

Yet another problem with the conventional terms *transcendence* and *immanence* is that much contemporary theological discourse places them in antago-

35. Ibid., 201.
36. Ibid.

nistic relationship. God's transcendence always comes at the expense of God's immanence and divine immanence only at the expense of transcendence. William Placher, borrowing Kathryn Tanner's terminology, calls this a "contrastive" account of transcendence. Placher recognizes that a contrastive account inevitably "makes divine transcendence and involvement in the world into a zero-sum game."[37] Placher shrewdly traces contrastive accounts of transcendence back to the fundamental error of taking God to be one being among others. He observes, "If God were one of the things in the world—as implied by the contrastive model of transcendence—then it would be natural to ask where God is located—in the world or outside it?"[38] And, quite naturally, either answer to the question militates against the other.

Both Tillich and Sankara reject this dualistic and reified conception of divinity. If meaningful discourse about transcendence and immanence is possible within a nondualistic theological framework, such talk will surely reject contrastive accounts altogether. Nondualistic theologies will likely upset some currently entrenched linguistic and theological habits. Fortunately, Placher traces these habits to the seventeenth century and not to Christian antiquity. Resorting to the language of transcendence and immanence without asking what meaning these terms acquire when they are inscribed within new theological and metaphysical frameworks can only lead to confusion. Given these dangers, readers must bear in mind that this book asks just precisely what transcendence and immanence might mean within a nondualistic framework. Consider, for example, the following: It may be possible to imagine that God is so near to me as to constitute my very being and yet for God to remain wholly beyond my ken, wholly beyond any conceptual apparatus by which I might seek to secure knowledge of the God. In such an unknowing knowledge of an immanent but nonetheless superabundant divine, East and West might find consensus. This book is a pilgrimage in search for just such a consensus.

---

37. See William C. Placher, *The Domestication of Transcendence: How Modern Thinking about God Went Wrong* (Louisville: Westminster John Knox Press, 1996), 111.
  38. Ibid., 112.

chapter two

Sankara on the Human Predicament

Diagnosis and Etiology

అఞఞ

"The Hindu Refuses to Call You Sinners": Opening the Question of the Human Predicament in Advaita Vedanta

In chapter 1, I noted that one obstacle to meaningful East-West conversation is the naïve preconception that Eastern traditions offer wholly positive accounts of human nature whereas their Western counterparts remain resolutely pessimistic. Readers who enjoy only a nodding acquaintance with Advaita Vedanta are often under the impression that it lacks theological resources for any serious analysis of the human predicament. Hence, it is taken for granted that the Christian doctrine of sin utterly contradicts the Advaita affirmation that the true Self is Brahman, the ultimate nondual reality. The famous Hindu sage, Swami Vivekananda, has done much to cultivate this impression of qualitative difference: "Yea, the Hindu refuses to call you sinners. We are the children of God, the sharers of immortal bliss, holy and perfect beings. Ye divinities on earth—sinners! It is a sin to call a man so; it is a standing libel on human nature."[1]

If the Swami's verdict is the final word on the matter, then this comparative project would fail to be interesting. A stark and uncomplicated opposition between Christian accounts of sin and Advaita's affirmation of the inherent divinity of the human would leave little for comparativists to do save to reaffirm and leave in place the radical dichotomy between East and West. But

---

1. Vivekananda, "Chicago Addresses," in *The Yogas and Other Works*, ed. Swami Nikhilananda (New York: Ramakrishna-Vivekananda Center, 1953), 188.

matters are not as straightforward as Vivekananda suggests.[2] Sankara does have an extensive account of the human predicament as caused by ignorance (*avidya*), and the consequences of ignorance are as painful and destructive as are the consequences of sin in Tillich's theology. That Sankara's nondualism includes an analysis of the human predicament suggests that general preconceptions about nondualism must be called into question. Nevertheless, central questions remain. If the true Self is Brahman, the absolute world-ground, how can life be characterized as predicament? Just how is ignorance possible? How is it that we who are Brahman fail to know what we are?

This chapter and the following begin the work of comparison by reading Sankara through the category of the human predicament. This chapter will focus on Sankara's diagnosis and etiology and chapter 3 will examine his prognosis and therapy for the human predicament. Chapters 4 and 5 will present a reading of Paul Tillich through those same categories.

Sankara's Anthropology: The Soul as Free Agent and Part of Brahman

Understanding Sankara is not just a straightforward matter of repairing to the relevant primary texts. Even those who are relatively unfamiliar with Sankara are likely to entertain presentiments and prejudices that strongly condition what they read. The Indologist Ronald Inden has argued that disproportionate Western interest in Sankara is motivated by the fact that Sankara can be employed to confirm Western stereotypes about the character of the Indian mind.[3] Two stereotypes deserve special attention. The first is the idea that Sankara is essentially an otherworldly thinker whose theological anthropology is fatally flawed because it does not recognize persons as agents who can engage in effective worldly action. On this view, Sankara is an unengaged quietist preoccupied solely with liberation from the cycle of reincarnation. A second, closely related idea is that Sankara is a mystic for whom liberating knowledge comes only in moments of mystical union, moments in which the world of ordinary experience is left behind.

Are these received notions about Sankara valid? What are the connections between Sankara's understanding of nondualism and the question of agency?

---

2. My intention here is not to set up Vivekananda as a straw man for ready dissection. Rather, I intend only to indicate that contemporary readers naturally tend to read Sankara in the light of Vivekananda's enormously influential and popular Neo-Vedanta. Moreover, as we shall see at the end of the next chapter, Vivekananda is by no means off the mark in every sense.

3. Ronald Inden, *Imagining India* (Cambridge, Mass.: Basil Blackwell, 1990), 105–8.

It is true that Sankara stipulates that seekers after liberation must renounce action as a precondition for liberating knowledge, but does that commitment impair or even neutralize the "realized capacity of people to act effectively upon their world?"[4] And does Sankara privilege any special mystical modes of experience in which the reality of the world is left behind?[5]

Addressing these preconceptions is by no means tangential to this project. Questions regarding agency, the reality of the world, and the nature of liberating knowledge are important to Tillich's understanding of Eastern religions in general and Hinduism in particular. Although Tillich recognized the affinity between his ideas and those of several Eastern traditions, Hinduism included, he remained convinced that Eastern traditions do not adequately recognize the importance of particularity precisely because mysticism is so dominant a strand in these traditions.[6] Tillich's convictions about mysticism in general and Eastern mysticisms in particular are clear: "Mysticism does not take seriously the concrete. . . . It plunges directly into the ground of being and meaning, and leaves the concrete, the world of finite values and meanings, behind."[7] Tillich is also concerned that the evanescent character of mystical experience leaves untreated enduring features of the human predicament that resurface as soon as mystical experience fades from immediacy. Tillich's understanding of Hinduism seems to be informed by just the kind of essentialist notions that scholars of Hinduism now stridently question. Given the tenacity of such stereotypes, it is unwise to leave them unexamined.

To counter effectively the charge that Sankara ignores ordinary life in the world, one must resist the temptation to move rapidly into Sankara's analysis of the human predicament. For Sankara, knowledge of life as predicament comes only at the final stage in the religious journey and not the first. Much comes before the turn to the ultimate truth of nonduality. Misconceptions about Advaita Vedanta flourish in part because interest in Sankara's understanding of ultimate truth (*paramarthikasatya*) trumps attention to

4. Inden is especially concerned about Indological projects that deny "human agency," by which he means, "the realized capacity of people to act effectively upon their world and not only to know about or give personal or intersubjective significance to it." Ibid., 23.

5. The question of agency will be treated in this chapter and the question of mysticism in the next.

6. Tillich seems to presume that Eastern traditions are mysticisms of some variety. Of course, Tillich is not alone in this regard. Richard King provides an invaluable critical discussion of the general phenomenon of the construction of the "mystic East." See Richard King, *Orientalism and Religion*, 118–42; 161–86.

7. Paul Tillich, *The Courage to Be* (New Haven: Yale University Press, 1952), 186. Hereafter, CTB.

his treatment of conventional truth (*vyavaharikasatya*).[8] It is true that in the brilliant light of ultimate truth, the empirical world is understood to be unreal, that is to say, subject to change and perishing. Brahman, the object of ultimate truth, is recognized as the eternal and unchanging ground for the world of flux. Sankara is indeed committed to teaching the ultimate truth of nonduality—that what we most truly are is Brahman—but he is also interested in teaching students how to understand ordinary experience rightly.

Sankara, unlike Tillich, is an exegetical rather than a systematic theologian; quite naturally he is interested in as wide an array of issues as are found in the Hindu scriptures. The Vedas and Upanishads treat a host of matters, including the right regulation of everyday life. In addition to teaching the ultimate nature of the true Self, the scriptures speak to purely conventional concerns, including the duties of class and stage of life (*varnasramadharma*). Indeed, the ritual portions of the Veda presuppose an altogether conventional anthropology in which the individual soul (*jiva*) is understood as knower (*pramatr*), agent (*kartr*), and experiencer (*bhoktr*). Scripture functions as a source of right knowledge about injunctions (*vidhi*) regarding the ritual and moral responsibilities of householders because it does not all at once overturn taken-for-granted notions about what the world is like.

Sankara believes that scriptural injunctions are irrelevant only for those who have come to know that they are not agents but changeless Brahman. But for those who have not yet attained to this culminating insight and so are concerned with action and its consequences, scripture has much to say about how to live life properly. Scripture thus plays a double role both as the source of knowledge about the right ordering of mundane life and as a source of the extramundane knowledge that leads to liberation. Sankara is concerned to bring reflection about conventional reality under scriptural provenance. Wilhelm Halbfass nicely captures Sankara's convictions regarding scripture: "Insofar as it speaks about transcendence, the Veda also speaks about what has to be transcended. There are no strict borderlines. The Veda 'reveals' reality as well as appearance in its soteriologically relevant details. . . ."[9]

When readings of Sankara ignore his treatment of action and the obligations of ordinary life—ingredients that make up the world of appearance—the

---

8. Sankara's thought is deeply influenced by Buddhist two-truth theory even though Sankara's version is quite distinctive. In Sankara's thought, each truth corresponds to a different order of reality. Conventional truth has to do with matters of worldly practice and everyday life. Ultimate truth, on the other hand, is the highest ontological truth of nonduality, the truth of Brahman.

9. Wilhelm Halbfass, *Tradition and Reflection: Explorations in Indian Thought* (Albany: State University of New York Press, 1991), 152.

long path seekers must travel *before* undertaking renunciation for the sake of an exclusive focus on liberation (*moksa*) fades from view. Key stages in Sankara's complex soteriological vision are inevitably neglected. These omissions lend credence to lingering assumptions about the putatively world-negating character of Sankara's theology. The result is that readers fail to see that Sankara takes pains to teach disciples how to live rightly in the world in order to put in place the foundation necessary for transition to the ultimate truth of nonduality.

For these reasons, a rudimentary sketch of Sankara's account of ordinary human life as rightly lived and understood must precede and prepare for descriptions of human life as predicament. Given limitations of time, no comprehensive account of Sankara's conventional anthropology is possible. His reflections on this matter are vast and include such topics as the relationship between individual soul and the Lord (*isvara*), the "dimensions of the soul," a comprehensive analysis of states of consciousness, and the relationship between the individual soul and its various organs, just to name a few. Though these and other matters merit consideration, time permits treatment of just two: the nature of the human being as free agent and the relationship of that free being with divinity.

Sankara's ultimate teaching regarding the nature of liberating knowledge is well known. The true Self is not the mind-body complex; rather, it is the light of consciousness that shines deep within the mind. This true Self is changeless, does not act, and so cannot be thought to be a free and purposeful agent. So how do persons come to think of themselves as agents with an assortment of responsibilities and obligations? And more importantly, why does scripture reinforce this notion of self as agent by specifying what persons should and should not do?

Sankara's answer to these questions begins with the notion of ignorance (*avidya*). Human beings are ignorant of their true identity as Brahman. Failing to understand Brahman's true nature, they are easily confused. The result is superimposition (*adhyasa*), which is the act of confusing two realities that are in truth utterly distinct, namely, the subject (*visayin*) and the object (*visaya*).[10] The subject is the Self that is by nature conscious (*cidatmaka*) and unchanging. By

---

10. *Vedanta-Sutras with the Commentary of Sankaracarya: Part 1*, trans. George Thibaut (Delhi: Motilal Banarsidass, 1988), 4. I shall refer to this text with the abbreviation VSBh 1. This text is a translation of Sankara's *bhasya* or commentary on the *Vedanta Sutras* also known as the *Brahma Sutras*. I also consult and cite from Swami Gambhirananda's translation, *Brahma Sutra Bhasya of Sri Sankaracarya* (Calcutta: Advaita Ashrama, 1993). The latter text will be abbreviated as BSBh.

object is meant the entire intrinsically unconscious realm of what is not the Self (*anatman*), which encompasses mind, body, and senses. In superimposition—and superimposition is how Sankara defines ignorance—persons impose the qualities or attributes of the mind-body complex onto the true Self and the attributes of the true Self onto the body-mind complex (BSBh 1; Introduction, 3). What results from this confusion called superimposition? Human beings come to think of themselves as finite, vulnerable creatures threatened by whatever poses a danger to the body-mind complex and driven by desire toward that which promises to complete the needs of body and mind. When persons confuse the true Self with what is not the Self, they attribute consciousness to mind and take it to be intrinsically, rather than derivatively, conscious and superimpose such attributes as vulnerability onto the true Self. More will be said later about superimposition as ignorance when we turn to Sankara's take on the human predicament. But before superimposition is understood from the perspective of liberating truth as a problem to be solved, it must first be understood as a relatively neutral description of life as ordinarily lived (ibid., 4.).

Identification of mind, body, and senses—Sankara calls these "limiting adjuncts" (*upadhi*)—with the conscious Self makes a person a knower and an agent. Only superimposition makes agency (*kartrtva*) possible. To conceive of oneself as a Brahmin who must perform the fire sacrifice or as a warrior obliged to fight in righteous battle is to superimpose onto oneself these contingent identities. The true Self is free from all attributes and is not a member of any class; it is free of all quality, activity, and relation. Superimposition is the source of all particular identities that derive from class membership, stage of life, and social relationships. In sum, only superimposition gives rise to the possibility of conventional experience. Superimposition, the very source of the human predicament when considered from the perspective of nonduality, forms the presupposition for conventional life with its multiple obligations.[11]

For a variety of reasons, despite his analysis of superimposition as cognitive error, Sankara does not believe that most human beings can simply and abruptly drop the habit of superimposition. A process of preparation customarily precedes introduction to liberating knowledge. Sankara believes that one must first understand conventional life rightly; only that will make it possible for persons to think and live in a manner that makes transition to ultimate truth possible. Human life must be brought under the normative

---

11. J. G. S. Hirst puts the point nicely when she writes that "while superimposition is the universal congenital fault to be overcome, it nevertheless forms the matrix which provides the very means of release." "The Place of Teaching Techniques in Samkara's Theology," *Journal of Indian Philosophy* 18 (1990): 140.

guidance of scripture. Given that persons believe themselves to be knowers, experiencers, and agents, how then should they live such that liberating transformation can eventually take place? Sankara believes that any understanding of conventional life that might interfere with liberating insight must be found wanting. Whether it be Buddhist proponents of impermanence who cannot account for the continuity necessary for the operation of causality or Buddhist idealists who deny the existence of an external world apart from mind, Sankara takes great care to dismiss misleading positions regarding the nature of everyday experience.[12]

Integral to understanding the ordinary world of experience rightly is to see that the world as experienced is unintelligible apart from a conscious and omnipotent creator. Sankara is wholly prepared to defend theism and argues that a creator God is necessary to make sense of the world as experienced. Ultimately, Sankara calls for a move beyond theism. His final position is that Brahman is not a personal Lord but, rather, the transpersonal ground of all reality, being-itself. Nevertheless, everyday notions of Brahman as conscious world-creator provide the foundation for Sankara's ultimate teaching of Brahman as absolute consciousness.

An important moment in Sankara's anthropology that demonstrates well his interest in conventional matters is his argument that the soul's capacity to act is dependent on the Lord. Having established that the individual soul in the state of ignorance, though not in truth, is an agent, Sankara raises the question about whether such agency is dependent on the Lord. The opponent argues that the soul, driven by its own faults, such as desire and aversion, is an independent actor and asks, "What has God to do with it?" In opposition to the claim that the individual soul is capable of acting on its own power, Sankara argues that the individual soul is not an agent in its own right:

> In the state of ignorance, the soul blinded by the darkness of ignorance, unable to distinguish itself from the collection of effects and instruments, derives its transmigratory state, consisting in its becoming agent and experiencer, from the behest of the supreme Self who presides over all activities and resides in all beings, and who is the witness [of all], imparts intelligence [to all], and is the supreme Lord. Liberation, too, results from knowledge that is caused by His grace.

12. For Sankara's argument against proponents of Buddhist impermanence, see BSBh 2.2.20, 406.

> Why? That is what is stated in the Vedic texts. Although the individual
> being is impelled by such defects as attachment and is endowed with
> accessories of activity, and although in ordinary experience, such
> activities as agriculture are not recognized as caused by the Lord, still
> it is ascertained from the Vedic texts that Lord is the efficient cause
> behind all activities. (BSBh 2.3.41, 504; translation modified)[13]

Here Sankara argues on Vedic grounds that human agency depends on the
Lord who is the witness and efficient cause of all worldly activities. Making
such an argument inevitably involves Sankara in theodicy problems. Despite
incurring the obligation to respond to the opponent's charge that such a Lord
would be guilty of cruelty and partiality, Sankara maintains that the soul is not
an agent in its own right. The soul's very capacity to act is derived from the Lord.
The charge of cruelty and partiality evoke from Sankara the response that the
Lord accords to each according to the merit and demerit each has accumulated
through past actions. The inequality that marks human experience is based on
karma and not divine arbitrariness. The opponent responds that this solution
is unworkable because the Lord causes each individual's action. To this argument, Sankara responds that each individual exercises responsibility for his
or her actions but that the Lord is the efficient cause making the actions of
each possible. The Lord's activity is compared to rain, which functions as the
general efficient cause supporting the growth of diverse plants, each according
to its own potentiality (BSBh 2.3.41–42, 503–6).

The details of Sankara's argument are not as important as the fact that
such an argument is ventured at all. Having established that, from the point
of view of ultimate truth, the Self is not an agent and that Brahman is free
from all causal relationships, Sankara nevertheless argues that conventional
action is grounded in the Lord's causal activity. The world of experience is

---

13. References to grace (*anugraha/prasada*) are not uncommon in Sankara's writings.
Naturally, they are likely to evoke serious interest on the part of Christian theologians. This
comparative project does not take up the question of grace centrally because Sankara ultimately believes that Brahman is not a gracious Lord but, rather, is unchanging and actionless world-ground. The proximate causes that give rise to knowledge are the Vedas and the
guru; the grace of revelation and the grace of the guru are in my estimate more important
to Sankara's thought than the notion of a gracious Lord. Moreover, the highest knowledge
offered by the gracious guru does not point to a gracious personal Lord but to the idea
that the true Self just is the Absolute (Brahman). The idea of Brahman as a gracious Lord
is only a conventional truth. For an alternative perspective that gives to divine grace a far
more central role in Sankara's work, see Bradley J. Malkovsky, *The Role of Divine Grace in
the Soteriology of Samkaracarya* (Boston: Brill, 2001).

unintelligible apart from our felt experience of ourselves as free and purposive agents. Sankara does not contest this. He is interested in teaching that the capacity for action derives from Brahman, here taken to be a personal and gracious Lord, despite knowing that such claims make him vulnerable to theodicy issues—issues that Sankara does not brush aside. On the contrary, Sankara takes these issues with the same seriousness that devotional Hindu theists do. That is why he takes special care to appeal to individual karma to refute charges of divine arbitrariness.

Sankara's willingness to argue that the soul's capacity for action comes from Brahman demonstrates that he has no trouble with the idea that agency derives entirely from divinity and yet that individual agents are nonetheless free. He sees no need to posit distance or separation as a precondition for freedom. To the contrary, Sankara follows up his argument for free agency with an argument defending the idea that human beings are part of Brahman. Sankara takes up two metaphors for the relationship between Brahman and individual souls: the relationship between a flame and its sparks and the relationship between a master and servant. Sankara opts decisively for the flame-sparks analogy as best suited for understanding the relationship between Brahman and individual souls because it best conforms to scriptural testimony and because it best conveys distinction without falling into duality (BSBh 2.3.4, 506–9).

The conclusions to be drawn are clear. A cogent and morally meaningful account of the world of conventional experience requires accepting a provisional vision of human beings as free agents. But such an account must not give the impression that human life is intelligible on its own terms apart from any relationship to Brahman. Human beings are free but they are also part of Brahman. Their capacity to be free agents is derived from Brahman in which they are always already rooted.

This view of the world is of course wholly preliminary. It is true but only conventionally so. After all, the ultimate truth about Brahman is that Brahman is *partless*. As such, human beings cannot really be a part of an indivisible reality. The ultimate truth is that the true Self just is Brahman *simpliciter*. Conventional truth is neither trivial nor false. It is worth defending by way of rigorous argumentation. Sankara believes that only a scripturally sanctioned reading of experience can prepare the way for nonduality. Leading people to a view of reality as essentially unified—the world and all that is in it is a part of Brahman—readies persons for the transition to ultimate truth of nonduality.

Sankara's arguments demonstrate the importance of agency for an adequate anthropology. The habit of superimposition taken as a given provides the epistemological foundation for conventional life. The confusion of the Self and nonself gives rise to the notion that one is a conscious embodied soul who is an agent, knower, and experiencer. This superimposition is not an errant cognitive event that occurs in the lives of individuals at some moment in time. There is no fall into this ignorance. Rather, ignorance is the root cause of the very process of beginningless transmigration and so is a congenital inheritance carrying with it accumulated results generated by innumerable actions performed over countless lifetimes. Action, whether Vedic or worldly, therefore, perpetuates transmigration. However, right action—action prescribed by the scriptures and traditional ethical treatises—sustains the good order of the world. The world is preserved and maintained by rites and duties of class and stage of life. Anything that can be enjoined—whether a rite, duty, or act of meditation—presupposes agency, which in turn takes superimposition for granted. Apart from the superimposition of consciousness onto mind and body, intentional experience and knowledge of the world as well as liberating knowledge are impossible.

Sankara makes it plain that this does not mean that the true Self is ultimately an actor, knower, or experiencer. To those who argue that scriptural injunctions require that the soul really is an agent, Sankara maintains that the scriptural injunctions merely take for granted conventional conceptions of the self created by ignorance but do not positively teach that the soul is in truth an agent (BSBh 2.3.40, 498–99). This qualification shows that the scripture does not contradict itself by teaching both that the soul is and is not an agent. By clearly distinguishing between what is *assumed* for conventional purposes and the ultimate truth expressly *taught* by scripture, Sankara demonstrates that the scriptures are not self-contradictory.

For Western readers of Sankara, what is important is not so much Sankara's defense of the internal consistency of Hindu scripture but rather Sankara's commitment to taking seriously action in the world. Sankara's willingness to defend an account of human agency as derived from Brahman belies the notion that Sankara is an otherworldly quietist wholly uninterested in action. There is indeed a place for engaged activity in religious life. In fact, most of human life is largely given over to transformative action in the world. Casual readers of Sankara can miss all this because Sankara takes the importance of action for granted. The focus of his theological energy rests on the final stage of religious life in which persons undertake renunciation in order to come to see the true nature of the Self as immutable Brahman. But transition to this final stage in religious life is impossible for those who have not lived a life of right action under the guidance of scriptural injunctions and prohibitions.

Sankara's Diagnosis of the Human Predicament: The Suffering of Samsara

Any comparative treatment of Sankara's diagnosis of the human predicament will have to face the fact that some features of his account are simply incomparable with Western accounts of the human predicament. One element in particular is absolutely singular: rebirth. The notion that human beings are caught in a beginningless cycle of transmigration is alien to Tillich's worldview but is central to Sankara's own. Great care must be taken to account for the ramifications of this basic difference. Such ramifications are manifold, especially with respect to the question of action. For Sankara, escape from the human predicament requires escape from the consequences of karma. Ultimately, this requires discarding the notion that persons are agents. Tillich's theology of ecstasy does allow for a special modality of action that is simultaneously human as well as divine and therefore different from mundane activity. In ecstatic action, there is a sense of "I and yet not I" generated by a special intimacy with ultimate reality, but there is never an outright rejection of agency.

It is possible to generate from Sankara's works an account of the human predicament as it is experienced within a single lifetime, that is to say, one that does not appeal to reincarnation. Such an account would focus on the cognitive and psychological faults and the way in which they compromise human life. An account of the human predicament that focused on such factors would be readily comparable with Tillich's reading of the human predicament as marked by unfaith, hubris, and concupiscence. Comparativists, however, must resist the temptation to ignore the idiosyncratic. An account of the human predicament that would be faithful to Sankara's thought must appreciate how these cognitive and psychological faults drive the cycle of rebirth. Only this dual focus on transmigration and the cognitive-psychological will do.

Sankara is part of a larger pan-Indic consensus—one that extends beyond Orthodox Hindu circles to Buddhists and Jains as well—that certain faults (*dosa*) or afflictions (*klesa*) compel persons to perform actions that lead to an accumulation of merit and demerit, which in turn generates rebirth.[14] Any list of faults common to several traditions would include desire (*raga*), aversion (*dvesa*), and delusion (*moha*). These three are among the basic factors that perpetuate bondage within the cycle of reincarnation. For those who seek liberation from transmigration, the most crucial questions are, "How do these afflictions come to be?" and "How can they be removed?" The answer to the first question is ignorance (*avidya*), which is the fundamental cause of the human predicament in Sankara's thought; ignorance gives rise to the afflictions that generate action. Such ignorance can only be removed by liberating knowledge.

Sankara develops his analysis of the human predicament by appeal to scriptural resources. Although Sankara does not explicitly state that an adequate analysis of the human predicament can be derived only from scripture, the conclusion follows from his position that the Veda is the only source of valid knowledge about the true nature of the Self.[15] Sankara's understanding of the human predicament can be characterized as retrospective in character: Only in the light of ultimate truth (*paramarthikasatya*) revealed by the Upanishads does the contrasting darkness of the human predicament become clearly manifest. Only revealed truth shows that ignorance is the act of superimposing the limiting adjuncts, namely the body and mind and their attributes, onto the true Self.

Identification with bodies gives rise to the notion that some things are intrinsically pleasant and desirable and others unpleasant and undesirable: Those things that generate pleasure are desirable and those that cause pain undesirable. Emotional afflictions such as desire and aversion have as their foundation superimposition. Indeed, superimposition does not end at the limits of one's body. Because every body is defined by its position in a vast matrix of obligations and relationships, superimposition also gives rise to one's unreflective attachment to children, wife, relatives, and friends, all those with whom one is in intimate relationship. Superimposition binds one's own identity and well-being to them as well. Sankara explains that the superimposition of self and other means that people are happy only when those whom they love are well and are unhappy when those whom they love are in pain.

---

14. Although lists of the various faults or afflictions vary across Indian traditions, Sankara draws no technical distinction between the faults and the afflictions. For our purposes, these terms are interchangeable.

15. The term *Veda* is used by Sankara to refer comprehensively to the entire collection of Vedic hymns, chants, and formulas; the ritual treatises (*brahmanas*); the forest treatises (*aranyakas*); and the Upanishads, which form the end (*anta*) of the Veda, the Vedanta. These texts are divided by Sankara into two sections, namely the ritual portion (*karmakanda*) and the knowledge portion (*jnanakanda*). For Sankara, only the knowledge portion, which teaches the true nature of the Self, is of ultimate importance.

Sankara goes so far as to say that human beings are like animals that turn away from persons wielding sticks and turn toward those offering grass (BSBh 1, 4). Human beings are driven by captivity to the same sort of instinctual aversions and desires. The point of Sankara's comparison is to establish that ordinary human behavior is very much like animal behavior and is constituted by an unreflective attachment to the mistaken sense of self generated by superimposition. Sankara is concerned that life must not be limited to pleasure-seeking and pain-avoiding behavior. Human desires may be more sophisticated; persons may long to attain the pleasures possible in heavenly realms, and such desires presuppose knowledge that the human soul is distinct from the body and will move on to other lives. Despite this difference in the degree and varieties of pleasures, for Sankara, human beings and animals are fundamentally similar with respect to the way in which superimposition generates essentially self-interested behavior. Ignorance prevents persons from understanding the fix they are in.[16] They cannot come to themselves spontaneously but need to hear revealed truth and to be taught the meaning of that truth by a guru before they understand the gravity of their situation.

Sankara's analyses of the human predicament vary in scope and detail. He provides several different lists of basic psychological faults.[17] He also offers several vivid metaphors and analogies to describe the character of the human

16. Halbfass has, on the basis of this discussion of animal behavior in Sankara's *Brahmasutrabhasya,* also concluded that Sankara rejects any fundamental distinction between human beings and animals that would be based on such conventional matters as rational capacity or foresight. Human beings are unique only because they have a distinctively human goal (*purusartha*) that animals in general do not, namely liberation. According to Halbfass, it is this "soteriological privilege" that distinguishes the human over against the animal. However, he also adds that there is nothing special about human nature that makes the human alone worthy of this privilege. Halbfass, *Tradition and Reflection,* 280–81.

17. Sankara occasionally uses the term affliction (*klesa*) but customarily employs the term *dosa,* which we have translated as "fault." It is difficult to determine whether and what kind of conceptual significance Sankara's choice of terms implies by way of contrast with the Yoga system to which Sankara often refers. Among the faults listed by Sankara are ignorance, desire, and aversion, three of the "afflictions" present in the *Yogasutras.* The classical Yoga of Patanjali and Vyasa, quite unlike Sankara's Advaita, invests tremendous energy on the question of mental states or operations and takes great care to distinguish between defiled (*klista*) and undefiled mental states. Yoga soteriology hinges on opposing the former with the latter and ultimately on bringing all mental processes to complete rest. Within such a context, attention to the precise nature and number of afflictions has signal importance. Sankara's soteriology, however, does not hinge on the quiescence of mental operations. Liberating knowledge does presuppose detachment and mental purity. Nevertheless, Sankara does not appear to be rigorously focused on providing a detailed or exhaustive account of the nature and number of faults.

predicament. His treatment of Upanishadic allegories about samsara is especially helpful in clarifying his understanding of the human predicament. Of these, two are particularly striking: the allegory of the transmigratory world as a vast ocean and the allegory of samsara as forced captivity in the forest of the body (*deharanyam*). An exploration of these allegories and of his many conceptual analyses of the transmigratory process will demonstrate that Sankara understands the working of samsara to be shaped by three basic causal factors, namely ignorance, desire, and action.

The most common among Sankara's many Upanishadic allegories is that of samsara as a vast ocean.[18] Sankara describes the world as

> a vast ocean that is filled with the water of suffering (*duhkha*) arising from ignorance, desire, and action (*avidyakamakarma*); that is infested with huge sea animals in the form of acute disease, age, and death; that has no beginning, end, and limit, and provides no resting place; that affords only momentary respite through the little joys arising from the contact of the senses and objects; that is full of high waves in the shape of hundreds of evils, stirred by the gale of desire for objects of the five senses; that resounds with the noise of cries and shrieks of "alas! alas!" etc. issuing from the beings condemned to various hells. . . .[19]

Readers acquainted with Buddhist texts will find Sankara's picture of samsara as an ocean full of the water of suffering and infested with disease, old age, and death very familiar. The very image of samsara as an ocean in which the raft of knowledge is the only available means for crossing over to the shore of liberation is central to Buddhist imagination.[20] Similarities between Buddhist and Advaita ways of imagining the human predicament point to deep thematic convergence. Although disagreement regarding ontological matters could not be sharper, they share the basic conviction that transmigration is characterized by suffering brought on by desire and ignorance.

Another vivid representation of samsara is found in Sankara's commentary on the *Chandogya Upanishad*. This text compares the predicament of the

---

18. I am grateful to Lance Nelson for bringing this passage to my attention.

19. Aitareya Upanishad Bhasya, *Eight Upanisads with the Commentary of Sankaracarya, Volume 2*, trans. Swami Gambhirananda (Calcutta: Advaita Ashrama, 1992), 1.2.1, 26–27; translation modified.

20. Sankara does in this very context speak of the "raft of knowledge which is furnished with such provisions for the way as truth, simplicity, charity, compassion, non-injury, control of inner and outer organs, fortitude and so on that are embellishments of the heart, and which has good company and renunciation of everything as its course and that has emancipation as its shore" (AUBh 1.2.1, 27).

transmigrator with that of a man from the country of Gandhara who is taken blindfolded from his native land and abandoned in an uninhabited place. Helpless and disoriented, the man can do nothing but cry out for help from some chance passerby. Liberation is then likened to the process whereby a person finds his way home after being unbound by a compassionate and intelligent person who sets him out in the direction he must travel. Just as the person seeking to find his way home gradually moves from village to village and eventually returns to his place of origin, so too the person desirous of liberation finds his way back to his own Self after he has been set free by his teacher.

In Sankara's hands, the Upanishadic analogy is developed into an extended allegory rich with details representing aspects of the transmigratory process. Sankara writes,

> So likewise, when a person is stolen from Being, the real Self of the universe, by thieves such as merit and demerit he is made to enter this forest of a body made of fire, water and food, full of air, bile, phlegm, blood, fat, flesh, bone, marrow, semen, worms, urine, and stool, subject to various types of miseries arising from opposites like heat, cold, etc. His eyes are bound by the cloth of delusion, fettered by thirst for many objects seen and unseen like wife, son, friend, animals, kinsmen and such. Being enmeshed by a hundred and thousand snares of misery, he goes on shouting, "I am his son, these are my friends, I am happy, I am in misery, I am deluded, I am wise, I am virtuous, I have friends, I am born, I am dead, I am emaciated, I am a sinner, my son has died, my wealth is lost; alas! I am undone, how shall I live, what will be my lot, what relief is there for me?" Somehow, because of surpassing merit, when he comes across a supremely compassionate knower of Being which is Brahman, freed from bondage, who is chief among the knowers of Brahman—and through his compassion, on being shown the path of knowing the objects of the world as full of defects, he becomes dispassionate towards all objects of the world, then he is told: "You are not a transmigrating soul possessed of such qualities as being the son of such and such a person, etc." What then? "You are that which is Being." Freed from the blindfold of the cloth of delusion which is ignorance, like the man from Gandhara, and attaining his own Self which is Being, he becomes happy and peaceful.[21]

---

21. *Chandogya Upanishad with the Commentary of Sankaracarya*, trans. Swami Gambhirananda (Calcutta: Advaita Ashrama, 1983), 6.14.2, 487–88; translation modified. Hereafter, CUBh.

Several features of this arresting constellation of images merit careful attention. Consider first the overall structure of forced captivity and return to native country that provides the narrative framework for Sankara's description of both samsara as well as liberation from samsara. The pedagogical efficacy of Sankara's allegory rests on this narrative frame. The language of returning home to Being suggests that liberation is not something absolutely new. Sankara often takes great pains to argue that liberation is instead just the true nature of the Self, and knowledge is merely the removal of superimposition and not a real transformation of the Self. The image of a return journey rather than travel to a new and foreign land nicely conveys this basic truth.

Sankara's vivid imagery also makes it plain that the journey home is impossible without external assistance. The conditions of captivity are so disorienting that the deluded are unable to find their way home under their own power. The compassionate and wise teacher must remove the blindfolds and fetters that keep a person imprisoned in the forest of the body with the help of scriptural sentences such as "You are that" (*tat tvam asi*) and point persons homeward to the Self. Lacking such assistance, one can do little else but cry out weakly for help.

This latter point deserves special attention as Sankara's nondualism is often misunderstood as an unrealistically optimistic account of the human condition. This judgment is most often a response to Sankara's contention that the Self, in truth, is never in bondage. His allegory, however, makes it unmistakably clear that an affirmation of the ultimate nondifference between the true Self and Brahman by no means amounts to naïve optimism about the human condition. Although it is true that from the perspective of ultimate truth, the Self is never captive to ignorance, this affirmation in no way minimizes the gravity of the human predicament as experienced. The true Self, which, for Sankara, is the absolute reality, may not be in bondage, but the conventional self most certainly is.

What Sankara's imagery makes most evident is that transmigration is explicitly understood as bondage within the body. If bondage is understood as forced habitation in the body, conversely, it follows that liberation is freedom from the body. Indeed, Sankara quite explicitly defines bondage as "embodiedness" (*sariratva*) and equates liberation (*moksa*) with disembodiedness (*asariratva*).

However, Sankara goes on to problematize this simple opposition between embodiedness and disembodiedness by arguing that the Self is, in truth, eternally disembodied, which is also to say eternally liberated (BSBh 1.1.4; 27–28). Likewise, the one who is liberated while living is said to be free of embodiment even though he appears to be embodied as before. This qualification of the rhetoric of the body as forest should remind readers that the Self in question is no mere isolated individual. The Self is the essence of all, the Absolute. This Self is not and never has been embodied.

Sankara's statements about the body should not lead readers to believe that he subscribes to a body-mind dualism; rather, he takes the mind-body complex to be a unity and understands superimposition to be the false identification of pure consciousness (*cit*) with the mind-body complex. The latter complex is not intrinsically conscious but only appears to be so when the light of consciousness shines therein. The relevant distinction to be drawn, the distinction that discloses the true nature of the Self as eternally liberated, is the distinction between *consciousness* and the mind-body complex and not between mind and body. Therefore, when Sankara speaks of karmically produced "association with the body," it should be understood that the entire mind-body complex is intended.

Furthermore, despite the strongly negative attitude toward bodily impurities evident in this text, the quest for liberation from embodiment is not motivated merely by aversion to bodily impurities.[22] On the contrary, for Sankara the mind-body complex in its entirety is problematic because it is the source of limitation, of finitude, to use a fitting term borrowed from Tillich's vocabulary. The Self that is in truth infinite and unlimited appears to be limited by way of its (apparent) association with the mind-body complex. In this connection, Sankara employs one of his favorite illustrations, namely, the example of air in a pot. As air in a pot appears to be limited and distinct from air outside the pot or the air in other pots, so too the all-pervasive (*sarvagata*) Self appears to be limited by individual mind-body complexes.

Lest the theme of embodiment be understood from too narrow a perspective, it is important to recognize that for Sankara all living beings, even the gods, are embodied. The case of the gods is particularly interesting and fruitful for reflection because it bolsters the argument that the quest for liberation is not motivated solely by an aversion toward impure human bodies but is instead a quest for the eternal and the infinite, a quest to transcend the limitations and relativities of existence altogether.

An important discussion about the embodiment of divine beings occurs in the context of a dispute between Sankara and his opponents as to whether

---

22. In fact, though not typical, Sankara does at times refer to the body as the city of Brahman (*brahmapuram*) and states that there is a connection between the body and Brahman because the body is the locus for the realization of Brahman (BSBh 1.3.14, 183–84).

the gods are eligible for liberation. Because the longing for liberation is one of three factors that make any being eligible (*adhikara*) for liberation, Sankara argues that the gods are embodied and therefore can and do wish to be disembodied.[23] This, of course, means that embodiment is a necessary precondition for the aspiration for liberation. That is to say, were it not the case that divine beings were embodied and thereby constrained by limitation, there would neither be the necessity nor the possibility of liberation.

The argument that even the divine beings are embodied forces Sankara to consider a number of complications. One such issue is the challenge posed by the fact that the gods must be present at a great many sacrifices simultaneously, an obligation that would appear impossible for an embodied being. Sankara responds by arguing that even as Yogins are capable of taking on multiple bodies (a matter on which all relevant parties agree), so too the gods can take on many bodies. Besides providing a window into some intriguing features of Sankara's cosmology, this argument indicates that Sankara is quite serious about divine embodiment and consequently willing to respond to obligations entailed by his position. His argument also demonstrates that even the gods long for liberation from finitude.

Because all beings are embodied, the various terms translated by the word *body* signify so broad a range of realities that it becomes apparent that embodiment functions for Sankara as a general principle of determination. In other words, for Sankara, to be embodied is to be limited, to be determinate, and all beings are, therefore, limited. Of course, the only reality that is disembodied and therefore beyond determination is Brahman.

From the point of view of conventional truth, bodily habitation does subject persons to the senses and so generates aversion to pain and lack and awakens desire for sources for pleasure and comfort. These aversions and desires prompt action, which in turn gives rise to the thieves of merit and demerit that perpetuate the transmigratory cycle. Because merit and demerit are the results of action, reference to this pair is also a reference to the binding character of action that keeps persons within the transmigration.

---

23. The other two conditions for eligibility are the capacity for liberation and nonprohibition from liberation (BSBh 1.3.33, 224). For example, quite apart from the question of desire and capacity for liberation, *sudras* are ineligible for liberation because they are prohibited from hearing the scriptures, the only right means of liberating knowledge. The *sudra* class, the lowest in the Indian class hierarchy that begins with Brahmins at the top, is obliged to serve all other classes. I follow current scholarly practice in not speaking here of "castes;" the latter term is restricted to naming the countless subgroups into which the four main classes are subdivided.

The basic image of the body as a terrifying forest provides Sankara with a great deal of freedom to describe the plight of transmigratory suffering. Whereas forests are infested with wild animals such as tigers and dangerous persons such as thieves, the forest of the body is filled with such vile things as phlegm, blood, urine, and stool. The impurity and dangers of the body are often lost on the transmigrator blinded by the force of desire. But this lack of awareness marks the distinction between the transmigrator and the man from Gandhara. The latter knows that the forest is not his true home and longs for return but deluded transmigrators do not appreciate their dire predicament.

This ironic contrast is what makes Sankara's treatment of superimposition and the identities generated by superimposition so striking. Within the allegory, ordinary expressions of identity such as, "I am his son, these are my friends, I am happy, I am in misery," and so forth are equated with the cries of the man bound in the forest hoping to attract the attention of the chance passerby. Of course, the man bound in the forest knowingly and voluntarily cries out for help. The person trapped in the forest of the body does not understand that his conventional self-identifications *are* cries for help. Quite remarkably, it follows that only the liberated teacher can understand these expressions for what they are in truth: expressions of distress.

The pedagogical function of Sankara's commentary is apparent. By employing Upanishadic metaphor, Sankara teaches readers that they are worse off than the man from Gandhara insofar as he knows that he is in a dangerous forest and must escape. Transmigrators not only ignorantly abide in the forest of the body but mistakenly accept identifications based on superimposition as their own genuine nature. The human predicament is here diagnosed as bondage within the cycle of transmigration generated by karma, produced by action, driven by desire, aversion, and delusion, which are in turn caused by ignorance.

Sankara's Etiology of the Human Predicament

What causes a person to be caught in the forest of samsara? What etiology explains why human beings find themselves in such a predicament? Sankara offers a number of different causal factors on different occasions. Some of these variations are due to the cyclical character of samsara. Because the causal factors that perpetuate transmigration operate cyclically, one can legitimately begin with any factor and eventually trace one's way back through to the others. As these causal links extend over multiple lifetimes, there can be alternative representations of the relevant causal connections. On some occasions, Sankara begins his account with the moment of death. At this juncture, the most significant causal factors are the consequences generated by past karma that give rise to the life to come. When causal analysis begins here, merit and demerit acquire signal importance. Consequently, the relevant questions for those interested in bringing rebirth to cessation are, "Can we insure that karmic consequences do not come to fruition and, if so, how?"

On other occasions, Sankara's causal analysis focuses on the connection between psychological factors, such as desire and aversion, and their root cause ignorance. Such an analysis provides a largely single lifetime account of the human predicament by temporarily bracketing from consideration the connection between these factors and past or future lifetimes. Sometimes when Sankara is engaged in this particular mode of analysis, he focuses not just on the single human being but also on the ways in which factors such as desire, aversion, and ignorance can have broad social and even cosmic consequences.

One of Sankara's most succinct statements about samsara and its causes can be found in the *Upadesasahasri*, his only authentic noncommentarial work. The account has appealing brevity and nicely illustrates the cyclical character of samsara by likening it to a wheel that rolls on endlessly. The account also takes up many of the causal factors considered in metaphorical fashion above.

> Actions produce association with a body. When there is association with a body, pleasant and unpleasant things are inevitable. From these result desire and aversion; from these actions. [From actions] virtue (*dharma*) and vice (*adharma*) result. From virtue and vice there results an ignorant man's association with a body in the same manner again. Thus this transmigratory existence rolls onward powerfully forever like a wheel. Since the root cause (*mula*) of the cycle of transmigration is ignorance (*ajnana*), its destruction is desired. Knowledge of Brahman is therefore commenced. The ultimate good results from this knowledge.[24]

This particular analysis of causal factors begins roughly where the earlier forest allegory does but with a minor modification; whereas the first allegory

---

24. *A Thousand Teachings: The Upadesasahasri of Sankara,* trans. Sengaku Mayeda (Albany: State University of New York Press, 1999), 1.1.3–5, 103. Hereafter, cited as U.

began with the two thieves merit and demerit, this account begins with the actions that produce merit and demerit. Actions in accord with one's proper duty (*svadharma*) produce positive consequences, such as birth in heavenly realms, and actions that violate the norms of duty yield negative consequences, such as rebirth in lower forms of life or even in various hells. For those seeking liberation from samsara, both sorts of consequences are unfortunate. For the person seeking liberation, any rebirth, no matter how blessed, is problematic.

Because of action's power to generate consequences that extend over the course of multiple lifetimes, Sankara argues that renunciation of action is a necessary prerequisite for liberation. If one is to bring action to a halt, one must find a way to overcome the force of such motivating factors as desire and aversion.[25] Any analysis of action as a link in the chain of causal factors must take care to consider agency (*kartrtva*) and desire (*kama*) as components in Sankara's very idea of what counts as action. According to Sankara, bodily or mental activity performed independently of the notion, "I am an agent," does not qualify as an action.

Action performed with the idea of agency in mind leads to rebirth in a hierarchy of embodied beings, a hierarchy of happiness and sorrow. That hierarchy is one in which human beings occupy the middle place. From "men to Brahma" and from "men to immobile and hellish beings," these are the two divisions to which Sankara refers (BSBh 1.1.4, 26–27). Whatever happiness there is on this scale of beings is the result of virtuous deeds, deeds in accordance with dharma, and whatever sorrow is the result of vicious deeds, deeds that violate scriptural prohibitions. Sankara states, "Thus it is well known from

---

25. It is important to note that, for Sankara, not all action is problematic. There are two important cases of nonproblematic action, namely, action performed without attachment to the fruits of action—that is to say, action performed as service to the Lord—and the "actions" of those who are liberated. As will be demonstrated in the following chapter, Sankara argues that liberated persons appear to act as they did before liberation in order not to mislead the ignorant or in order to maintain the integrity of the world. However, Sankara argues that these persons are, in truth, beyond action because they are fully aware that the Self is not an agent. Consequently, these persons, even in the midst of bodily activity, know that they are in truth beyond all activity and change and are therefore actionless. Also important for Sankara is the case of action performed without attachment to the fruits of action, which Sankara understands as action performed in service to or in worship of the Lord. In this case, the actor under the power of superimposition continues mistakenly to conceive of himself as an agent. However, because these actions are not motivated by desire for pleasurable consequences or by aversion to disagreeable ones, they serve to diminish the force of desire and aversion and so purify the mind and in this way prepare persons for liberating knowledge.

the Vedic texts, Smrtis,[26] and reasoning that this transient world is constituted by a gradation of happiness and sorrow, that this gradation occurs to persons who are subject to such faults as ignorance (*avidyadidosa*), and that it comes to them after their birth and in accordance with the gradation of their virtuous and vicious deeds. . . . In support of this there is the Vedic text, 'For an embodied being there can be no eradication of happiness and sorrow'" (BSBh 1.1.4, 27).

Action, therefore, determines one's location within the chain of beings. Regardless of how high in this chain of being one moves, all are "subject to such faults as ignorance." Just as there is no qualitative distinction between the behavior of animals and the behavior of human beings with respect to desire generated by superimposition of the body, there is no qualitative distinction between human beings and deities who are also subject to ignorance and therefore confined to their own particular varieties of embodied, relative existence.

The next pair of factors in the causal chain discussed above is desire and aversion, which emerge as a consequence of embodiment. Sankara argues that for embodied beings, contact with things pleasant and things unpleasant is inevitable. These contacts give rise to fundamental motivations, drives, habits, and emotions. These factors, namely desire and aversion, as well as a number of others of which Sankara speaks (delusion, sorrow, and fear), are too varied to allow for exhaustive enumeration. Though one might choose to highlight particular dimensions of each fault, all include affective, volitional, and cognitive dimensions. Because ignorance is the root cause of all others, the cognitive dimension enjoys special significance.

Some of Sankara's most fruitful reflections on the human predicament can be found in his commentary on the *Bhagavad Gita*. The *Bhagavad Gita* is the record of Lord Krishna's teaching to Arjuna, a teaching occasioned by the warrior-prince Arjuna's incapacity to carry through with his decision to fight in a just war, an incapacity resulting from overwhelming grief at the knowledge that he will have to kill beloved relatives and revered teachers. For Sankara, this is not the tale of one man's failure. Krishna's advice to Arjuna on how to overcome confusion and paralysis in this particular crisis is meant really as a teaching for all humanity. Sankara maintains that Arjuna's situation serves the Lord's larger

---

26. The term *smrti* refers to such texts as the *Mahabharata*, the *Bhagavad Gita*, and the *Ramayana* that enjoy a secondary scriptural status when compared to the *Vedas* and *Upanishads*, which are accorded the highest degree of authority. The *smrti* texts are "remembered" texts, texts of authoritative tradition, rather than texts that are revealed or "heard" (*sruti*) as are the Vedas.

purpose, which is to favor the whole world (*sarvalokanugrahartham*) with the knowledge that provides release from the human predicament.[27]

Sankara begins by stipulating that the entire dramatic introduction to the *Gita* up to eleventh verse of the second chapter, at which point Arjuna falls silent after telling Krishna that he will not fight, must be "explained as revealing the cause of the origin of faults such as grief and delusion which form the seed of the cycle of transmigration of all living beings."[28] This extremely dense phrase presents yet another account of how Sankara understands the human predicament.

In this account, the faults said to be responsible for perpetuating transmigration are grief (*soka*) and delusion (*moha*), not desire and aversion. Sankara refers to this pair as the seed of the cycle of transmigration (*samsarabija*).[29] As signaled earlier, it would be inappropriate to conclude prematurely that we have here a contradiction. Sankara shows considerable flexibility on this question within a single work and mentions several other factors besides these two pairs. Sankara simply recognizes that there are several faults that motivate action. It is also worth noting that Sankara does not often define these terms and takes their meanings to be obvious. There is no reason to believe that these faults have any special or distinctive function in Advaita. Likely Sankara makes no special effort to define these terms because they are shared across a number of religious systems. In this instance, he just proceeds to explain how these faults arise by using Arjuna as his illustration.

Sankara explains that Arjuna's sufferings, the sufferings that have brought on his paralysis in time of crisis, are caused by affection and fear of separation from those whom he loves. He goes on to add that both affection and the fear of separation are caused by mistaken notions (*bhrantipratyayanimitta*) about the Self of the sort, "I belong to them" and "They belong to me." The discussion of superimposition presented above indicates that these phrases, "I belong to them," and "They belong to me," serve for Sankara as a handy reference to the confusion of the subjective and the objective, the Self and the not-Self.

27. *Bhagavad Gita with the Commentary of Sankaracarya*, trans. Swami Gambhirananda (Calcutta: Advaita Ashrama, 1991), 36.

28. BGBh 2.10, 35; Gambhirananda's translation modified.

29. The frequent occurrence of biological metaphors of seed, root, soil, fruition, and growth in Sankara's thought is worth highlighting. Such images, present in many Indic traditions, play a significant role in both Yoga and Advaita traditions. Also common is the metaphor of burning or roasting seeds so that they no longer have the capacity to germinate. In order to bring samsara to an end, Sankara will argue that the seeds that perpetuate the transmigratory process must be burned.

Sankara argues that these mistaken notions render Arjuna vulnerable to grief and delusion that in turn cause Arjuna's erratic behavior, behavior that threatens to bring about dire social consequences.

> Thus indeed, Arjuna's own grief and delusion, caused by the ideas of affection, parting etc. originating from the mistaken notion, "I belong to them"; "They belong to me," with regard to kingdom, teachers, sons, allies, friends, kinsmen and relatives, have been revealed by him with the words, "How can I [fight] Bhisma in battle?" etc. His discriminating knowledge (*vivekavijnana*) overcome by grief and delusion, he desisted from war even though he had entered into a war of warrior's duty of his own accord, and set out to perform the duties of others (*paradharma*) such as living the life of a renunciant. Likewise, all living beings, their minds filled with such faults as grief and delusion will quite naturally abandon their own duties (*svadharma*) and resort to prohibited ones. Even when they perform their own duties, the activity of their speech, mind, body, etc. is motivated by a desire for reward (*phala*) and egoism (*ahamkara*). That being the case, because of the accumulation of virtue (*dharma*) and vice (*adharma*), the cycle of transmigration, characterized by desirable and undesirable births and the acquisition of pleasure and pain, continues without ceasing. Therefore, grief and delusion are the seeds of transmigration. Their cessation comes from nothing other than the knowledge of the Self, preceded by the renunciation of all action.[30]

What is most apparent in this version is the interplay between cognitive and emotional factors. The faults of grief and delusion are caused by ideas of affection and parting, a clear reference to the reality of superimposition. Here superimposition is not merely the confusion of pure consciousness with one's own mind-body complex but a confusion of the Self with an extended network of social relationships within which one is located. Superimposition of the Self with the body-mind complex gives rise to complex identities that are taken exhaustively to fix persons within limited social networks, limited when the resultant identities are compared with the true reality of the Self, which is infinite, changeless, eternal, and pure. Because of such ignorance, human beings come to think of themselves as finite, vulnerable embodied creatures whose identities are exhaustively captured within such particular identifications. Precisely such notions of vulnerability and finitude give rise to powerfully disorienting faults such as grief and delusion.

---

30. BGBh 2.10, 35–36; Gambhirananda's translation modified.

What, according to Sankara, are grief and delusion? How does he understand desire and aversion? Though Sankara employs both pairs throughout his works, grief and delusion seem to be more pervasive. This is not surprising, as Sankara shows a decided preference for Upanishadic terms. The relevant verse from the Isa Upanishad is one that Sankara cites frequently: "When to the man of realization all beings become the very Self, then what delusion, what grief can there be for that seer of oneness?"[31] Sankara says very little by way of commentary on this verse but merely indicates that grief and delusion "come to the ignorant man who does not perceive the seed of desire and activity" and labels them the effects of ignorance.

To find definitions for these terms one must turn elsewhere. Sankara's commentary on the *Bhagavad Gita* is particularly helpful. Sankara maintains there that delusion is caused by separation from the pleasant and that grief is caused by contact with pain (BGBh 2.14). These brief definitions are offered after Sankara notes that even a knowledgeable person who has been freed from the delusion that the Self is subject to destruction (because he knows the Self to be eternal by way of scriptural teaching) may be, and indeed often is, seen to be deluded by contact with heat, cold, pain, and pleasure. As the overall flow of the *Gita* makes clear, the knowledge that the Self outlasts death does not necessarily free persons from delusion occasioned by such factors as cold, heat, pleasure, and pain. From these comments, we can conclude that delusion (*moha*) refers to the partly cognitive and partly emotional obfuscation of the mind caused by separation from something desirable. The cognitive component of *moha* is the lack of clarity that sets in under such circumstances, a lack that prevents one from deciding what course of action to follow.

Still later in his commentary on the *Bhagavad Gita*, Sankara speaks about the relationship between desire (*kama*) and suffering (*duhkha*). He maintains that the ignorant man, when consumed by longing, regards desire as a friend. Only after he experiences the suffering that is the inevitable effect of desire does he come to see that his pain was brought on by his longing (BGBh 3.39). From these contexts and many others, one can legitimately conclude that grief and delusion, like desire and aversion, are effects of ignorance understood as the mutual superimposition of the Self and the body. Faults such as desire and aversion can only be removed once the true nature of the Self is understood. The mistaken notion that the Self is embodied and so vulnerable must be dismissed if one is to transcend desire, aversion, grief, delusion, and fear.

---

31. Isa Upanishad Bhasya, *Eight Upanisads with the Commentary of Sankaracarya: Volume I*, trans. Swami Gambhirananda (Calcutta: Advaita Ashrama, 1991), 7, 14; Gambhirananda's translation modified.

Anyone who does not know the Self to be different from the ultimately unreal body, senses, and mind will be easily overwhelmed by identification with such all-consuming faults. In Arjuna's case, Sankara argues that the force of grief and delusion overwhelms his discriminating knowledge (*vivekavijnana*), which, in this context, appears to be a kind of discriminating practical wisdom about where duty lies. Sankara also maintains that delusion can also be defined as the muddying of the distinction between the Self and the not-Self, a confusion that directs the mind outward toward the sense objects (BGBh 2.52). Once knowledge is overcome by grief and delusion, occasioned by his attachment to family and teachers, Arjuna lacks the clarity to follow through on his proper responsibility to fight in a just war that he had entered into by his own volition.

Sankara's analysis of Arjuna's predicament points to aspects of the human predicament that were not mentioned in the selections considered thus far. What is new in this account is that Sankara indicates that these faults have the power not just to bring about negative karmic consequences for Arjuna's next life but also to bring about larger communal or social repercussions. Not just his private karmic lot is at stake. Because these faults have the power to cause persons to violate the moral order, Sankara argues that human inclinations must be controlled by bringing actions under the province of scriptural authority. To follow the inclinations of one's own deluded nature is to be overcome by faults such as grief and desire and thereby to bring about moral and social ruination (BGBh 3.34).

Bringing human action within scriptural compass, however, does little to address the root cause of the human predicament, the unrelieved and congenital conviction on the part of human beings that they are merely finite beings defined without remainder by their particular identities as those are constituted by the limiting adjuncts of mind, body, and senses. So long as this problem remains unsolved, even action in accordance with scripture is performed only for the sake of the limited and egotistic interests of the finite self.

This is why Sankara argues that there can be no solution to the question of action and rebirth without addressing the prior construction of the self as an agent. So long as a person entertains the notion, "I am an agent," action is inevitable and so long as actions continue to be performed, rebirth will continue. Earlier in the chapter, the argument was made that Sankara's conventional anthropology left in place the notion that the individual soul is an agent with the important qualification that the individual soul must rely on the Lord who is the ultimate cause of all action. However, it was also noted that Sankara took great care to indicate that the Self, in truth, is not an agent. He writes,

> [W]e say that it is not possible for the soul to have natural agency, for that would lead to a negation of liberation. If agency is the very nature of the Self, there can be no freedom from it, as fire can have no freedom from heat. Moreover, for one who has not got rid of agency, there can be no achievement of the highest human goal, for agency is a form of suffering. . . . Moreover, it has been stated that liberation stands established from the fact that the soul has been expounded . . . to be eternally pure, enlightened, and free. But the presentation of such a soul cannot be logically justified if agency is natural. Hence the agency of the soul arises from the superimposition of the attributes of the limiting adjuncts; it is not innate.[32]

Plainly then, Sankara contends, the problem of transmigration is fundamentally connected to an ontological and anthropological question regarding the nature of the Self. If the Self is really an agent, action and its consequences are inescapable, and there is no possibility of rest, of cessation from action. Escape from samsara is possible only if the Self is in truth beyond action. Otherwise action and its consequences would continue to perpetuate the cycle without end. Sankara believes that the Self can only rest from its (apparent) labors like a carpenter who leaves his tools in his workshop and then returns home contented if and only if the Self is distinct from such tools as mind, body, and senses, and therefore intrinsically free from agency. That the Self is intrinsically free from agency is known on scriptural grounds. Revealed texts that state that the Self is eternal and changeless rule out for Sankara any possibility that agency can be attributed to the Self.

The intimate connection here between soteriology and ontology is worth emphasizing. Because he believes that one must escape action in order to escape transmigration, it is essential for Sankara to conceive of the Absolute Self as unchanging. One can escape action only if the Self is not an agent. Consequently, Sankara conceives of Brahman as an unchanging absolute rather than as dynamic creativity. This conception of being-itself differs significantly from Paul Tillich's conception of God as living.

---

32. BSBh 2.2.40, 498–99; Gambhirananda's translation modified.

The Impossible Possibility of Ignorance

The preceding discussion of Sankara's conception of the human predicament ought to have demonstrated that it is one thing to maintain that Being, the true Self of the universe, is eternally beyond change and suffering and another matter entirely to say that the category of the human predicament is inapplicable to life as ordinarily lived. On the contrary, according to Sankara, human beings from time without beginning have been subject to deep and pervasive ignorance regarding their own true nature. There is no fall into ignorance in Sankara's thought but, rather, only the beginningless round of birth and death.

The human predicament can also be described not just in terms of rebirth and death but also in terms of the many faults and afflictions to which human beings are subject, namely, aversion, grief, delusion, and fear. These faults compel human beings toward self-centered action. Even when action is in accord with scriptural norms, those actions are almost always performed in the interests of the finite self, the false creation of superimposition. Even actions in accord with dharma do not fundamentally alleviate the pain of the human predicament, although it is true that scripturally sanctioned actions must trump those that threaten or violate cosmic and social order. All beings on the scale of transmigration are subject to such relativities as pain and pleasure, happiness and sorrow. All alike are subject to ignorance. Manifestly, ignorance understood as superimposition is the primary etiological cause of the human predicament.

But suppose inquiry proceeds still further by asking, where does ignorance itself come from? Put more abstractly, what is the cause of the cause of the human predicament? Just who is ignorant? "Whose is *avidya*?" These questions have been bracketed from all that has thus far been said about the human predicament with good reason. For quite some time, Sankara scholars have known, thanks especially to the work of Daniel H. H. Ingalls, that Advaitins find questions regarding the origin and ontological status of ignorance vexing. Ingalls has also shown that Sankara's own approach to the question differs considerably from those of both his predecessors and his disciples.[33]

The problematic character of questions of origin can be expressed simply. For the nondualist who maintains that only the Self is ultimately real, the question "Whose is *avidya*?" is not easily answered. On the one hand, the eternal Self is beyond ignorance and cannot be deluded. On the other hand, there is

---

33. See Daniel H. H. Ingalls, "Sankara on the Question: Whose Is Avidya?" *Philosophy East and West* 3, no. 1 (1953): 69–72.

really no other knower who can be deluded, particularly as the very idea of individual selfhood is a product of ignorance. So then, whose is *avidya*?

As Ingalls has demonstrated, Sankara steadfastly refused to answer this question. Sankara insists on treating ignorance as a practical and pedagogical matter. To the student who asks, "Who is ignorant?" Sankara answers that the student himself is ignorant as his very question reveals. If, on the contrary, the student claims that the scripture teaches that he is Brahman and therefore not ignorant, then Sankara responds that the student ought not to pose the question if he already knows that no one in truth is ignorant.[34]

Does Sankara's strategy amount to mere sophistry? I think not. Sankara's response to students suggests that there is no way to account rationally for the irrational let alone to give ignorance proper accommodation within a nondualist ontology. To suggest that ignorance is real as Brahman is real is immediately to lapse into dualism—something that Sankara refuses to do. Ignorance remains an empirical given; people suffer because they do not know their true nature to be Brahman. Despite the somewhat humorous nature of Sankara's dialectical play with the student, he does not frivolously dismiss the pain and sorrow that marks the human predicament. Rather, Sankara is primarily concerned to eliminate such suffering rather than theorize its sources.

Readers familiar with Tillich will recognize in Sankara's rejection of a theoretical explanation for ignorance a deep similarity with Tillich's refusal to provide a rational account for the fall. Any such explanation runs the risk of making sin seem a necessary part of the divine plan. "Symbolically speaking, sin would be seen as created, as a necessary consequence of man's essential nature" (ST 2:29). The same may be said of ignorance in Sankara's thought. He refused to provide a logical explanation for the existence of ignorance. Any such account would give to ignorance an ontological status and so make it real as Brahman is real. One would then have to speculate about the kind of reality ignorance has and how that reality is related to the being of Brahman. Sankara adopts instead an alternative strategy, one that allows that ignorance is an indisputable fact of experience but refuses to give ignorance any ontological status whatsoever.

At this juncture, the medical model is strained by the ingenuity, novelty, and theological subtlety of Sankara's thought. Sankara's refusal to explain how ignorance is possible is tantamount to admitting that there can be no finally satisfying etiology for the human predicament. We cannot finally say

34. See BSBh 4.1.3.

why human beings are ignorant and so suffer the pains of the cycle of rebirth. We can point only to what observation shows: People suffer due to ignorance. To say anything more would be rule out what Sankara goes on to affirm. In truth—that is to say from the perspective of ultimate truth—there is no ignorance and no one who is ignorant. Only Brahman is, and Brahman is most assuredly not ignorant. At this level of argumentation, the medical model is not just strained but transcended. Sankara's ontological soteriology requires persons to surrender conventional identity and to identify themselves wholly with Brahman. Once knowledge of one's identity with Brahman is established, one realizes that Brahman can in no sense fall victim to the disease of samsara caused by ignorance.

This situation is only apparently analogous to the following medical scenario: Doctors can often trace a set of symptoms back to a disease, know enough about the disease to treat it, and yet be unable to determine how the patient came to have the disease in the first place. But Sankara's soteriology is still more radical. When one comes to know oneself as Brahman, the very idea of disease and ignorance is abandoned as Brahman cannot be ignorant. That is why Sankara rigorously rejects any explanation that would give to ignorance any ontological standing. Perhaps a more appropriate medical analogy is to be drawn from Munchausen syndrome. Patients display all the symptoms of a given disease and are genuinely miserable, so much so that physicians can be misled by presenting symptoms. But, in truth, the patient is not ill, or at least not ill as he or she believes. In Sankara's case, once persons come to know that they are in truth Brahman, it becomes quite clear that Brahman is wholly and eternally free from disease.

Like Sankara, Tillich does not want to make sin an ontological inevitability; whether he succeeds in accomplishing what he intends is a matter of debate. For Tillich, sin is the result of finite freedom. In Tillich's words, "man" chooses to actualize his own finite freedom and stand on his own ground at the cost of estrangement from the ground of being. Tillich's language is the language of volition, not of cognition. This emphasis on volition introduces weighty differences between Tillich and Sankara. Tillich argues that creaturely freedom requires that the creature enjoy substantial independence over against God. There must be, Tillich insists, some distance between creature and creator if the creature is to be free. This distance is the condition for the possibility of human sin, but the choice to actualize that freedom in separation is in part a contingent decision. Nonetheless, because Tillich posits an ontological distance between the divine and the human as the necessary precondition for the possibility of choice, Tillich shows not only how human fallenness is possible but also that it is *empirically* inevitable. When human beings choose to actualize autonomous freedom, they introduce a real separation between themselves and their divine ground. For Tillich, such separation is ontologically real and not merely a matter of felt experience.

Sankara posits no such distance. From the point of view of ultimate truth, there is no distance between the persons and Brahman, and there is no ignorance. Even from the point of view of conventional truth, human freedom is said to be possible only because Brahman as Lord makes freedom possible. Human freedom is assumed and does not presuppose any distance or separation; on the contrary, it is precisely because Brahman as Lord is the material and efficient cause of creatures that freedom is even a possibility. Clearly, there are important differences between Sankara and Tillich regarding the etiology of the human predicament despite a common commitment to the premise that ignorance and fallenness are not logically necessary.

Much more work, however, remains to be done before sustained reflection on these deep affinities and apparent differences can begin. Sankara's understanding of the human predicament is incomplete without an appreciation of the true nature of the Self together with an account of how that true Self is discovered. Such an account must of necessity clarify ontological convictions regarding the reality of the Self and the "unreality" of what is other than the Self. Only then can we bring Tillich and Sankara together for fruitful and illuminating conversation.

chapter three

Sankara on Liberation from the Human Predicament

Prognosis and Therapy

❧❧❧

Is Healing Available Premortem or Only Postmortem?

The previous chapter read Sankara through the category of the human predicament. In Sankara's own terms, the human predicament is diagnosed as
bondage to the cycle of transmigration. That cycle is perpetuated by action
and its consequences, namely merit and demerit. Human beings who seek liberation from samsara must renounce action. But persons cannot simply stop
acting; they are compelled to activity by such faults as desire, aversion, delusion, and fear. So long as these forces remain active, no attempt to refrain from
action can succeed. These faults can only be eliminated once their root cause
is removed.

The root cause of desire and action is ignorance, ignorance concerning the
true nature of the Self. Human beings fail to understand that their true nature
is Being (*sat*), which is, in Sankara's language, the true Self of the universe.
Instead they believe that their identities are exhaustively defined by body, mind,
and senses. Such identification gives rise to the notion that human beings are
nothing more than individual actors, knowers, and experiencers. These identities, however, are transitory and so by definition ultimately unreal.

Given the centrality of action's role in perpetuating transmigration, the
notion of agency is especially problematic; so long as persons take themselves
to be agents, they cannot escape the force of action, just as fire cannot be free
from light or heat. To remove ignorance is to remove the false notion that
one is an agent. To be free of false identifications is to realize that the true
Self is identical with Brahman, the absolute world-ground. Such knowledge

removes desire, aversion, fear, and other faults that arise from identification with embodiment. It is the cure for the disease of ignorance.

How can curative knowledge of nonduality be attained? Is such knowledge the product of exceptional mystical intuition or insight? What role, if any, do ritual and meditation play in the process of coming to knowledge? What does the human being who is free from bondage to faults such as desire, aversion, sorrow, and delusion look like? Answers to these questions will generate an account of Sankara's therapy and prognosis for the human predicament.

I begin this investigation by posing a troubling preliminary question. Is it reasonable to expect from Sankara a description of human life as it is apart from such faults? If the human predicament is understood as bondage to rebirth, the most basic meaning of liberation must be escape from transmigration. If liberation is so understood, can Sankara's work yield a vision of human wholeness since the ultimate goal is not so much a fault-free human life as it is escape from life altogether? In brief, is the desired prognosis of complete healing available premortem or only postmortem?

I argue that Sankara's work, particularly his vision of the person who is liberated while living (*jivanmukta*), provides rich resources for a compelling premortem vision of human healing. Indeed, because the Self is ultimately never in bondage but only ignorantly construed so to be, liberation (*moksa*) is not in fact a thing to be achieved but is rather the Self's true nature. In the final analysis, Sankara maintains that *liberation* is just another word for Brahman. Knowledge of Brahman is nothing but the removal of the ignorant notion that the eternal Self is embodied, finite, and subject to transmigration. Consequently, there can be no final ontological difference between the self of the liberated person and postmortem reality of the Self beyond transmigration.[1]

Knowing and Not Knowing Brahman:
On Why Sankara Is Not a Mystic

Is healing knowledge of Brahman to be attained by way of mystical experience? As has already been noted, the category of mysticism is frequently and even routinely applied to Sankara's thought. I shall argue that Sankara is no

---

1. For a more extensive treatment of the theme of living liberation in Sankara, see Lance E. Nelson, "Living Liberation in Sankara and Classical Advaita: Sharing the Holy Waiting of God," in *Living Liberation in Hindu Thought*, ed. Andrew O. Fort and Patricia Y. Mumme (Albany: State University of New York Press, 1996), 17–62. See also Andrew Fort, "Knowing Brahman While Embodied: Sankara on *Jivanmukti*," *Journal of Indian Philosophy* 19 (1991): 369–89.

mystic if the term is taken to refer to someone who knows ultimate reality by way of epistemologically extraordinary experience. Sankara rejects the possibility of epistemologically extraordinary experience of the sort that modern thinkers typically categorize as mystical. For Sankara, scripture is the only valid source of liberating knowledge.[2] So long as Sankara continues to be misread as a mystic committed to experiencing Brahman, his commitment to Brahman as radical mystery will go unappreciated.[3]

Sankara should be read not as a mystic but rather as an apophatic theologian. The term *apophasis* is regularly defined in multiple and incompatible ways. Often apophatic theology is equated with negative theology, which affirms that language stipulating what God is not is truer than positive language about what God is. Apophatic theology is more accurately characterized as theology that knows ultimate reality as language-transcending mystery beyond either positive or negative description. Apophatic discourse—the very term bespeaks a conundrum—proclaims that the ultimate reality is beyond good, beyond being, beyond all predication.[4]

The relationship between mystical experience and apophatic theology is complex. It is often assumed that every apophatic theology is rooted in and calls for a mystical experience of union with divinity beyond language. Sankara, on the other hand, is an apophatic theologian who rejects the idea that ultimate reality can be experienced.

A compelling treatment of the relationship between apophasis and mystical experience is to be found in Denys Turner's *The Darkness of God*.[5] Turner argues that patristic and medieval apophatic theologians are regularly misread as mystics who have extraordinary experiences. The negative language they employ to deny the possibility that God can be experienced is regularly mis-

---

2. The most vigorous defense of the final authority of scripture and a challenge to the so-called priority of mystical experience in Sankara's thought can be found in the work of Anantanand Rambachan. The argument presented here is indebted to Rambachan's work. See *Accomplishing the Accomplished: The Vedas as a Source of Valid Knowledge in Sankara* (Honolulu: University of Hawaii Press, 1991).

3. As noted in chapter 2, the task of confronting and ultimately deconstructing the mystical Sankara is important to this project because Tillich understood Hinduism, and in particular Vedanta, as compromised by its quest for mystical experience. An accurate reading of Sankara should help to demonstrate that Tillich's reservations regarding mystical experience are inapplicable to Sankara's theology.

4. The font of apophatic theology in Christian tradition is Pseudo-Dionysius. See *Pseudo-Dionysius: The Complete Works*, trans. Colm Luibhéid and Paul Rorem (Mahwah, N.J.: Paulist Press, 1987).

5. See Denys Turner, *The Darkness of God: Negativity in Christian Mysticism* (New York: Cambridge University Press, 1995), 4–5.

read as descriptions of a peculiar language-transcending negative experience. Turner names this error "experientialism." Such "experientialist" patterns of misreading are not limited to Christian circles. Sankara is regularly misread in the same way.

Just what then does it mean to know Brahman? Brahman is not an entity characterized by genus, quality, activity, or relation. Consequently, it cannot be known as conventional realities are known. Sankara maintains that although Brahman cannot be known, scripture teaches that Brahman is the innermost Self (*pratyagatman*). By stripping away mistaken notions that arise when persons confuse the innermost Self with mind, body, and senses, the nonduality of the Self (Atman) and Brahman can be taught. The content of liberating knowledge is the insight *that* one truly is Brahman. *What* Brahman is—both despite and because of its radical immanence—remains unknowable.

The most important textual locus in which Sankara addresses knowledge of Brahman is in his commentary to the *Kena Upanishad* (KeU). The KeU sounds a strongly apophatic note regarding Brahman. Sankara shows that the KeU takes up and resolves the potentially crippling problem posed by its own radical insistence on the unknowability of Brahman: Liberating knowledge might be rendered impossible. Consider the dilemma: If the fundamental etiological problem is cognitive in nature—we do not know what we truly are—then what would follow if Brahman cannot be known? The human predicament might then be irresolvable, a disease without a cure. The Upanishad acknowledges that the mind (*manas*) cannot know Brahman because as the innermost Self, it is the mind's own ground. However, the innermost Self does not need to be cognized because it is self-luminously present as the light of consciousness in the midst of each and every cognition.

Sankara bases his position on the following verses: "The eye does not reach there; neither does speech nor mind. We do not know, we do not understand how It can be taught."[6] "It is known to whom it is unknown; he does not know to whom it is known. For whom it is understood, it is not understood; To whom it is not understood, it is understood."[7] These verses appear to dismiss the possibility that Brahman can be known and instead maintain that only those who do not know, that is to say, only those who know that Brahman cannot be known, can be said to understand in truth. But these verses, Sankara argues, also point the way to the knowledge of Brahman as the innermost Self (*pratyagatman*), the unchanging ground of all changing cognitive states. The

---

6. KeU 1.3, 48; translation modified.
7. KeU 2.3, 65; translation modified.

Kena speaks of this innermost reality with a host of expressions, such as "ear of the ear," "mind of the mind," and "eye of the eye" (KeU 1.2). Sankara explains that such expressions are necessary because the innermost Self is not a substance endowed with attributes. If the Self were such a reality, then it could be designated directly apart from its association with activities of eye, ear, and mind. But the "changeless, undecaying, immortal, fearless, and unborn" reality is beyond all attribution (KeUBh 1.2, 45).[8] Speech about the Self is possible only by means of indirect communication.

Precisely because Brahman is the innermost Self, the mind is unable to know that by which it knows. Contrary to conventional appearances generated by superimposition, Sankara argues that the mind is not conscious in and of itself. The mind's capacity (*samarthyam*) to carry out its functions is contingent on illumination provided by the infinite and unconditioned light of consciousness (*cit*), which is the light of the Self (*atmajyoti*) (KeUBh 1.2, 44).[9] However, the mind so illumined is unable to turn back on the light on which it depends; this, Sankara argues, is an outright impossibility. Just as fire cannot burn itself or the point of the sword cut itself, the Self cannot know itself (KeUBh 2.3, 48). Sankara makes the point concisely: "For the knower cannot be known by the knower, just as fire cannot be consumed by the consuming fire; and there is no other knower different from Brahman to whom Brahman can become a separate knowable" (KeUBh 2.1, 59).

8. Rambachan provides a helpful and compact account of Sankara's strategies of indirection for teaching nonduality; *Accomplishing the Accomplished*, 68–70.

9. Readers acquainted with Augustine will recall the Saint's discussions of the light within. See Augustine, *Confessions*, trans. Henry Chadwick (New York: Oxford University Press, 1998), 123. In Book VII, he writes, " I entered and with my soul's eye . . . saw above that same eye of my soul the immutable light higher than my mind. . . . It transcended my mind, not in the way that oil floats on water, nor as heaven is above earth. It was superior because it made me, and I was inferior because I was made by it. . . . When I first came to you, you raised me up to make me see that what I saw is Being, and that I who saw am not yet Being. And you gave a shock to the weakness of my sight by the strong radiance of your rays, and I trembled in love and awe." The similarities and differences between Augustine and Sankara on divine light are telling and worth exploring. Both agree that this light that illumines the mind is not the mind but is far above it. Both agree that this light is immutable and is Being. The difference is that Sankara would have seekers identify themselves with the light and see the light and not the mind-body complex as the true Self. Augustine, on the other hand, contends that creatures are neither Being as God is nor nonbeing; they are contingent, created beings who are illumined by light and participate in it but are not that light itself. Sankara would regard such claims as close to the mark but finally inadequate to the ultimate truth of nonduality. As creatures have no being or consciousness apart from the divine light, Sankara believes that it would be truer to regard that divine light as their true being, their true Self.

Does this epistemological obstacle mean that liberating knowledge of the Self is impossible? Not at all. Liberating knowledge consists just in knowing that one's true Self is Brahman. The knowledge that the Self is Brahman brings an end to the disciple's desire to know Brahman as though it were an external reality to be sought after (KeUBh 1.4).

In what sense can the person who knows that Brahman is the light of consciousness claim to know Brahman? Sankara notes that some may mistakenly come to believe that consciousness is an essential and defining property of Brahman and thereby labor under the impression that to know Brahman is to know Brahman as a substance that has consciousness as its essential attribute. He dismisses such claims and argues that even in scriptural accounts about Brahman, terms such as *consciousness* are used with reference to Brahman as associated with mind and body. Even consciousness ought not to be understood as describing the essential nature of Brahman. Brahman, as it is apart from all conditioning or limiting adjuncts, cannot be positively designated by any term or concept (KeUBh 2.1). Unconditioned Brahman is utterly unknowable.

If Brahman is completely unknown, then what differentiates liberated knowers of Brahman from those who are just plain ignorant? After all, both do not know Brahman (KeUBh 2.4).[10] To resolve this conundrum, Sankara must show that the not-knowing of the knowers of Brahman is different from sheer ignorance such that the former is productive of liberation while the latter obviously is not.

Sankara understands the *Kena* to resolve this dilemma by stating that Brahman can be known only with each cognition as the very Self of those cognitions.[11] Although Brahman cannot be known in itself, it can be known

---

10. That Sankara feels compelled to acknowledge and respond to this extreme possibility is an indication of how seriously he takes the Upanishad's assertion that Brahman is unknowable.

11. Sankara's resolution to the dilemma posed by the need to know Brahman and the constraints imposed by the unknowability of Brahman cannot be understood apart from his interpretation of KeUBh 2.4, especially the key phrase "*pratibodhaviditam matam.*" The great burden of Sankara's exegetical efforts hinge, in particular, on a proper interpretation of the key term *pratibodha*. Olivelle's much acclaimed translation of the Upanishads renders the phrase as follows, "When one awakens (*pratibodha*) to know (*viditam*) it, one envisions (*matam*) it. . . ." *Upanisads*, trans. Patrick Olivelle (New York: Oxford University Press, 1996), 228. Sankara does not interpret the verse in this way; indeed, he takes particular care to dismiss "awaken" as a possible interpretation of *pratibodha*. Instead, he renders *pratibodhaviditam* to mean "*bodha bodha prati viditam,*" a rather surprising and unlikely grammatical analysis that means "known (*viditam*) with each cognition (*bodha*)." This analysis provides the basis for Sankara's argument that Brahman is known only when it is known as the Self of each cognition.

indirectly as the illuminating light present in each cognitive event. Knowledge of Brahman amounts to a scripturally generated conviction *about* Brahman, namely that Brahman is the Self of all cognitions. Direct cognition of Brahman is ruled out as an epistemological impossibility.[12]

Knowledge that Brahman is the Self suffices for liberation because it brings an end to the false notion that human beings are nothing but ignorant, finite, and suffering creatures, the notion that is the root cause of transmigration. Because a false notion is the root cause of all human misery, only a true one can bring misery to an end. The wisdom of the wise consists in this knowledge of nonduality. Sankara states,

> The Self, that encompasses all cognitions as its objects, is known in relation to all these cognitions. Being the witness of all cognitions (*sarvapratyayadarsi*), and by nature nothing but the power of Consciousness, the Self is indicated by the cognitions themselves, in the midst of the cognitions, as pervading [all of] them. There is no other door to Its awareness. Therefore when Brahman is known as the innermost Self . . . of cognitions, then is It known, that is to say, then there is Its complete realization (*samyagdarsanam*).[13]

This brief but crucial statement is Sankara's most precise description of what knowledge of Brahman is and is not. To know Brahman as the unchanging witness that is the ground for all cognition is to know it as the eternal, unconditioned, innermost Self. By teaching that Brahman is this witness, the scriptures make it known that the Self is radically distinct from all that

---

12. This point has been considered with great insight in Paul Hacker's important article, "*Cit* and *Noûs*, or the Concept of Spirit in Vedantism and in Neoplatonism," in *Philology and Confrontation: Paul Hacker on Traditional and Modern Vedanta*, ed. Wilhelm Halbfass (Albany: State University of New York Press, 1995), 214. Hacker writes,

> That principle which makes knowledge possible—knowledge of all kinds, sensorial perception as well as mental insight and discursive thinking—cannot naturally be grasped or comprehended by that of which it is the very basis of existence. Whatever names we may give to the principle that makes both mental and sensuous acts or events possible, whether we call it consciousness or spirit or thought or knowledge, it is absurd to assume that this principle should need an act of knowledge in order to attain that status which we call "to be known" or "to be manifest."

13. KeUBh 2.4, 66–67; Gambhirananda's translation modified.

is witnessed and so bring an end to superimposition. Knowledge is just this removal of superimposition and nothing more. Persons who truly understand that the Self is the eternal witness no longer seek to know the Self in any other way because such knowledge is impossible: "He who knows that the vision of the seer is eternal, does not wish to see It in any other way. The wish to see the seer comes to an end because of its very impossibility, for nobody longs for a thing that does not exist."[14]

Wilhelm Halbfass nicely sums up the import of this discussion concerning the nature of liberating knowledge: "Sankara does not invoke any extraordinary 'psychological events,' and he does not try to validate the truth of non-dualism by referring to 'visionary' or 'mystical' experiences of extraordinary persons. Instead, he reflects on the nature of self-awareness and immediacy, as it is present even in ordinary life, and he tries to find in it what the Upanishads teach explicitly. However, he insists that without the guidance of revelation such reflection would not be able to uncover the true, i.e., non-dual nature of 'experience' and the self."[15] What seekers need is not a special set of *experiences* but an understanding of the very character of *experiencing* as such. What is nearest to hand, however, is too near to be known. Scripture accomplishes what experience cannot. It teaches us that Brahman is the light of consciousness that illumines the mind and so is the true Self. That knowledge is the cure for the disease of suffering caused by ignorance.

On Knowing Brahman as Being, Nonbeing, and Beyond Being

This treatment of liberating knowledge in Sankara's thought has largely proceeded by appeal to the notion of consciousness. However, the concept of being (*sat*) also plays an important role in Sankara's Advaita. An adequate understanding of his theology is impossible without a careful scrutiny of his many approaches to being. As being-itself is also at the heart of Tillich's theology, the work of comparison requires a careful consideration of being in Sankara's thought.

Of central importance here is an inquiry into the ontological and soteriological motivations behind Sankara's radical assertion that the everyday world

---

14. BUBh 1.4.10, 109; translation modified.

15. Wilhelm Halbfass, *India and Europe: An Essay in Understanding* (Albany: State University of New York Press, 1988), 390.

is unreal. Without a doubt, this claim of unreality is what most Western readers find objectionable. I shall demonstrate that in the final analysis Sankara's true goal is not so much to deny the reality of conventional experience as it is to establish the absolute ontological priority of Brahman. The contention that the world of name and form has no independent reality, no being of its own, is but one half of an argument that aims to establish that the being of conventional realities is simply Brahman understood as being-itself.[16]

Sankara scholars have long recognized that the Advaitin exercises considerable reserve when employing the term *being* to speak of Brahman.[17] Put simply, the reality of Brahman exerts pressure on being that the term cannot readily bear. The inadequacy of language in general and being in particular does not mean that Sankara summarily abandons being as an unusable notion. Rather, Sankara believes that one's conception and use of the term *being* must change as preliminary ideas about Brahman are adopted and eventually discarded in favor of more nearly adequate ones. Consequently, for Sankara, when *sat* is used to speak of Brahman, the term bears the following meanings: (1) being as the material and efficient cause of beings; (2) being as unchanging ground and substratum for changing projections; and (3) being proper, a notion applicable only to the unchanging reality of Brahman and inapplicable to the (questionable) reality of the world. Even this last meaning is ultimately inadequate to the reality of Brahman, which transcends all conceptualization, even the thought of pure being. Sankara will eventually go so far as to say that Brahman is beyond being. Taken together, these uses of being as well as his claim that the term is finally inadequate to the reality of Brahman constitute a set of pedagogical strategies that teach the liberating truth of nonduality by progressively employing and then discarding guises that Brahman appears to wear. For Sankara, Brahman is always the primary object of theological interest and not being as such. That is why "being" must be sacrificed when its meanings threaten to obscure rather than illuminate understanding of Brahman.

16. That a discussion of ontology is essential to Sankara's theological anthropology should not be surprising. Consider Halbfass's apt observation that Sankara's "concept of liberation, that is, of coinciding with the absolute reality and identity of Brahman has an undeniably ontological dimension. Familiar distinctions of 'philosophical theory' and 'soteriological practice' are not well-suited to describe Sankara's peculiar 'soteriontology.'" Wilhelm Halbfass, *On Being and What There Is: Classical Vaisesika and the History of Indian Ontology* (Albany: State University of New York Press, 1992), 39.

17. On Sankara's reservations about applying the term *sat* to Brahman see Paul Hacker's "Sankara the Yogin and Sankara the Advaitin," in Halbfass, ed., *Philology and Confrontation*, 111–12.

Being as Material and Efficient Cause of the Universe: Isvara

The most rudimentary understanding of Brahman as being in Sankara's thought defines being as that from which the manifest universe is born, a notion that finds classical expression in the *Chandogya Upanishad* (CU). In these verses, being is understood as material and efficient cause of the manifest universe. When Brahman is considered under the rubric of causality, Sankara takes Brahman to be the conscious and personal Lord who creates, sustains, and finally destroys the manifest universe. At this level of discourse, Sankara can be read as a theologian for whom being and Brahman as Lord are one and the same.

The relevant Upanishadic verses in which this notion of being finds expression are as follows:

> My dear, in the beginning all this was being alone, one only without a second. With regard to that, some say all this was nonbeing alone, one only without a second. Therefore, from nonbeing was born being. "But, my dear, how indeed can that be?" he said. "How can being be born from nonbeing? My dear, this was indeed being alone, one only without a second." (CU 6.2.1-2)[18]

In his commentary, Sankara glosses the word *sat* as follows: "The word *sat* means mere existence (*astitamatram*), a reality (*vastu*) that is subtle, without distinction, all-pervasive, one, taintless, partless, consciousness, which is known from all the Upanisads."[19] In his subcommentary on Sankara, Anandagiri explains that Sankara's gloss on the term *being* dismisses the notion that the word *being* has for its object the highest universal.[20] Religious life as envisioned by Sankara is not oriented toward an abstraction. Rather, the word *sat* refers to a positive reality that is pure being described as all-pervasive, one, taintless, and so forth.

The process of creation is described as the transformation of undifferentiated, pure being into particular "name and form" (*namarupa*) realities. Sankara offers the supporting example of a man who sees a potter lay out a lump

---

18. The translation is mine; I have consulted and appropriated elements from both Patrick Olivelle's and Swami Gambhirananda's translations.

19. CUBh 6.2.1, 413; translation modified.

20. *sacchabdasya samanyavisayatvam vyudasyati.* See *Chandogyopanishad: Upanishadbhashyam Volume Two with the Bhashya of Shri Shankaracharya Adorned by the Commentaries of Acharyas Shri Narendra Puri, Shri Ananda Giri, and Shri Abhinava Narayananandendra Sarasvati* (Varanasi: Mahesh Research Institute), 214.

of clay in the morning and upon his return later in the day sees pots and plates and infers that the pots were made from the clay he had seen earlier in the day. In the case of creation, being is without a second. Unlike clay, which requires the potter to serve as efficient cause, being is without a second and so must be both material and efficient cause of the manifest universe.

For Sankara, the pots and plates are merely the contingent names and forms taken on by the clay. The *Chandogya* is quite illuminating in this regard: "It is like this, son. By means of just one lump of clay one would perceive everything made of clay—the transformation is a verbal handle, a name—while the reality is just this: 'It's clay.'"[21] In his commentary on this verse, Sankara argues that an effect can be known by knowing its cause because an effect is not different from its cause. It is a basic premise of Advaita thought that the effect preexists in the cause (*satkaryavada*). This notion provides the conceptual foundation that gives the clay pot analogy its efficacy within Sankara's overall argument. Transformation is but a name; it does not ultimately refer to an independent reality over and above clay. Just as a pot is really just clay, so too all existents are nothing other than transformations of being, qualified by contingent name and form. As evanescent transformations of being, they have no independent ontological reality.

Sankara also maintains that the idea of Brahman as material and efficient cause can be shown to be rationally defensible. His willingness to argue for the rational defensibility of an understanding of being as material and efficient cause is important because it helps to root out representations of Sankara as a subjective idealist for whom the world has no extra-mental reality. Sankara rejects that notion without qualification: "That omniscient and omnipotent source must be Brahman from which occur the birth, continuance, and dissolution of this universe that is manifested through name and form, that is associated with diverse agents and experiencers, that provides support for actions and results, having well-regulated space, time, and causation, and that defies all thoughts about the real nature of its creation" (BSBh 1.1.2, 14).

Despite his arguments for a theistic conception of Brahman or being as material and efficient cause of the world, Sankara eventually goes on to argue that Brahman cannot be understood adequately by appeal to causality. At the heart of the matter lies Sankara's commitment to the position that Brahman does not and cannot undergo transformation. His ontology leaves room neither for creation out of nothing (*creation ex nihilo*) nor for creation out of God

21. Olivelle, *Upanisads* (CU 6.1.4, 148).

(*creation ex deo*). If every effect must preexist in its cause, the world as effect must preexist in Brahman. It follows that a causal account would require Brahman to undergo transformation. To maintain that Brahman as being suffers change is to implicate Brahman in the world of movement and flux, the world of transmigration, and thereby to undermine the possibility of liberation. Sankara has his opponent raise the critical question: "How is it logical for partless being [to have] a transformed state?"[22] By way of his response to this question, Sankara makes a fundamental shift away from the language of causality to a language of imagination and ignorance. This shift signals a move to a fundamentally different understanding of being. Henceforth, being is understood not as material or efficient cause but instead as the real and eternal substratum for impermanent and ultimately unreal beings.[23]

Being as the Real Substratum for Unreal Name and Form

In response to the opponent's question about how partless being can undergo transformation, Sankara maintains that just as a rope can appear to be a snake without undergoing change, so too changeless and partless being can appear to undergo a transformation that results in the manifestation of the universe. From the point of view of ultimate truth, only partless and nondual being is. Sankara writes, "Being alone is truly real according to the scriptures. Even when one has the idea of 'this,' ultimately [only being is] One only without a second."[24]

How are readers to understand Sankara's language about illusion? Does the snake-rope analogy suggest that world is itself an illusion? Especially puzzling is the apparent conflict between Sankara's commitment to divine creation as expressed in the clay pot analogy and the very different implications of metaphors of illusion. For Hindu-Christian dialogue, few points are as decisive: The question of the world's reality is a make-or-break issue for Christian theologians and so must be treated with utmost care.

---

22. *niravayavasya satah katham vikarasamsthanam upapadyate? Chandogyopanishad,* CUBh 6.2.2; the translation is mine.

23. Paul Hacker nicely summarizes Sankara's approach to the idea of creation: "for S, cosmogony was only of very minor importance. For him it was not much a matter of concern exactly how the events of creation are presented or conceived nor, certainly, which terms are used. The account of creation in his system has only the propaedeutic function of drawing attention to the unity of being." Halbfass, ed. *Philology and Confrontation,* 84–85.

24. CUBh 6.2.2, 422; Gambhirananda's translation modified. The term *this* (*idam*) is Sankara's way of referring to any empirical given that can be designated as a particular this.

The snake-rope analogy is not the only example of illusory transformation to which Sankara appeals. Elsewhere he also offers the example of the desert mirage. He writes, "As the spaces within pots or jars are non-different from the cosmic space or as water in a mirage is non-different from a . . . desert—since they sometimes appear and sometimes vanish away, and as such their nature cannot be defined, even so it is to be understood that this diverse phenomenal world of experiencers, things experienced, and so on, has no existence apart from Brahman" (BSBh 2.1.14, 327–28).[25]

What do these analogies of illusion have in common with real transformation analogies? What comes into focus in Sankara's analysis is that both present a common idea: the absolute ontological dependence of the world on Brahman. Pots and jars cannot be apart from the clay, just as the snake and the mirage cannot be apart from the rope and the desert. It is a more complicated matter to establish that whereas clay is real, pots and plates are only relatively so, but Sankara works hard to make precisely this point. He argues that every effect is unreal apart from its material cause because the effect cannot exist apart from its cause. The cause, however, does not need the effect to be. Neither pots nor mirages are independently real.

By employing these analogies, Sankara wants to make absolutely clear that Brahman is ultimately real, but the manifest realm of conventionality is not. What the second kind of analogy does over and above analogies of real transformation is that it illustrates how the world can depend on Brahman while Brahman remains unaffected by that relation of dependence. Because Sankara maintains that only the changelessly eternal is real from the point of view of ultimate truth, anything that suffers change is by nature inconstant and so ultimately unreal.[26] The scriptures teach that Brahman does not suffer change. Consequently, analogies of apparent transformation must trump analogies suggesting real transformation even though both support Sankara's primary pedagogical aim: to demonstrate the world has no reality apart from Brahman.

25. We shall not explore herein the analogy of the space in pots but will focus instead on the example of the desert mirage. Clearly, the former analogy attempts to speak of how Brahman can pervade everything without becoming conditioned thereby.

26. See for example, Sankara's commentary on the *Taittiriya Upanishad*. "As for *satya*, a thing is said to be *satya*, true, when it does not change the nature that is ascertained to be its own; and a thing is said to be unreal when it changes the nature that is ascertained to be its own. Hence a mutable thing is unreal." *Eight Upanisads: Volume I with the Commentary of Sankaracarya,* trans. Swami Gambhirananda (Calcutta: Advaita Ashrama, 1991), 308–9.

At stake is a key point that is at once ontological, soteriological, and anthropological. Sankara intends to establish beyond question that liberation is not a state or a condition that can be brought about by any sort of action. Liberation comes through hearing the words of scripture alone and not by action. The words of scripture serve to teach that the Self is always already liberated because liberation *is* the Self's ownmost nature. The Self just is Brahman. To suggest that Brahman undergoes real transformation is to suggest that something must be done to effect a reversal of the process of cosmic evolution. When liberation is conceived as an inversion of such a process, liberation becomes a thing to be accomplished and so no longer eternal.

The soteriological advantage of analogies of apparent transformation are obvious in this context.

> This identity of the embodied soul [with the self which is Brahman] . . . is a self-established truth, not something to be accomplished through extraneous effort. From this it follows that like the idea of the rope removing the ideas of snake etc. . . . The acceptance of the unity of the Self and Brahman, as declared in the scripture, results in the removal of the idea of an individual soul bound up with the body. . . . (BSBh 2.1.14, 328)

By affirming that the true Self is always already changeless Brahman, Sankara shows that liberation is not something to be brought about by ritual or ethical action. Seekers after liberation need not *do* anything. What is required instead is a deep transformative knowledge that one just *is* Brahman.

At what price is this soteriological gain purchased? Does Sankara gain the Self at the cost of the whole world? Are not the charges of world-denial levied against Sankara by his contemporaries and by history justified inasmuch as the Advaitin maintains that "unity alone is the ultimate truth and multiplicity is conjured up by ignorance?"

These charges must be answered in the negative even though the Advaitin provides ample opportunity for misunderstanding. Among the reasons for misunderstanding are precisely his analogies. One such analogy is his claim that understanding the truth of nonduality is like waking up from a dream. With respect to such an analogy, the distinction between saying that the liberation is *like* waking up from a dream and saying that the world itself *is* a dream, though enormously significant, is often overlooked.

The strongest evidence for the claim that Sankara does not believe the world to be a dream are his arguments against Buddhist idealists. The idealists that Sankara has in mind contend that only consciousness is real. They maintain also that objects given in experience have no being apart from mind as is the case in dreams. Against them, Sankara insists that waking and dream experience are fundamentally different in nature (*vaidharmyam*). When pressed to specify the nature of the difference between waking and dream experience, he states that the ideas or cognitions of dream experience are unlike those of waking experience. Whereas the former are sublated, the latter are not. He quite definitively asserts, "a thing seen in the waking state, a pillar for instance, is not thus sublated under any condition" (BSBh 2.2.29, 423).

What is at stake in Sankara's disputations with Buddhist proponents of the idea that only consciousness is real is the extramental status of the world. Sankara regards their position as scurrilous. By attempting to equate waking experience with dream experience, Sankara argues that Buddhist idealists attempt to deny what is readily apparent. When Buddhists say that the world only appears to be external to the mind, he argues that they engage in mere sophistry (BSBh 2.2.28, 419).[27] The world of waking experience is unsublatable in the way dream experiences are; waking experience, unlike dream experience, is based on the perception of objective realities and is not a fiction produced by anyone's mind. Whatever Sankara may mean when he speaks of conventional experience as conjured up by ignorance, he does not mean to say that the waking world *is* a dream.

Because Sankara believes that the experienced world is neither a mere production of the mind nor a dream, he cannot be charged with world-negation. And yet he maintains that the world of conventional experience is revealed to be "unreal" in the light of scriptural teaching! Sankara's theology presents an apparent paradox: The conventional world has extramental existence but is nonetheless unreal. The appearance of paradox is diminished when one remembers that, in the final analysis, the term *real* or *true* (*satya*) is reserved only for that which is eternal and changeless. The things of conventional experience perish almost as soon as they appear; such evanescent realities are not real.

---

27. Because Sankara's own position is so often mistaken for a kind of subjective idealism by nonspecialists, it is worth citing one of Sankara's pointed repudiations of Buddhist idealism: "How can a man's words be acceptable who while himself perceiving an external object through sense-contacts still says, 'I do not perceive, and that object does not exist,' just as much as a man while eating and himself experiencing the satisfaction arising from that act might say, 'Neither do I eat, nor do I get any satisfaction'?" (BSBh 2.2.27, 419). Sankara clearly believes that the Buddhist position is truly incredible.

Between Brahman and the world, there is an absolute asymmetry. The world depends upon Brahman as its ground but Brahman in no way depends upon the world. The asymmetry is so radical that even the world-grounding character of Brahman is ultimately unreal. To avoid drawing Brahman into the world of change, Sankara's thinking about the relationship between Brahman and the world is constrained by the following unstated axiom: There can be no real connection between the real and the unreal.

Operating under the constraints imposed by this axiom means that Sankara must reinterpret all Upanishadic passages that speak of creation. His strategy is to explain that creation texts are intended to serve only as a means (*upaya*) to the realization of Brahman. Creation texts, properly understood, lead persons to the truth of nonduality by way of teaching the nondifference of effect and cause. The attribution of causality and transformation to Brahman is later shown to be provisional in the light of texts that teach that Brahman does not change. Creation texts serve as a way station toward the truth of nonduality; Brahman does not really become the world as clay is really transformed into pots.[28]

The language of apparent transformation is pressed into service to specify the nature of the relationship between the world and Brahman. Sankara needs a way of showing that the world is dependent on Brahman without the latter being affected by that dependence. Causal representations will not do: Something that causes an effect acquires the character of becoming the cause of just that effect. If Brahman really causes the world, then Brahman acquires the character of being the world's cause. The rope-snake and the desert-mirage analogies are helpful because they are everyday examples in which two orders of reality are asymmetrically co-present. The snake and the mirage need the rope and desert to be. However, the rope and the desert are in no way changed or conditioned by serving as the substratum for the unreal snake and mirage. Likewise, the world needs Brahman to be, but the nature of Brahman is in no way affected by serving as the ground or substratum for the world. Indeed, it is precisely because Brahman transcends its character as the world's ground that the notion of being is finally inadequate as a way of speaking of Brahman.

The question can be raised, How do the terms of the analogy correspond to the things that the analogy is meant to explain? In the rope-snake and the

---

28. Readers familiar with Tillich will remember—and here we anticipate the discussion to follow—that he argues that *creatio ex nihilo* ought not to be understood to mean a real generation of the world out of nothing. Instead, the idea of creation out of nothing is a way of teaching that creation depends on nothing other than being-itself. For Tillich, creation symbolizes the "participation" of beings in being-itself whereas for Sankara creation is a means to teach the truth of nonduality. The relationship between participation and nonduality will be central to the comparative work to follow.

desert-mirage analogies, someone's ignorance regarding the true nature of the rope and the desert gives rise to an illusion projected on to a real ground. When these analogies are employed to clarify the nature of the relationship between Brahman and the conventional diversity, Brahman plays the role of the rope and the desert and the unreal world plays the role of the snake or mirage. But "Whose is *avidya*?"[29] Whose ignorance is responsible for this whole operation? Surely not Brahman, for then Brahman would be ignorant!

As the previous chapter demonstrated, Sankara refuses to answer the question and refuses to advance a theory of ignorance. The root problem Sankara faces is this: Were he to treat ignorance as real, his system would, strictly speaking, no longer be nondualistic. Ignorance would then be a second reality that stands over against Brahman. To surmount this obstacle, Sankara contends that ignorance is experientially real but cannot be ontologically real.

Whereas Sankara's successors seek to resolve epistemological questions raised by the application of illusory manifestation analogies, Sankara's thought is given over to the question of asymmetric co-presence. He is more interested in determining how the snake can be said to be by virtue of the rope without giving to the rope a snake-generating character than he is in determining whose ignorance is responsible for the said manifestation. The world of diversity is said to be illusory not because it is imagined by someone but because of its mutable and unreal-apart-from-Brahman character.

Sankara's refusal to take up epistemological questions indicates an awareness that analogies of cognitive error must finally break down. He understands that analogies drawn from conventional experience cannot literally apply to the question of the very status of the conventional world. From the ultimate perspective, no one is ignorant.

Sankara seems to have believed that the quest to explain the status of ignorance is neither philosophically necessary nor salvific. Ingalls argues,

> One must realize that *avidya* is not an inherent characteristic of the self or the soul. As soon as it is seen not properly to belong to the self, the true nature of the self will be realized and *moksa* will be obtained. The question of the exact modality of *avidya* is inconsequential. One

---

29. Here, I am referring to Daniel H. H. Ingalls' seminal article, "Samkara on the Question: Whose Is Avidya?" *Philosophy East and West* 3, no. 1 (1953): 69–72.

is reminded of the words of another religious teacher of India. The Buddha was asked a number of metaphysical questions by the fool Malunkyaputta. His answer was to liken Malunkyaputta to a man struck by an arrow, who would not let the surgeon draw the arrow till he discovered the name of the man who shot it and the wood of which it was made.[30]

Ingalls's observation redirects attention to the medical model where it squarely belongs. He quite rightly suggests that Sankara shares with the Buddha a passion for alleviating suffering and is prepared to leave aside questions that distract aspirants from the therapeutic process.

In likening the relationship between the world and Brahman to the relationship between an unreal illusion and its real ground, Sankara is manifestly wrestling with a problem familiar to Christian theologians: What is the relationship between the world of change and immutable ultimate reality? This problem is perhaps even more acute for Christian theologians who are obliged to reckon with scriptural testimony and the credal confession that the Word *became* flesh. Much in the history of Christian theology can be read as a series of attempts to account for the becoming of the *logos* without giving up on the principle of divine immutability.

Whereas Christian theologians are forced by christological and soteriological considerations to take seriously the reality of change, in Sankara's case, soteriological considerations compel him to adhere rigorously to the immutability of Brahman. Sankara must affirm divine immutability because he wants to maintain that human beings are eternally liberated because they are Brahman. There is nothing they need to do to become something other than what they already are.

That human beings can do nothing to bring about salvation is a deeply held Christian conviction. But in the Christian case, that conviction is rooted not in an identity already given—the identity between the soul and divinity—but rather on the priority of divine initiative. God's saving action precedes and empowers any capacity for human response, and that is why Christians have typically maintained that salvation is not fundamentally a matter of human action. Nonetheless, a deep kinship is present, one in which action plays a secondary role in the process of coming to union with divinity.

30. Ibid.

The meaning of Sankara's move away from transformation metaphors to illusion metaphors can now be summarized. The clay pot metaphors indicate that each being given in experience is a transformation of being. Just as a pot remains essentially clay, so too, all things are essentially being even in their particularity. Such particularity is but name and form, a mere verbal designation, that has no reality apart from its material cause. Much the same point is made with metaphors of illusory transformation except that these metaphors make clear that being remains unchanged. Being is now identified as the unchanging substratum for fluctuating name and form. As name and form realities have no being of their own, the being that they appear to have is just Being as such.

Brahman as Neither Being nor Nonbeing

Of even greater importance are those passages in Sankara's writings in which the term *being* is recognized as inadequate to the reality of Brahman. Here Sankara's apophatic commitments are most evident. One such discussion occurs in Sankara's commentary on *Katha Upanishad* 6.12. The verse reads, "Not by speech, not by mind, not by sight can he be grasped, how else can that be perceived, other than by saying 'He is!'"[31]

Sankara begins by observing that although Brahman is beyond cognition, nevertheless Brahman is. The reason Sankara offers is that Brahman is known as the root of the world. In his commentary Sankara gives voice to the apprehension that the radical unknowability of Brahman may lead some to the mistaken conclusion that the root of the world is nonbeing or, rather, that there simply is no root to the world. To establish his own position, Sankara argues, "If the world had no root, this creation would be filled with nonbeing and would be perceived as non-existent (*asat*). But in fact, this is not so; it is perceived as existing (*sat*), just as a pot, etc. produced from clay etc., are perceived as permeated by clay. Therefore, the Self, the root of the world, is to be realized as existing."[32]

However, asserting that being is the root of the world only brings one to a knowledge of Brahman as conditioned by the world for which it serves as root. Brahman unconditioned by limiting adjuncts (*nirupadhika*) is "free from becoming an object of such concepts as being and nonbeing" (KaUBh 2.3.13, 227).[33] Brahman is known as being only insofar as it serves as the substratum for existent things. The true nature of Brahman free of limiting adjuncts is to

---

31. KaU 6.12, 246; Olivelle's translation.
32. KaUBh 2.3.12, 226; Gambhirananda's translation modified.
33. *sadasadadipratyayavisayatvavarjita* . . . ; Gambhirananda's translation modified.

be known by means of scriptural texts that describe Brahman as, "changeless, bodiless, inexpressible, unsupporting" (ibid., 228).

Sankara makes the same argument in his commentary on the *Bhagavad Gita*. The critical verse is the following: "I shall teach you what is to be known; for knowing it, one attains immortality; it is called the supreme Brahman, beginningless, neither being nor nonbeing."[34] The opponent argues that it is not appropriate to say that Brahman is neither being nor nonbeing. He maintains that anything to which being cannot be attributed must be nonexistent. The opponent quite reasonably asks, "Do not all cognitions truly involve the idea of existence (*astibuddhi*) or non-existence (*nastibuddhi*)?" Sankara responds,

> No, as a sense-transcending [reality], it is not an object of cognition involving either of the two ideas. Indeed, any object perceivable by the senses, such as a pot etc., can be either an object of cognition involving the idea of existence, or it can be an object of cognition involving the idea of non-existence. But this reality to be known being sense-transcending and known from the scriptures, which are the sole means of [its] knowledge, is not, like a pot etc., an object of cognition involving either of the two ideas. Therefore, it is said to be "neither being nor nonbeing."[35]

Sankara's argument is that Brahman is not the sort of thing that can be said either to exist or not because it is not any sort of thing at all. It is real but it does not exist as pots do. Words can only be used to speak of Brahman as conditioned by limiting adjuncts.

Strikingly, Sankara goes so far as to say that reality of the Self is "ultimately beyond the scope of the concept and the word 'Self'" (BUBh 1.4.7, 95). The concept of *Self* is absolutely fundamental for Sankara's soteriology. By denying that even the concept *Self* is adequate to the reality of Brahman, Sankara makes it patently clear that one should not labor under the impression that one has come to know the ultimate reality of Brahman by knowing it as the Self. To know Brahman as the Self suffices for liberation but only because it removes the mistaken notion that persons are finite transmigrators. However, one should not thereby presume to know Brahman.

This rigorous emphasis on the ineffability and unknowability of Brahman makes it appropriate to characterize Sankara's theology as culminating in

---

34. Barbara Stoler Miller translates Brahman as "infinite spirit." I leave the term untranslated. *The Bhagavad Gita: Krishna's Counsel in Time of War* (New York: Bantam Books, 1986).

35. BGBh 13.12, 529; translation modified.

an apophatic anthropology that combines an absolute immanence with an equally radical transcendence. As the being of beings, Brahman is the Self of all; indeed, apart from Brahman nothing can be. In that sense, Brahman is absolutely immanent to the human being as its very ground. And yet what is one's very Self cannot be known. The source of knowledge cannot itself become an object of knowledge. Brahman is utterly unknowable and radically transcends the mind.

For Sankara, therefore, the essence of human being is mystery. Any attempt to define the human being would necessarily fall short of the reality of the Atman as revealed by scripture. Human nature as determined by the mind-body complex is no different from animal nature. Both are equally driven by faults such as desire and aversion. Both are marked by transitoriness and so are ultimately unreal. When liberating knowledge arises and one comes to see that Brahman is one's true Self, another dimension of identity comes to view, a view of the human being in its transcendent character as absolute mystery. Here one is reminded of the words of twentieth-century Catholic theologian Karl Rahner:

> We can say what man is only if we say what he has to do with and what concerns him. But in the case of man who is a transcendental subject this is something which is boundless, something which is nameless, and ultimately it is the absolute mystery whom we call God. In his *essence*, in his nature, therefore, man himself is the mystery, not because he is in himself the infinite fullness of the mystery which concerns him, which fullness is inexhaustible, but because in his real essence, in his original ground, in his nature he is the poor, but nevertheless conscious orientation to this fullness.[36]

Despite noteworthy differences, Sankara's insights resonate profoundly with Rahner's convictions. Sankara would agree that human being as a particular finite reality is, ontologically speaking, nothing in itself. But precisely because the human qua human is nothing apart from being, Sankara would argue that what the human being truly is is Brahman, something Rahner would not affirm. For Sankara, scripture reveals that the mystery that concerns human beings, the object of ultimate concern (*paramapurusartha*) is the Self but that liberating knowledge does not in the slightest do away with the mystery of Brahman.

---

36. Karl Rahner, *Foundations of the Christian Faith: An Introduction to the Idea of Christianity*, trans. William V. Dych (New York: Crossroad, 1987), 216.

Here also Rahner's words about the beatific vision are richly appropriate: "The immediate vision of God which is promised to us as our fulfillment is the immediacy of the incomprehensible. It is, then, the shattering of the illusion that our lack of total comprehension is only provisional. For in this vision we shall see in God himself, and no longer merely in the infinite poverty of our transcendence, that God is incomprehensible."[37] Sankara would refuse the possibility of vision, but he would readily agree that ultimate reality is and must necessarily remain wholly incomprehensible.

The possibility of an apophatic anthropology as raised by Sankara will be considered in further detail in our discussion of Paul Tillich's theological anthropology. A critical question to be taken up then is whether Tillich's attitude to Sankara's Advaita might have been modified had he appreciated its essentially nonmystical and apophatic character. Other critical questions for further consideration include the following: Can Tillich's theology of participation by beings in being-itself allow for a radically apophatic anthropology? How nearly does his ontology of participation approximate Sankara's theology of the nondifference of Self and Brahman? Can one envision, however dimly, an apophatic anthropology drawn from both Hindu and Christian sources that maintains both divine transcendence and immanence within a nondualistic ontology?

Sankara on Therapy: Preparing For and Becoming Established in Liberating Knowledge

A careful reading of Sankara's writings suggests that he was beset constantly by opponents who persisted in questioning the efficacy of scriptural knowledge to bring about liberation; they insisted that something above and beyond the mere hearing of scripture is necessary. For some, these arguments were based on conviction that meditation is necessary for that mystical insight that alone would suffice to bring about liberation. Still others believed that only knowledge in combination with ritual action would suffice for liberation. What makes the arguments of Sankara's opponents appear plausible is a rather simple observation: No one is seen to be liberated by hearing scripture alone.

Sankara rejected this claim. As was demonstrated earlier, he refused to stipulate that only some special sort of knowledge would bring about liberation. Some do understand the meaning of scripture from a single hearing. Still

37. Ibid., 217.

others may require indefinitely many hearings so that some aspect of superimposition is removed each time. However, Sankara uncompromisingly rejected every claim that sought to maintain that some mode of action, whether ritual, worldly, or meditative was necessary for liberation. The reasons for Sankara's insistence are quite clear: Liberation is not a thing to be achieved but something that is eternally the case. Knowers of Brahman do not become Brahman. They only come to know that their true nature is Brahman.

Once this ontological and soteriological commitment to the efficacy of knowledge alone through scripture alone is rigorously established, Sankara does allow action—ritual, worldly, and meditative—a preliminary role in the process of preparing persons for liberating knowledge. Sankara even recognizes that meditation may be necessary after the arising of liberating knowledge, not in order to transform scriptural knowledge into some form of mystical knowledge but rather to secure firmly knowledge already gained. Sankara is quite scrupulous about this latter point lest in acknowledging a place for meditation in the lives of those for whom liberating knowledge has already dawned, his opponents find reason to argue that meditation is necessary for liberation itself. Finally, although Sankara usually speaks of the liberated person as transcending action and the errant notion of agency altogether, he acknowledges that action remains a possibility even for the liberated.

In what ways must persons be transformed in order to be open to liberating knowledge? How are persons transformed by that knowledge? How can such knowledge be secured? By answering these questions, one gains an understanding of the ramifications of the cognitive center of Sankara's thought throughout other dimensions of personal and social life. Only in this way can we come to an adequate understanding of Sankara's therapy and expected prognosis for recovery from the illness of ignorance.

How does a person habitually motivated by ignorance, desire, aversion, and delusion come to know that the innermost self is Brahman? Is such knowledge possible for one who is plagued by these faults? Because liberating knowledge can be gained only by understanding the meaning of scripture, scripture is plainly of unparalleled importance in Sankara's soteriology. Also critical is a teacher who embodies the truth of nonduality. The teaching of scripture properly interpreted by an authoritative teacher can direct the student's attention away from the external to the internal. Desire, aversion, and delusion are eliminated in those who come to know themselves as Brahman. But in order for scriptural teaching to be efficacious, the student must be properly prepared.

Those who are not transformed by hearing scripture fail not because of any inefficacy on the part of scripture but because they are inadequately prepared. Detached action and meditation prepare persons for the rise of knowledge.

Sankara argues that persons who seek to know Brahman must possess certain attributes without which knowledge cannot arise. These attributes are "discrimination between the eternal and the non-eternal, dispassion for the enjoyment of fruits [of actions] here and hereafter, a perfection of such practices as tranquility, restraint and so on, and the desire for liberation."[38] Would-be students of Advaita face stiff admission requirements before they can begin inquiry into Brahman. These dispositions are clearly opposed to ignorance, desire, aversion, and delusion and seek to diminish their hold on the mind. Only a mind free of these faults is capable of understanding that its true nature is other than the ephemeral constructs of superimposition that ordinarily define identity.

Action and meditation are important to Sankara because they are the means by which the aforementioned qualities of mind and heart are generated. Sankara teaches that the disciplined performance of action free from attachment to the fruits of action leads to the purification of the mind. Such disciplined action is called *karmayoga*. What does the practice of *karmayoga* look like, and how does it lead to purity of mind? Sankara describes the process as follows: "That duty, characterized by action and enjoined for different castes and stages of life, even though it is meant for achieving prosperity and attaining heaven etc., yet when performed with the thought of dedication to the Lord and without desire for results, leads to the purification of the mind. And, for a person with a purified mind it becomes the cause of the supreme good by becoming the means for the attainment of fitness for steady adherence to knowledge."[39]

Sankara also states that *karmayoga* is "the performance of action with detachment after destroying the pairs of opposites for the sake of worshiping the Lord (*isvararadhanarthe*)" (BGBh 2.39, 85). These statements demonstrate that Sankara envisages *karmayoga* as an activity that is devotional in nature. *Karmayoga* is action performed in a spirit of selfless sacrifice to God. According to Sankara, *karmayoga* does not lead independently to liberation because, like action in general, *karmayoga* also generates karmic fruits. Objecting to an opponent who suggests that action performed in a spirit of devotion to the

---

38. BSBh 1.1.1, 9; translation modified. Rambachan provides a helpful and compact discussion of these prerequisites for knowledge. See *Accomplishing the Accomplished*, 85–92.

39. BGBh, Intro, 7; translation modified.

Lord will not generate karmic consequences, Sankara argues that such action will produce still more abundant fruit than self-centered action (BGBh, 6). For Sankara, *karmayoga* only enables progress toward liberation by purifying the mind of the performer so that he is ready for knowledge. Only knowledge liberates. The purification of the mind is contingent on an attitude of strict detachment from the results of action. Sankara warns the performer of *karmayoga* to be so detached that he must even abandon the thought, "The Lord will be pleased with me."[40] The performer of *karmayoga* is permitted to entertain the thought, "I am an agent, and I work for the Lord as a servant."[41]

Karmayoga generates purity of mind because it counters the customary passions that drive human activity. Whereas action is ordinarily motivated by desire, aversion, and the like, actions performed in devotion to the Lord are not so motivated. Consequently, *karmayoga* cultivates tendencies that oppose those generated by actions motivated by faults or afflictions. Only a mind so transformed is genuinely open to transforming knowledge. Thus, knowledge is not entirely free of any connection with action. A preliminary and preparatory course of *karmayoga* treatment may be necessary for the medicine of knowledge to be efficacious. Although once knowledge has arisen, it is quite capable of bringing about its result (liberation) independently, knowledge depends on detached action for its own arising.

Sankara's Prognosis: On the Liberated Person and the Possibility of Action after Liberation

What are the qualities of the liberated person who, after having acquired the qualities of mind and heart necessary for knowledge through *karmayoga*, is established in the knowledge of Brahman?[42] Given the already remarkable qualities of the ideal student, in what way is the liberated person different? Also, what does it mean to be liberated while living?

Lance Nelson and Andrew Fort have demonstrated that if liberation is understood as emancipation from samsara, living liberation would be a contradiction in terms; such emancipation must necessarily be a postmortem condition. Every transmigrating being is an embodied being and embodiedness is constitutive

---

40. *isvaro me tusyati iti tyaktva* (BGBh 2.48).

41. BGBh 3.30, 162; translation modified.

42. The following presentation of living liberation is greatly indebted to the work of Andrew Fort and Lance Nelson. See Andrew Fort, "Knowing Brahman While Embodied." See also Lance E. Nelson, "Living Liberation in Sankara and Classical Advaita," in *Living Liberation in Hindu Thought*, ed. Fort and Mumme.

of the false identities of transmigrating beings. Liberation from transmigration is, therefore, liberation from embodiedness. If liberation is so understood, liberation while living is impossible.

Sankara, however, redefines liberation not as a thing to be achieved but rather as just another way of speaking of Brahman. Liberation is an eternal verity, not a future possibility. What is necessary then is knowledge about what is eternally the case, and such knowledge can only be gained while living. However, Sankara still faces the task of reconciling his ontological definition of liberation with the notion of liberation as freedom from transmigration and freedom from the body. Here, Sankara makes the bold claim that the Self has never been and never will be embodied. In response to the opponent's contention that disembodiedness only occurs after the body falls, Sankara responds, "Not so, for the idea of embodiedness is a result of false nescience. Unless it be through the false ignorance of identifying the Self with the body, there can be no embodiedness for the Self. And we said that the unembodiedness of the Self is eternal, since it is not a product of action" (BSBh 1.1.4, 40). By arguing that the Self is eternally disembodied and so never subject to samsara, Sankara reconciles his ontological definition of liberation as Brahman with ordinary definitions of liberation as freedom from transmigration. Were it not the case that the Self is disembodied, no knowledge event could make it so.

Sankara's basic thesis is that the liberated person knows that the Self is, in truth, not embodied. Because of that knowledge, even when alive, his knowledge gives him a radical detachment from the body. Sankara concludes, "Thus since embodiedness is the result of a false perception, it is established that the enlightened man has no embodiedness even while living. Thus about the knower of Brahman occurs this Vedic text, 'Just as the lifeless slough of a snake is cast off and it lies in the ant-hill, so does this body lie . . .'" (BSBh 1.1.4, 42). The knowledge that gives rise to such detachment sets one free from agency and every fault-generated motivation for action.

Among the many clues about the character of the liberated person, one in particular is invaluable because it provides a key interpretative principle. Sankara writes, "For in all the scriptures about the supreme Self, whatever are the characteristics of the man of realization are themselves presented as the disciplines for an aspirant, because these [characteristics] are the result of effort. And those that are the disciplines requiring effort, they become the characteristics [of the man of realization]."[43]

With this principle in hand—what the seeker aspires for is what the liberated person possesses—any description of the qualities of the ideal student

---

43. BGBh 3.30, 162; translation modified.

can be applied to the liberated person with the proviso that, in the liberated person, these are settled qualities no longer in need of disciplined cultivation. Knowledge brings about the cessation of the faults, such as grief and delusion, that cause samsara. Although the discipline of action purifies the mind of these faults, only knowledge can finally render them powerless.

Rather than provide an extensive catalogue of the various virtues attributed to the liberated person, we will focus instead on the connection between Sankara's ontology and the qualities of the liberated person. Because the faults are caused by a fundamental error about the true nature of the Self, the virtues of the liberated person are based on the elimination of that very error. The person who has realized the Self has transcended desire. Such a one lacks nothing and so is free from compulsions. Sankara maintains, "For a thing that is known as other than oneself may become an object of desire. But such a thing does not exist for the knower of Brahman, the objects of whose desires have all been attained. He to whom all objects of desire, being but the Self, are already attained, is alone free from desires, is without desires, and does not desire any more; hence he attains liberation. . . . Since a man who has realised his identity with all has nothing to desire, he cannot perform actions. . . ."[44]

This last statement concerning action raises a critical question about the nature of the liberated person: Can liberated persons act? Can liberated persons who are unreservedly detached from the body act once they know they are not agents? Sankara ordinarily represents the liberated person as a renunciant who has transcended the activities of conventional life. By coming to understand himself as actionless Brahman, he knows definitively that he is not an agent. Not surprisingly, Sankara does allow that liberated persons engage in minimal activity for the sake of sustaining the body.

Sankara makes a particularly illuminating and comprehensive statement about the possibility and nature of action after liberation in his commentary on BG 4.22. The *Gita* verse reads as follows: "Content with whatever comes by chance, beyond dualities, free from envy, impartial to failure and success, he is not bound even when he acts" (BG 4.22, Miller's translation). In his commentary, Sankara makes it plain that he believes the verse to be a description of the liberated person (BGBh 4.22, 206). Sankara characterizes the liberated sage as one who

> in the course of going about for alms, etc., for the bare maintenance
> of the body, is ever clearly conscious of the fact, "I certainly do not
> do anything; the qualities of nature (*guna*) act on the qualities," he,

44. BUBh 4.4.6, 499–500; translation modified.

realizing the absence of agency in the Self, certainly does not do any
actions like going about for alms etc. But when, observing similarity
with conventional activity, agency is superimposed on him by ordinary people, then he [apparently] becomes an agent with regard to
such actions as moving about for alms, etc. But from the standpoint of
his own realization which has arisen from the scriptures which are the
right means of knowledge, he is surely not an agent. . . .[45]

Remarkably, Sankara finds a way to reconcile both the actionlessness of the
Self and the observed actions of the liberated person. Liberated persons perform actions even if the actions are only those of a renunciant who begs for the
food necessary for his continued existence. Having abandoned his ordinary
sense of self, the realized person no longer confuses his true nature with the
activities of his body. However, from the conventional perspective of unen-
lightened observers, the realized person appears to be an agent even though
the liberated sage is established in the truth that the Self does not act.

Moreover, conventional action need not be restricted solely to minimal life-
sustaining activity. Sankara leaves room for other more robust forms of action.
Sankara envisages the possibility that persons caught up in the flow of active
life may in the midst of such activity find themselves transformed by insight.
On one occasion, Sankara describes the situation of a person who is impelled
to action by such faults as ignorance and desire who, because of the purification of the mind that occurs in the midst of detached action, comes to the
truth of nonduality.[46] Sankara suggests that for such a person action and the
conventional motivations for action are no more. The private desires for the
sake of which ritual practice and other forms of action are usually performed
cease to exist. He has even come to know that the Self in truth is not actor.
But that knowledge does not mean that the liberated person simply ceases to
act. On the contrary, he may continue to act deliberately as before, only now
his reasons for action are no longer private: He now acts for the welfare of the
world (BGBh 2.11, 42–43).

The activity of liberated persons is different in kind from actions performed
by those committed to the discipline of action (*karmayoga*). Liberated persons
do not entertain the thought, "I am an agent," because they know that they are
the actionless Self. Liberated persons enjoy freedom from desire and freedom

---

45. BGBh 4.22, 206; translation modified.

46. Sankara gives as an example a person who, in the midst of the *agnihotra* sacrifice,
suddenly finds himself free of those desires that prompted the ritual in the first place but
nonetheless proceeds to complete the ritual in question.

from the notion of agency. Performers of *karmayoga* may be relatively free from desire, but because they still believe that they are agents, they remain burdened by karmic consequences. The liberated are not. Liberated persons who know, "I am not an agent," are free to engage in action without fear of accruing merit or demerit. As these persons are free of egoism and are not motivated by the faults, their motive for action can only be the welfare or integrity of the world.

Sankara goes so far as to state that some liberated persons may have a special eligibility or responsibility (*adhikara*) to continue activity even in other lifetimes. Citing traditional texts in which liberated sages are said to have many lifetimes, he maintains, "Apantaratamas and others, though they are divine, are entrusted with their respective responsibility by the Lord; and hence though they are possessed of full vision, leading to liberation, they continue in their bodies so long as their responsibilities demand this and so long as their actions are not completed; and when that is fulfilled they become freed."[47]

Clearly, Sankara's understanding of Brahman's actionlessness does not compel him to adopt a quietist conception of human life in which all action must inevitably be renounced. True, he does generally envisage living liberation as a possibility for renunciants who have surrendered the conventional duties of class and stage of life and after liberation maintain a minimal level of activity. But he acknowledges that, for some, living liberation is not incompatible with a life of action. It is tempting to say that liberating knowledge gives to such active persons a certain poise. Being established in wisdom, the living liberated can work for the welfare of the world without being plagued by merely private or egotistical concerns. Indeed, like Mahayana bodhisattvas, liberated persons may take on multiple lifetimes in order to fulfill their unique responsibilities. Sankara's employment of two-truth theory makes it possible to affirm both ultimate actionlessness and conventional activity. The person of steady wisdom is able to keep his vision open to both truths without confusing each with the other.

Despite the remarkable capacities attributed to the *jivanmukta*, the person who is liberated while still living, Sankara acknowledges the possibility that even a knower of Brahman may become confused and so may need to exercise meditative discipline. The possibility of ongoing spiritual practice even for liberated knowers raises provocative questions. Why is such discipline necessary?

47. BSBh 3.3.32, 703; translation modified.

Are such disciplines the spiritual equivalent of ongoing therapy as might be the case with those who, after having recovered from a disease, may still need treatment to prevent recurrence? Or is it the case that the illness in question is chronic and lifelong such that constant treatment is mandatory and complete recovery impossible?

Sankara acknowledges that the liberated person's knowledge of nonduality can be obstructed by the same forces that perpetuate his continued existence. Meditation may be necessary to prevent such obstructions.

> Since the resultant of past actions that led to the formation of the pres-
> ent body must produce definite results, speech, mind and the body
> are bound to work even after the highest realisation, for actions that
> have begun to bear fruit are stronger than knowledge; as for instance
> an arrow that has been let fly continues its course for some time. . . .
> Therefore there is need to regulate the train of remembrance of the
> knowledge of the Self by having recourse to the means such as renun-
> ciation and dispassion. (BUBh 1.4.7, 93)

Sankara states that sustained and unobstructed knowledge would be inevitable were it not for the interference of karma that has already begun to bear fruit (*prarabdhakarma*), which generates the body of the liberated person. Because such karma can interfere with the constant remembrance of Brahman, meditation may be necessary. Meditation is not mandated but may prove to be helpful on occasion. Sankara affirms that knowledge can prevent the germination of karma that has not yet begun to bear fruit. Sankara's argument, therefore, has a temporal element; *prarabdhakarma* is a matter of the past and of the unfolding present, of karma that is already in operation, and knowledge can do nothing about that. However, it can prevent what has not yet come to be.

By acknowledging the possibility that the operations of *prarabhdakarma* can interfere with knowledge, does Sankara undercut his claim that the medicine of knowledge alone suffices for liberation? To ward off this possibility, Sankara argues that once knowledge has been obtained, it cannot be lost. He gives the example of someone who, upon realizing that a shiny object on a beach is not silver but just mother-of-pearl, cannot again be in error. But Sankara allows that another kind of error is possible. Sankara gives the example of an outdoorsman, who although he is "familiar with the points of the compass sometimes all of a sudden gets confused about them" (BUBh 1.4.10, 116).

The example of the knowledgeable outdoorsman who momentarily becomes disoriented serves to illustrate how one who knows himself to be the Self can momentarily become confused. Presumably then, even the knower of Brahman can lapse back into confusing his finite, superimposition-generated contingent identity with his true Self. Meditation and other disciplines (*sadhana*) such as renunciation and dispassion can prevent such false impressions from arising. Despite the extraordinary virtues of the liberated person and his transformative knowledge of Brahman, Sankara allows that even the liberated person is not wholly free from the force of karma even though he is established in the knowledge of nonduality. Recurrence of disease is impossible, but health may need to be maintained by spiritual discipline.

Sankara's picture of the liberated person is rich and nuanced. He is not merely a treasure chest of superior virtues, the idealized opposite of the ordinary transmigrator. Although Sankara's normative conception of the liberated person is that of a wandering actionless renunciant, he allows that reality may be more complex. Sankara concedes that liberated persons may instead be settled, active, and engaged. Such a person may engage in action for the sake of the world's welfare. Although the liberated person is free of the notion, "I am an agent," he is not restricted from acting for the sake of others and even on occasion engaging in meditation as spiritual discipline.

Recognizing the complexity of Sankara's understanding of living liberation, particularly in the light of his concessions about *prarabdhakarma*, Lance Nelson asks a brief but pointed question, "Is *jivanmukti* complete liberation?" Nelson offers the following reflections on his provocative question: "In several of the passages in which he discusses *prarabdha*, Sankara suggests something very much like the later Advaitin's concept of *videhamukti*. That is, he introduces the idea of a literally disembodied, post-mortem liberation that he appears to think of as a soteriological advance over the state enjoyed by the living Brahman-knower."[48]

Nelson admits that it is unclear how statements that suggest that liberation occurs only after the body falls can be reconciled with the ontological affirmation, "The liberated sage is Brahman while living; he does not have to attain Brahman after death."[49] He suggests that although there is no ontological gain to be had, there is the practical advantage that after the fall

---

48. *Videhamukti* literally means bodiless liberation. See Lance Nelson, "Living Liberation in Sankara and Classical Advaita," 28.

49. Ibid., 29.

of the body, finitude is altogether transcended with the complete cessation of karmic operations. Despite his rigorously ontological understanding of liberation, Sankara appears to leave room for a more conventional definition of liberation as escape from the sufferings and ambiguities of finite existence.

Immanence and Transcendence in Sankara's Theology: On Apophatic Anthropology

Sankara is a single-minded thinker committed to teaching that liberation, the supreme goal of human existence, is attainable in this very life. He readily acknowledges that life is most often given over to penultimate pursuits such as wealth, pleasure, and obligation that are by nature impermanent (*anitya*) whereas liberation is eternal (*nitya*). What is eternal is neither a product of human effort nor a state brought about by meditation. Whatever is produced is necessarily impermanent. Liberation seems like a goal to be accomplished only for those in bondage (BSBh 4.4.2, 897). In truth, liberation is but another way of speaking about ultimacy. Liberation is Brahman.

Sankara aims to teach persons what they truly already are. He seeks to show human beings that the truth taught by scripture requires jettisoning conventional notions about identity. Human beings innately reject the true Self and cling to finite identifications and thereby fall victim to faults such as desire, aversion, grief, delusion, and fear. These faults fuel action, and the accumulated results of action fuel rebirth. Even if one finds the idea of reincarnation unconvincing, the insight that fault-generated action creates subtle predispositions that bind persons to the habitual performance of fault-based actions is plausible and compelling.

Through an exposition of scripture, Sankara teaches that human beings belong to two orders of reality, one conventional and unreal and the other ultimate and eternally real. To transcend the human predicament, one must realize what is always already the case. However, to receive this knowledge as transformative wisdom rather than as mere information, a process of preparation is customary. A variety of disciplines makes possible purity of mind. The grace of the teacher, scripture, and even the grace of Brahman understood as Lord prepare the way for knowledge.

To know the truth about the Self is to know that action can be altogether transcended. Some individuals continue to act for the world's welfare even though they are beyond injunctions and prohibitions. They have transcended the sphere of conventional moral obligation. These liberated actors are neither immoral nor amoral. On the contrary, because the violation of obligations is prompted by faults such as desire, aversion, grief, and delusion, liberated actors who have overcome ignorance are free from addictions that motivate self-seeking action. To borrow Pauline language, liberated persons have died to their conventional selves and so are dead to the law.

The most paradoxical and intriguing feature of Sankara's thought is his claim that human beings cannot cognize their essential nature. His teachings suggest that the famous Delphic and Socratic dictum, "Know thyself," cannot be fulfilled. At best, knowledge of self means recognizing that the true Self is mystery. Words such as *consciousness*, *being*, and even *Self* are inadequate to the deepest truth about one's innermost nature. Sankara's teaching regarding the nonduality of the Self and Brahman culminates in an absolute immanence that nonetheless preserves the most rigorous transcendence. The truth of nonduality does not violate the mystery of divinity. Rather, nonduality, as Sankara understands it, culminates in apophatic anthropology. I cannot know what it is that I most truly am. My being comes from Brahman and is Brahman, but Brahman utterly exceeds me.

This is not to deny the validity of psychology, sociology, or any other mode of investigating persons as emotional, social, and biological beings. Sankara's anthropology does not prohibit such inquiry. But these are preliminary and cannot penetrate to the ultimate mystery that is at the core of the human being. Sankara's theological anthropology concludes with the knowledge that the human being is not just a temporally distended being whose nature is encompassed in the time between birth and death or even past and future lifetimes. The Self is in truth eternal.

What is, nonetheless, deeply problematic about Sankara's vision is the presence of the unresolved residual dualism between a changeless and eternal Brahman and the changing world of impermanence. Lance Nelson speaks of this phenomenon as the "dualism of nondualism." He rightly maintains that Advaita "cannot accept the world as identical with Brahman, for that would admit change into the spirit. It therefore . . . wants to keep the world outside the Absolute."[50]

---

50. Lance E. Nelson, "The Dualism of Nondualism: Advaita Vedanta and the Irrelevance of Nature," in *Purifying the Earthly Body of God: Religion and Ecology in Hindu India*, ed. Lance E. Nelson (Albany: State University of New York Press, 1998), 72.

Bound by a theory of karma that makes action problematic, Sankara insists that Brahman is unchanging. The claim that Brahman is unchanging is the single attribution about ultimate reality that Sankara never qualifies in any way. It marks the one moment in Sankara's theology wherein the logic of apophasis is abrogated. The Christian theologian Pseudo-Dionysius enacts that logic by claiming that God is "beyond assertion and denial."[51] In this spirit, he writes of God as "not immovable, moving or at rest."[52] Sankara negates movement alone. The result is an unbridgeable gap between the moving world of name and form and immovable Brahman. Sankara avoids dualism by specifying that the material realm of name and form has no intrinsic reality, but a practical dualism remains. This dualism is apparent in Sankara's theological anthropology wherein the liberated person is required to act with the idea that he does not truly act. He is encouraged to recognize that only the constituents of material nature do.

Tillich's theology is motivated by a search for an ecstatic account of action in which dualism between ultimate reality and human beings is undercut. Tillich is not hamstrung by a commitment to a vision of ultimate reality as inactive. This allows him to affirm the possibility that human action can be simultaneously the action of God. Tragically (as we shall see), such a possibility is only allowed a fragmentary and fleeting position in Tillich's theology because he too backs away from nondualism. Only occasionally are human beings transparent to the divine depths in such a way that human activity can at once be divine activity. In Sankara's case, failure to adhere rigorously to nondualism gives rise to a tendency to define away the world as unreal. In Tillich's case, his belief that freedom requires separation between God and creature gives rise to a tragic vision of human life as inevitably compromised by ineradicable ambiguity. It is worth asking whether a nondualism that borrows conceptual resources from both thinkers can overcome their respective inadequacies without sacrificing the tremendous theological promise of each vision.

For the constructive theologian in search of resources for a Christian nondualism, several components of Sankara's theology hold great promise. Sankara's rejection of any fundamental ontological divide between human being and Brahman suggests that human life need not be marked by a perpetual and inevitable brokenness. Tillich, on the other hand, is forced to posit a distance between human beings and God in order to make room for freedom. The

---

51. Pseudo-Dionysius, "The Mystical Theology," in *Pseudo-Dionysius: The Complete Works*, 141.

52. Ibid.

room necessary for freedom is what makes sin possible, even inevitable. Tillich gives an ontological account that explains *why* sin as separation is unavoidable. Sankara, on the other hand, is content to leave ignorance largely unexplained and inexplicable. The Advaitin knows that any explanation of ignorance would likely make ignorance seem real. That is something Sankara will not do as he is absolutely keen to deny to ignorance any ontological status. To do so would give the lie to nondualism.

Sankara's theology is also promising because it retains a surprisingly strong sense of transcendence despite the fact that there is no distance between Brahman and beings. The absolutely immanent divine can in no way be imaged as transcendent by way of spatial metaphors. Brahman does not transcend me by being elsewhere than where I am. The transcendence in question is cognitive or epistemological in character. I cannot know what it is that I truly am and must remain content to know that my true being is mystery.

But in order to affirm nonduality Sankara is forced to define away conventional identity defined by factors such as age, gender, class, and stage of life as ultimately unreal albeit existent. He does not deny altogether the importance of finite or determinate identity; rather, he intends to teach that finite identity, though important to matters of ordinary life, is not the true or essential Self. Sankara seeks to effect in persons a fundamental cognitive transformation—a transformation with profound affective consequences—in which persons come to see themselves as not-other than Brahman, the Self of the universe. Nonetheless, the question remains: Can we imagine a nondualism that affirms identity with Brahman but does not in the process deny the reality of ordinary identity and experience?

The idea that finite or determinate reality has no being apart from being-itself need not be problematic for Christian reflection. If calling the world unreal is but a way of stipulating that the world cannot exist apart from divinity, Christian theologians can live with such a proposition, terminological nuances notwithstanding. More problematic is Sankara's fundamental disjunction between human activity and an unchanging absolute. On this account, there can be no sense in which human action can be at once also divine action. Christian experiences of being prayed through by the Spirit—experiences central to Tillich's own theological vision—do not register in a system that requires ultimate reality to be utterly inactive in order to ground escape from the transmigratory process.

In sum, despite the difficulties posed by conceptions of an inactive absolute, Sankara offers a great many insights regarding the connection between ontological nondualism and apophatic anthropology. Sankara provides theological evidence for the claim that an uncompromising affirmation of divine immanence need not lead to impoverished conceptions of transcendence. A deep sense of mystery remains at the heart of Sankara's theology. Moreover, precisely because nondualism means that the being of ultimate reality is not-other than one's own being, Sankara's theology allows for a vision of human life that promises the possibility of relative freedom from what Tillich would call the ambiguities of existence. If one rejects the notion that there must be a fundamental chasm or divide between ultimate reality and human beings, then one can embrace an alternative vision in which human beings are not inevitably bound to estranged existence. Experience may well be marked by tragedy but such tragedy is never rendered necessary. Sankara's theology provides for an intriguing combination of radical immanence, a strong sense of transcendent mystery, and a robust hope for the possibility of sanctification. These are rich resources that Christian reflection cannot do without.

chapter four

Tillich on the Human Predicament

Diagnosis and Etiology

໑໑໑

The mind is able to turn away from what is nearest to the ground of
its own structure.

—Paul Tillich[1]

Priming the Comparative Pump: Where Do We Begin?

Paul Tillich and Sankara share a fundamental conviction: Ultimate reality
is not a being, not even the supreme being, but rather being-itself.[2] This
deep resonance of thought presents itself as an obvious starting point for
comparison. But why believe that a twentieth-century German Christian
existentialist émigré to America means the same thing by "being" as does the
eighth-century Hindu theologian? To minimize the risk of mistaking formal similarity with substantial convergence, we must ask different questions:
How does ultimate reality come to beings caught up in the midst of predicament? How does being function to remedy the ills that afflict persons captive
to sin and ignorance? If the God who is being-itself enables persons to cope

---

1. Paul Tillich, *Theology of Culture* (New York: Oxford University Press, 1959), 15. Hereafter TOC.

2. As the preceding chapter has shown, Sankara's apophatic commitments mean that
even the notion of "being" is ultimately inadequate to the reality of Brahman. Tillich is
more comfortable with the notion that God is being-itself. Nonetheless, he too acknowledges the mystery of being-itself and argues that all talk about God must be symbolic. In
the final analysis, Tillich too is an apophatic theologian.

with the human predicament in a very different manner than does Brahman, then, likely, each thinker has in mind very different conceptions of being.

Tillich's own theological method insists that theology must begin with the questions posed by the human predicament. The answers provided by revelation will remain unintelligible if they are not correlated with and addressed to concrete existential questions posed by the place and time in which the theologian lives. We have already seen how Sankara, like the Buddha, has little patience for speculation that fails to treat the fundamental problem of ignorance.

Moreover, comparison faces special dangers when it takes up notions veiled in mystery. Comparativists are more likely to conclude that ultimate realities compared—in this case Brahman and God—are identical inasmuch as they both transcend knowledge and even language. But just because religious conceptions of ultimate reality share certain formal properties such as ineffability, ultimacy, and unity need not mean that the realities in question are in fact identical.[3] Beginning with the human predicament helps to minimize the risk of being so misled.

One final note: After reading Sankara through the category of the human predicament, it would be exceedingly difficult to postpone comparison when employing the same category to read Tillich. Hence, this chapter and the one to follow will offer an explicitly comparative reading of Tillich. My hope is that reading Tillich with Sankara in mind will yield fresh perspective on Tillich's theology and shed light on fundamental questions that arise in the course of East-West conversation.

Preliminary Reflections on Courage:
Arjuna's Courage and the Courage of Faith

In keeping with the commitment to begin with existential matters, we turn to a notion central to Tillich's theology but largely unthematized in Sankara's

---

3. This argument has been made vigorously in the field of comparative mysticism. See especially Steven Katz's prudent contention that in the formal statement, "x transcends all empirical content, is beyond space and time, is ultimate reality, gives a sense of joy, is holy, can only be expressed in paradoxes and is actually ineffable," the placeholder x "can be replaced by several, radically different, and mutually exclusive candidates, e.g. God, Brahman, *nirvana*, Nature." See Steven T. Katz, "Language, Epistemology, and Mysticism," *Mysticism and Philosophical Analysis,* ed. Steven T. Katz (New York: Oxford University Press, 1978), 47.

works: courage. To begin with courage is to follow through on comparative reflections inaugurated by Tillich himself. With the Indian context in mind, Tillich posed the question, "Can courage be united with mysticism in any way?" He suggests that courage in India is primarily a martial virtue, the disposition of warriors (*kshatriya*), and is not to be associated with religious figures. The virtues displayed and cherished by mystics and ascetics, he argues, transcend the warrior's courage.

But such religious transcendence, Tillich goes on to say, is itself a form of courage:

> It is courage in the larger though not in the narrower sense of the word. The ascetic and the ecstatic mystic affirms his own essential being over against the elements of nonbeing which are present in the finite world, the realm of Maya. It takes tremendous courage to resist the lure of appearances. . . . The mystic seeks to penetrate the ground of being, the all-present and all-pervasive power of the Brahman. In doing so he affirms his essential self which is identical with the power of Brahman, while all those who affirm themselves in the bondage of Maya affirm what is not their true self. . . . (CTB, 157–58)

In this remarkable reflection on the nature of mystical courage in Advaita, Tillich provides a sensitive account of basic Advaita convictions and provides an opening gambit for our comparative labors.[4]

The importance of Tillich's intuition about courage in Advaita Vedanta can be confirmed by a brief examination of courage as treated in Sankara's commentary on the *Bhagavad Gita*. In that eminent text, Lord Krishna chastises the warrior Arjuna for the timidity (*kasmalam*) and cowardice (*klaibyam*) that cause him to shrink from righteous battle. Krishna enjoins Arjuna to act courageously, remembering that Arjuna's true Self is "indestructible, enduring, unborn, unchanging" (BG 2.20, 32). Sankara regards this teaching regarding the true Self as the very essence of the *Gita*. He argues that Arjuna

---

4. The term *Maya* we now know is relatively unimportant to Sankara's thought though central to Advaita as a whole. That discrepancy does not compromise Tillich's reading because he is not referring here to any particular thinker but to a generalized "Hinduism," which in most instances appears to be Advaita. Our interpretation of Sankara as a nonmystical Advaitin must also be distinguished from the Advaita Tillich has in mind. Nevertheless, it must be said that although Tillich had only a rudimentary acquaintance with Advaita, he learned a great deal from the sources available to him. For a more extensive analysis of Tillich's acquaintance with Hinduism in general and Advaita in particular, see the work of Terence Thomas, *Paul Tillich and the World Religions* (Cardiff: Cardiff Academic Press, 1999), 101–22.

is overcome by grief and delusion because he does not know his true nature. Arjuna can find courage to reenter battle only by coming to see that he is not, in truth, merely the finite self he believes himself to be. Knowledge of the Self's identity with being-itself, with Brahman, will provide Arjuna with the courage he needs.[5]

Sankara's exegesis indicates that he does not subscribe to the relatively sharp distinction between martial and mystical courage that Tillich takes to be a central feature of Eastern traditions. For Sankara, the latter grounds and makes possible the former. This point of disjunction notwithstanding, Sankara's commentary confirms that Tillich is right to see in Advaita's detachment from quotidian forms of identity a form of courage.

The trouble with mystical courage, as Tillich sees it, is that it is limited and incapable of functioning as an adequate source of genuine healing. In Tillich's estimate, mystical courage cannot overcome two serious and intrinsic limitations. First, mystical experience is temporary: "The mystical courage to be lasts as long as the mystical situation. Its limit is the state of emptiness of being and meaning, with its horror and despair" (CTB, 159). Put simply, the mystical situation proper is short-lived and is subsequently followed by the deepest negativities. Tillich clearly has in mind the dark night of the soul experiences of John of the Cross and others.

Our reading demonstrates, however, that what Tillich calls "mystical courage" is by no means an evanescent phenomenon for Sankara. After all, his theology is not founded on fleeting mystical experiences. Hence, Tillich's notion of mystical courage is, strictly speaking, inapplicable to Sankara's thought. The Advaitin believes that one can be *established* in the knowledge of Brahman. A genuine teacher is a person of firm and stable wisdom, not someone who has experienced episodic glimpses of nonduality. Knowledge that one is Brahman is derived solely from the Upanishads. No epistemologically exceptional experiences are necessary.

If anything, the charge of an unwarranted dependence on temporary religious states may be more accurately leveled against Tillich's theology, a theology that maintains that human beings can experience ecstatic union with the ground and power of being-itself but only "fragmentarily" so (ST 2:140). Tillich believes that experiences of the Spiritual Presence are given only partially

---

5. Sankara does not regard the warrior Arjuna as the ideal student capable of understanding the truth of nonduality. He is only qualified for *karmayoga*. Nonetheless, Sankara claims that the Lord uses Arjuna's crisis to reveal the highest teaching of *jnanayoga*, the discipline of knowledge. He goes so far as to say, "Lord Vasudeva found that for Arjuna, whose mind was confused about what ought to be done and who was sunk in a great ocean of sorrow, there could be no rescue other than through the knowledge of the Self" (BGBh 2.10, 45).

in time and space and cannot be sustained. Hence, they are fragmentary. For Tillich, the "fulfilled transcendent union" between God and humanity must remain "an eschatological concept" (ibid.). Sankara's nondualism holds open the possibility of sustained and enduring knowledge of one's true identity as the Self of all in this life and not merely in a postmortem eschatological state, something that Tillich's ontology does not permit.

Tillich levels a second and still more serious charge against the mystical courage to be. He writes, "Mysticism does not take seriously the concrete and the doubt concerning the concrete. It plunges directly into the ground of being and meaning, and leaves the concrete, the world of finite values and meanings, behind" (CTB, 186). Mysticism does not interrogate the ordinary; it relativizes it. By leaving behind the concrete realm of everyday experience, Tillich believes that mysticism leaves itself open to a deeper threat: the threat of meaninglessness (CTB, 177–78). What is needed is a more radical form of courage called "faith" or "absolute faith." The courage of faith has an "in spite of" character. This form of courage finds a way to affirm finite values *after* having passed through an experience of radical meaninglessness regarding those very values and meanings. Mystical courage does not face up to this threat: "The experience of meaninglessness is more radical than mysticism. Therefore it transcends the mystical experience" (CTB, 178). Faith is the courage to affirm the meaningfulness of the finite realm of particulars despite a radical skepticism about those very meanings. Mystical courage neither questions finitude as radically nor affirms it as deeply as faith does, or so Tillich contends.

Does Sankara's Advaita fail to take finitude seriously? With what measure of seriousness should one approach finite identities, concerns, and values? If both Tillich and Sankara agree that finitude is not exhaustive of human identity because our being is grounded in being-itself, then where does this leave the world of finite meanings and concerns? These questions must play a prominent role in the constructive theological reflection that follows after comparison. One cannot help but hear in these queries the fundamental motifs of East-West conversation. Western thinkers have persistently charged their Eastern counterparts with recklessly diving headlong into the mystical abyss and forsaking particularity and individuality in the process. The countercharge typically leveled by Eastern thinkers is that the West is too much enamored of safeguarding the ego albeit in the name of defending particularity. Bringing Sankara and Tillich together in conversation helps us to get at these large cultural questions and concerns by way of patient attention to particular thinkers rather than by way of unwieldy generalities.

Our present task is to appreciate Tillich's vision of faith and the relationship between that form of courage and the power of being-itself. After all, Tillich clearly maintains that both forms of courage (mysticism and faith) enjoy a unique relationship with being-itself. Faith, for Tillich, is the most radical form of the courage to be because faith does not bypass anxiety; precisely this power of faith to reckon with anxiety, even the anxiety of meaninglessness, gives to faith its "in spite of" character.

For Tillich, anxiety is ultimately an ontological phenomenon. Far from being an accidental psychological peculiarity of the neurotic, anxiety is the manifestation of nonbeing intrinsic to finite being.[6] Anxiety is finitude come to self-awareness. Courage cannot eliminate anxiety but it can take this anxiety within itself. The crucial question that Tillich poses is, From whence does this courage come? If anxiety is an essential and invariant mark of finitude, the courage capable of overcoming such anxiety must originate from a source that transcends finitude. Tillich argues that the courage of faith is the manifestation of the power of being-itself grasping the anxious self and driving it ecstatically beyond itself without destroying the centered self. My courage in the face of anxiety is my own and not someone else's. But my courage is also *not* my own. This courage is generated in me by the power of being-itself. To say that the source of the courage to be is not at my own disposal does not mean that I am possessed by that which is alien to me, but it does mean that, with St. Paul, I can only say about the source of this courage, "I and yet not I." The courage to be is produced by the power of being-itself, a power to which human beings essentially belong and in which they participate but from which they are nevertheless estranged. That power is experienced most clearly in ecstatic moments in which the power of being overcomes nonbeing and makes it possible for human beings to actualize their essential being unambiguously albeit fragmentarily under the conditions of existence.[7]

How is this self of the "I and yet not I" that is in ecstatic union with being-itself to be compared with Sankara's nondual self? What is the relationship between the ecstatic self and the nondual self? What are the similarities and differences between these two conceptions of the authentic or true self? These are among the most compelling and captivating questions to be addressed in the conversation between Sankara and Tillich.

---

6. Of course, Tillich does not deny that there are also neurotic forms of anxiety.

7. The meaning of these technical terms (essence, existence, unambiguous, fragmentary) will be explored in some depth in this chapter and the following.

Without entirely giving away the conclusion of this tale, I offer the following general summary of similarities and differences. Sankara's nondual Self is the eternal, unchanging Brahman. As a rule—a rule that does allow for exceptions—persons who have realized their true identity as Brahman do not act. Such persons become renunciants. Even the rare exception to the rule is instructed to bear in mind that he does not really act. Rather, only the qualities of material nature (*gunas*) act on each other. The result is a recalcitrant dualism within Sankara's purported nondualism: the divide between an unreal (in Sankara's very distinctive sense) but active conventional self and a real but actionless ultimate Self.

Tillich's doctrine of the ecstatic union of God and human being suggests the possibility of a more dynamic nonduality—a nonduality in which my ecstatic action is both my doing and God's as well—than Sankara can permit. However, such nonduality is given only fragmentarily in Tillich's account. Ecstatic union is not a securely established ontological fact but is instead an event that breaks into human experience. Of course, Tillich did not himself employ the language of nonduality. Consequently, it would be wiser to speak more cautiously at this juncture by using Tillich's own vocabulary of union, especially because union suggests the reunion of two distinct realities whereas nonduality does not.

This provisional statement of some comparative differences that will emerge in the course of this chapter and the following raises critical questions that we will employ to subject Sankara and Tillich to mutual critique. What are we to gather from the fact that both theologians in the end either fail to deliver (Sankara) or refuse to embrace (Tillich) a thoroughgoing nondualism? Is there a lesson to be learned here, a lesson regarding the impossibility of theological nondualism? Or is it the case that each theologian was prevented from arriving at a deep and robust nondualism because of unfortunate and avoidable errors?

Both Sankara and Tillich share a deep conviction: Human well-being is the result of divine immanence. We are healed and made whole when we encounter the radical proximity of ultimate reality in human experience. Divine healing is never action at a distance, a mere juridical declaration of absolution pronounced from on high by a remote and removed divine being. Only the immanent divine saves.

Unfortunately, Sankara gives us immanence at very great expense: We must come to think of the mind-body complex as ultimately unreal. And Tillich gives us a dynamic and ecstatic union, but such union never endures. It remains at best fragmentary and fleeting. Might it be possible to accept Sankara's strong sense of nondual identity while rejecting his commitment to the idea that Brahman is unchanging? And can one generate a dynamic nondualism by appeal to Tillich's notion of ecstasy while rejecting the latter's characterization of ecstasy as unavoidably episodic? Can theological reflection that emerges after comparison generate new possibilities for constructive theology, options that make creative use of each theologian's best insights and central convictions while purging what is problematic and unsustainable?

The remainder of this chapter will explore Tillich's understanding of the human predicament. One overriding concern will animate this exploration: Why must ecstatic union with being-itself necessarily be fragmentary and episodic in Tillich's vision of life? Why does Tillich believe that all healing is at best partial and always subject to subsequent disruption? Should not Tillich's own vision of divine immanence allow for a stronger and more promising vision of divine-human union? Must one make do with a courage that always includes the "in spite of," or can one hope for a deeper peace beyond the perpetual conflict against nonbeing? Using a more traditional Christian theological vocabulary, the question can be framed as follows: Can we hope for a more robust account of sanctification than Tillich is able to offer?

This chapter will demonstrate that Tillich's vision of fragmentary ecstasy derives from his conviction that something is ontologically awry. The human predicament is not just the product of ignorance or choice but the product of a universal—even nature is included—fall away from what we truly are and so are meant to be. In Tillich's technical language, this rupture is the fall from essence to existence. As we have shown in chapters 2 and 3, although Sankara generates at least as devastating picture of the human predicament as does Tillich, he accomplishes this without positing a fundamental ontological fault or rupture. Sankara does not need something to be ontologically rotten to give an account of the human predicament. Ignorance has no ontological standing in Sankara's thought but is deeply troubling nevertheless. Because he does not posit a rupture or divide between human being and the Absolute, Sankara is able to offer a far more optimistic account of human possibilities. The *jivanmukta* has largely overcome the problems posed by the human predicament. That Sankara leaves open the possibility that even liberated persons are vulnerable to disorientation suggests that he, like Tillich, recognizes the depth and severity of the human predicament. Nonetheless, Sankara is far more open to the radical possibility that human beings can in principle and in practice overcome bondage to the faults and afflictions that plague human life.

Introducing Tillich's Ontological Apparatus

As the preceding two chapters have demonstrated, Sankara's theology is worked out with great conceptual economy: One concept, namely Brahman, encompasses Sankara's soteriology, anthropology, and theology. Tillich's theology, on the other hand, employs a far more complex ontological architectonic. Tillich's vocabulary, shaped by both the existentialist and psychoanalytic traditions, is also particularly luxuriant in its description of the human predicament. The key terms Tillich employs include anxiety, despair, doubt, estrangement, unbelief, hubris, and concupiscence. According to Tillich, every aspect of human nature, every human activity, every province of meaning, including culture, art, and religion, is compromised by what the classical Christian tradition calls sin and what Tillich calls estrangement. A comprehensive description of the human predicament would have to enumerate the consequences of estrangement in each of these areas. Such a task is vastly beyond the scope of the present chapter.[8] Indeed, Tillich calls it an "infinite task" (ST 2:68). The present analysis will focus instead on Tillich's diagnosis, etiology, and prognosis of the human predicament.[9]

Tillich identifies "four levels of ontological concepts" (ST 1:164). The first level names the "basic ontological structure" of being and consequently of human experience as well. This basic ontological structure is the self-world polarity. "The self having a world to which it belongs—this highly dialectical structure—logically and experientially precedes all other structures" (ibid.). This means that "Man experiences himself as having a world to which he belongs" (ST 1:169). Outside the realm of human experience, the ontological structure indicates that everything is both self-related and related to some environment of which it is a part. Only human beings are consciously aware of this double-relatedness, and it is the human experience of this structure that most interests Tillich. Speaking of human experience, Tillich writes, "Without its world the self would be an empty form. Self-consciousness would have no content, for every content, psychic as well as bodily, lies within the universe. There is no self-consciousness without world-consciousness, but the converse is also true. . . . Both sides of the polarity are lost if either side is lost. The self without a world is empty; the world without a self is dead" (ST 1:171).

---

8. These omissions demonstrate that even a comparative project that focuses on just two thinkers rather than on entire traditions cannot possibly strive for comprehensiveness. Every act of comparison is necessarily and unavoidably selective.

9. We shall attend to Tillich's understanding of therapy as well but not extensively. A complete treatment of Tillich's understanding of healing the human predicament would require an extended foray into Christology, which is beyond the scope of this comparative venture.

The implications of Tillich's understanding of the self-world polarity are far reaching and appreciated best by contrast with Sankara. On the one hand, Sankara is largely in agreement with Tillich's description of the self-world relation if that description is taken to be about our everyday experience. Within that context we do confuse the subjective and the objective realms; the self that emerges from such confusion belongs to the world and is defined by that belonging. Sankara's position is formally equivalent to Tillich's understanding of the self-world polarity. The *conventional* self is contentless apart from the world to which it belongs; it knows itself only through relation to this world.

There appears to be a point of fundamental difference, however. For Sankara, the ultimate Self transcends conventional experience and stands beyond the self-world polarity. The true Self can never be objectified and is not part of the world. Consciousness as it is drawn into the subject-object world is always a consciousness of something and never pure. But Sankara understands the light of consciousness that makes experience possible to be a transcendent reality. Though this light is only known in and through each act of consciousness, this light is the eternal nondual Self. It does not need the world to give it content. For Sankara then, Tillich's treatment of the self-world polarity is valid so far as it goes. But if this account of selfhood is taken to be true without remainder, then human beings remain exhaustively and mistakenly defined by finitude.

How might Tillich respond? He is prepared to acknowledge the immediate presence to mind of certain "transcendentalia," such as *esse, verum,* and *bonum,* which are the presupposition of all thought (TOC, 22–23). But for Tillich these realities, although they form the ground of the mind's own structure, are not the self. Consciousness in Sankara's thought certainly functions in part as these transcendentalia do in Tillich's thinking. More precisely, Sankara's understanding of consciousness (*cit*) is similar to Tillich's notion of the divine *logos* in which these transcendentals are grounded. For Sankara, consciousness is indeed the immanent reality that illuminates the mind and makes mental functions possible, but Sankara takes the added step and argues that one's true Self is not the evanescent mind-body complex but rather that without which the mind and body could not be, namely consciousness. Tillich resists this further step. Such a self is likely to strike Tillich as a dangerous abstraction from finite particularity. For Tillich, the self cannot be separated from the world of which it is a part. As for the question, "What precedes the duality of self and world of subject and object?" Tillich insists that that "is a question in which reason looks into its own abyss—an abyss in which distinction and derivation disappear. Only revelation can answer this question" (ST 1:174). So, there is indeed something that precedes the duality of self and world, but what that is is not the self but unnameable divinity.

Both substantive and terminological differences are at stake in this conversation, though on balance, the differences are not as stark as they first appear to be. Sankara is arguing that what precedes and grounds the subject-object structure of conventional reality, Tillich's abyss, is the true Self. Sankara does not come to this insight by means of a rational deduction. He would agree that only revelation can disclose the nature of that which precedes "the duality of self and world." Sankara's conclusion that Brahman is the true Self rests precisely on his conviction that the only viable interpretation of revelatory statements such as "That thou art" is an uncompromising nondualism. Tillich objects to the notion that the divine reality that is prior to the subject-object distinction is the true Self. We belong to that reality, we cannot exist apart from that reality, but we are not that reality *simpliciter*.

We shall make one further observation before moving to the second level of Tillich's ontological concepts: Whereas Sankara's theology has a fundamentally *hierarchical* structure, Tillich's ontology is *polar* in character. Sankara's theology is hierarchical because of the pervasive influence of two-truth theory. In two-truth theories, certain truths have a preliminary and restricted validity that is subsequently corrected by a higher and more final truth. For example, Sankara allows that the world of change and multiplicity is really given in experience, but then he goes on to argue that from the point of view of ultimate truth, only Brahman is real. A polar theory of reality, on the other hand, tries to hold opposing polarities in dynamic tension. Elements in a polar view of reality are never subordinated to or reconciled by some higher truth, nor is one pole given priority over the other. In Tillich's words, "the loss of either pole means the loss of both" (ST 1:199). Many of the tensions between these two theologians have to do with differences between polar and hierarchal accounts of reality.

The second level of Tillich's ontological concepts has to do with the "elements that make up the basic ontological structure." These elements consist of three pairs of polarities that characterize everything that is. These polarities are individualization and participation, dynamics and form, and freedom and destiny. No understanding of Tillich's anthropology or theology is possible apart from a grasp of these polarities.

The first pair of these polarities are individualization and participation (ST 1:174–78). Tillich writes, "Individualization is not a characteristic of a special sphere of beings; it is an ontological element and therefore a *quality* of everything. It is implied in and constitutive of every self, which means that at least in an analogous way it is implied in and constitutive of every being" (ST 1:174–75). To say that individualization is a quality of everything is to say that every reality, from the smallest of inorganic particles to the human being, is characterized by distinctive particularity no matter how relatively trivial that particularity might appear to be. For Tillich, individualization reaches its peak with the human person who is an absolutely centered being. Whereas individualization might be trivially true of leaves of the same tree, the significance of individualization is most apparent in the human being. Here, individualization culminates in absolutely distinctive personhood. But self-relatedness cannot be separated from the element of world-relatedness. Because these polarities make up the self-world structure of being, the first self-related polar element is a mere abstraction apart from its world-related partner. Consequently, individualization is contentless apart from its opposite pole, namely participation.

Now, participation is arguably the single most important concept in Tillich's system. There is no way to appreciate in depth the range of meanings that the concept bears without knowledge of Tillich's entire corpus. For the purpose of understanding participation as part of the ontological structure, however, more limited remarks will do. To say that participation is a quality of everything is to say that everything is what it is by being part of a larger context. To be is to be something particular but every particular is related to "universal structures, forms, and laws" (ST 1:176). To be is to participate in an environment or world. "Without individualization nothing would exist to be related. Without participation the category of relation would have no basis in reality. Every relation includes a kind of participation. . . . The element of participation guarantees the unity of a disrupted world and makes a universal system of relations possible" (ST 1:177). Tillich's understanding of participation rules out a nominalistic ontology in which reality consists solely of individual things. With the element of individualization, Tillich acknowledges the distinctiveness of each thing. With the element of participation, Tillich rejects an atomistic conception of reality.

The second pair of ontological elements is dynamics and form. Form is easily defined: The form of anything is its essence, its determinate nature. "The form of a tree is what makes it a tree, what gives it the general character of treehood as well as the special and unique form of an individual tree" (ST 1:178) The real challenge is to understand what Tillich means by "dynamics." Dynamics refers to "potential being," namely that which receives form. The problem is that what is as yet unformed cannot be defined. "If it could be named properly, it would be a formed being beside other beings instead of an ontological element in polar contrast with the element of pure form" (ST 1:179). To overcome this problem, Tillich employs a broad range of concepts drawn from several languages and the technical vocabularies of specific thinkers such as Henri Bergson and Friedrich Nietzsche in order to indicate what he means. Among these terms are *me on*, *élan vital*, and will. Each of these terms symbolically points to the creative, energetic, and active dimension of reality—that which is formed, that which gives content to any form, but also that which breaks old forms and drives reality toward novelty.

The meaning of these highly abstract ontological notions becomes evident when Tillich turns to explain how these polarities are experienced in human life.

> The polarity of dynamics and form appears in man's immediate experience as the polar structure of vitality and intentionality. . . . Vitality is the power which keeps a living being alive and growing. *Élan vital* is the creative drive of the living substance in everything that lives toward new forms. . . . Vitality, in the full sense of the word, is human because man has intentionality. . . . Man's vitality lives in contrast with his intentionality and is conditioned by it. . . . Man's dynamics, his creative vitality, is not undirected, chaotic, self-contained activity. It is directed, formed; it transcends itself toward meaningful contents. There is no vitality as such and no intentionality as such. They are interdependent, like the other polar elements. (ST 1:180–81)

In human life, dynamics is experienced as vitality and form as intentionality. The energy for life is paired with purpose and meaning that derives from form. Neither can be separated from the other although both are joined together always in creative tension. Tillich's use of vitality and intentionality also calls to mind the traditional medieval scholastic distinction between will and intellect, terms that figured both in anthropological discussions and in medieval disputes regarding the nature of God. In Tillich, these terms are abstracted and generalized so that they no longer refer to faculties but refer instead to qualities of being as such. When related to human experience, the terms become readily comprehensible. A flourishing human life is marked by vitality, energy, and dynamism; but any such dynamism that is not in polar union with meaning, structure, purpose, and form, would be undirected randomness. The converse also obtains. A life oriented wholly toward structure and form would tend toward ossification apart from a dynamism that animates and drives structure toward change and renewal.

The third and final pair of polar elements are freedom and destiny. This pair, as we shall see in the section to follow, plays a fundamental role in Tillich's analysis of the human predicament. For the moment, we need only to highlight certain distinctive features of Tillich's understanding of freedom. First, freedom "is not the freedom of a function (the 'will') but of man, that is, of that being who is not a thing but a complete self and a rational person" (ST 1:183). To be human is to be free, to choose, and to decide. But freedom is not the capacity to act arbitrarily. My freedom is precisely my freedom because of the specific choices and options available only to me because of the particular circumstances of my life, circumstances that are in many ways given to me apart from my choosing. Destiny refers to this situated character of all freedom. "Destiny is not a strange power which determines what shall happen to me. It is myself as given, formed by nature, history, and myself. My destiny is the basis of my freedom; my freedom participates in shaping my destiny" (ST 1:185). This pair of polarities also characterizes not just human beings but reality as a whole. In subhuman realms, Tillich indicates that it is experienced as the tension between "spontaneity and law."

Tillich maintains that because God is not a being, God is not subject to the ontological structure or its polarities. However, God is the ground of this structure and so the God-human relation is inevitably shaped by the structure that God grounds. Given this axiom, it also follows that God cannot be nearer to one element in a polar pair than to another. If God is the ground of both dynamics and form, then it will not do to conceive of God solely in static terms. When the pole of dynamics is employed to symbolize the divine, then God is imagined as "living." Of course, Tillich believes the term to be deeply symbolic; God is not *a* being, living or otherwise. The term signifies that the ground of life processes cannot itself be fixed, immobile, or dead. It also follows that when God is understood by appeal to form, we see that the divine is not arbitrary creativity but that which structures reality and can even be said to be the ground and structure of reality itself.

The implications for comparison with Sankara are extensive. Sankara understands Brahman as eternal, without internal distinctions, and unchanging—the stable ground for a radically unstable world. Tillich would contend that Sankara misrepresents divinity by privileging form at the expense of dynamics. Clearly, we shall have to revisit this important difference when we take up Tillich's doctrine of God.

It also follows that the relationship between humanity and divinity will be misunderstood if individualization is privileged at the expense of participation or vice versa. When individualization assumes priority in imagination, then the relationship is conceived mistakenly as a person-to-person relationship. God is individualized and is taken to be one being among others with whom one has a personal relationship. When the pole of participation assumes lopsided priority, then the God-human relation takes on an exclusively mystical character. God fails to be imagined as personal in any sense, and so God is taken to be an impersonal principle or Absolute. As no relationship is possible with an impersonal reality, the divine-human relation is characterized as immersion into the Absolute, an immersion in which personal identity is lost. Tillich rejects both these models for imagining the divine-human relationship.

The polarities also play a fundamental role in understanding Tillich's account of the human predicament. When human beings are separated or estranged from the ground of being, they fall into self-contradiction. They fail actually to be what they are essentially. This estrangement from essential nature ruptures the balance between these basic polarities. Each element in a polarity acts against the other, and the creative tension between them is disrupted. As the polarities make up the basic self-world structure, this disruption leads to self-destruction and world-loss.

This discussion of estrangement and disruption brings us to the third level of Tillich's ontological concepts: the difference between essential being and existential being. Tillich affirms that the distinction between essence and existence, or in theological terms, the distinction between the created world and the fallen world is "the backbone of the whole body of theological thought" (ST 1:204). Indeed, the human predicament for Tillich can be described as the split between essence and existence. Consequently, this third level of ontological concepts will be a primary focus of attention in the remainder of this chapter. The fourth and final level of ontological concepts in Tillich's architectonic is "the categories of being and knowing" (ST 1:164). Tillich is referring here to the basic categories of time, space, causality, and substance that structure experience. These categories will also be considered in the course of the following treatment of the human predicament.

Ontology and the Human Predicament: Tillich's Etiology

Tillich's theology can be compared fruitfully with Sankara precisely because he believes that the human predicament must be described and analyzed in ontological terms. If talk about the human predicament were to be confined exclusively to the symbolic language of Christian *mythos*—as disobeying the dictates of a divine being, for example—then comparison would fail to be interesting. Tillich, however, does not think of human evil and suffering as the consequences of a ruptured relationship between humans and a lordly divine being. On the contrary, Tillich insists on differentiating between the mythological framework of biblical language and the ontological meaning of myth and symbol. The theologian's task is, in considerable measure, a hermeneutical one: He or she prevents philosophical and theological absurdity by showing what is at stake in myth and symbol by translating symbolic language into a properly ontological register.[10] For Tillich, the human predicament must be understood as a tragic and universal estrangement from what human beings essentially are. In fact, human beings suffer from a triple estrangement: They are separated from their own essential being, from each other, and from the ground and power of being-itself to which they belong. It is at this precise juncture that the shared ontological focus in both thinkers makes for comparability. The task at hand is to distinguish between Sankara's claim that human beings are *ignorant* of our essential nature as divine and Tillich's notion that human beings are *separated* from our essential nature because we are separated from divinity.

Sankara and Tillich both face a special challenge in accounting for the sheer possibility of human fallibility, a challenge that is the natural consequence of a strong affirmation of divine immanence. If human beings have no being apart from the being of being itself—a point on which both Sankara and Tillich agree—then just how is ignorance or estrangement possible? Just how is it that "the mind is able to turn away from what is nearest to the ground of its own structure" (TOC, 15)? How can human beings act against and so contradict their own essential nature?

Readers should recall that the question about the cause of the human predicament is not easily resolved in Sankara's thought. Though it is a simple matter to cite ignorance as the cause of the human predicament, things become more complex should questioners press further and ask after the cause of

---

10. Tillich is altogether aware that this translation comes with gains and losses. Religious power and efficacy reside in symbol and not in the concept. In this regard, Tillich is not Hegel as Tillich rejects the Hegelian priority of the concept over the symbol. Clarity and precision comes at a cost.

ignorance itself. For Sankara and Advaita as a whole, there is no cause for ignorance. The insolubility of the problem is suggested by the traditional assertion that ignorance is beginningless. Moreover, Sankara's pragmatic focus does not lead him to inquire after the cause of ignorance. As we have noted, he focuses instead on teaching the liberating truth of the Upanishads. The truth of one's essential nature as Brahman—as taught by the guru who understands scripture rightly—brings the person home to his true nature.[11] The return back to one's self cannot be accomplished by the individual alone despite the fact that one always already is Brahman.

The gravity of Sankara's analysis of the human predicament can only be appreciated adequately when one understands that *avidya* does not signify a mere cognitive error, though it most certainly is that as well. Ignorance is instead a congenital condition that causes human beings to remain hopelessly bound to a mistaken notion of finitude. The vocabulary of error is inadequate to Sankara's vision of the human predicament even though it does speak to the question of how ignorance is ultimately to be rooted out. As there is in Sankara's thought no error-free moment in which human beings were once aware of their true nature, human experience is fundamentally distorted from time out of mind. Not only are we ignorant about our true identity, but we are also fundamentally bound by the push and pull of compulsive desire and aversion. Put differently, not just the intellect but the will too is compromised. Therefore, when the term *ignorance* is employed, it should be understood broadly as signifying more than an error of the intellectual apparatus. And yet, despite the gravity of ignorance and its consequences, it must also be remembered that ignorance finally has no ontological standing.

Whereas Sankara's analysis of the human predicament has a predominantly though not exclusively cognitive focus, Tillich's analysis of the human predicament emphasizes the language of freedom. Tillich is careful to specify that freedom is not the operation of an isolated function of the human personality. For him, the human being just *is* finite freedom. Tillich believes that the human predicament cannot be understood as caused by the fault of a single function of the human being. To link the human predicament with a distortion of freedom is therefore to speak of the distortion of the entire human personality.

The ramifications for comparison of a volitional rather than cognitive focus will be significant. Though Tillich does note that estrangement distorts reason

---

11. Recall again that the use of the masculine gender is deliberate and refers to Sankara's own commitments, which explicitly affirm that only men are eligible to pursue liberation.

as well as freedom, there is no question that Tillich's analysis of the human predicament hinges on the human freedom to "turn away" from the divine. Just as a distortion of reason does in fact lead to a distortion of the will in Sankara, so too a distorted will leads to a distortion of reason in Tillich's theology. Despite important ontological differences, there are deep resonances between their diagnoses of the human predicament. Both would agree that whether due to ignorance or a turning away from the divine, the fundamental error is that human beings mistakenly take themselves to be the centers of their own world. Therein rests the fundamental problem.

Tillich's emphasis on freedom does ultimately signify fundamental ontological differences, however. For Sankara, healing the human predicament requires only that human beings come to know their true Self. Within an allegorical space, it is possible to speak of a separation and return from one's true nature, and yet, ontologically speaking, what the human being needs to realize is that he has never ceased to be Brahman. The familiar Vedanta tale of the prince who is reared from childhood by commoners better serves Sankara's ontology than the Upanishadic allegory about the man who is bound and taken away from his home village and abandoned in a forest. Regardless of his errant belief that he is only a commoner, the young prince has never ceased to be a prince. For Tillich, on the other hand, the freedom to turn away from one's divine ground presupposes a real "distance" between the human and the divine. Tillich's analysis of estrangement and salvation from estrangement hinges on a dynamic of separation and union, a vocabulary that is inconceivable except as metaphorical, within the framework of a strict nondualism. But just how are separation and union even possible within the framework of Tillich's theology? After all, he, like Sankara, strongly rejects conventional forms of theistic dualism. Only a careful exploration of the ontological implications of freedom in Tillich's system can show how it is possible for human beings to be separated from God who is the ground of being.

Despite the work that remains to be done to clarify the nature of this separation, it is worthwhile to restate a comparative observation offered earlier. For Sankara, there is nothing ontologically awry about the human predicament. It is true that the human predicament is caused by ignorance of ontological nonduality, but ignorance itself has no ontological status in Sankara's system. It is at best (and at worst) an existential and experiential truth. For Tillich, on the other hand, the human predicament is due to a fundamental ontological disruption, the universal rupture between essence and existence. This ontological analysis is both the greatness and the tragedy of Tillich's system. By rooting the human predicament in ontological dislocation, Tillich avoids a narrow moralism characteristic of those who believe that the human predicament is caused by a violation of divine commandments. On the other hand, emphasizing the universal separation of human beings from divinity results in a tragic vision in which salvation is always given only fragmentarily under the conditions of existence. Human life remains always and everywhere compromised and inevitably so.

In Tillich's theology, freedom plays the fundamental role in actualizing the transition from essence to existence. His analysis of freedom's role in bringing about the human predicament is rather subtle. For Tillich, freedom is not so much the *cause* of estrangement as it is the very *condition* for the possibility of estrangement. Freedom, by its very nature, includes the capacity for self-contradiction, but freedom does not make such self-contradiction necessary. Tillich writes, "man is free, in so far as he has the power of contradicting himself and his essential nature. Man is free even from his freedom; that is, he can surrender his humanity" (ST 2:32).

That we are free to take leave from our essential humanity does not mean that there once was a time of original perfection from which human beings subsequently fell away. Tillich rejects this idea without qualification. Tillich rightly parts company with literalistic readings of the myth of Adam and Eve: "Theology must clearly and unambiguously represent 'The Fall' as a symbol for the human situation universally, not as the story of an event that happened 'once upon a time'" (ST 2:29).

If there is no temporal fall from perfection, if the biblical account of the fall is symbolic of the "human situation universally," then in what sense is the category of etiology or causality relevant to an analysis of the human predicament? Put otherwise, if the fall is not an event but a fact that is universally true, how can a causal explanation be proffered? Causal accounts customarily explain some spatio-temporal event Y by appealing to a certain factor, or set of explanatory factors, X, that precede Y, but if what must be explained is not an event at all, then how can a causal account be generated? We appear to be in the same position with Tillich's fall as with Sankara's beginningless ignorance. Tillich is clear: "The transition from essence to existence is the original fact. It is not the first fact in a temporal sense or a fact beside or before others, but it is that which gives validity to every fact. It is the actual in every fact.... It means that the transition from essence to existence is a universal quality of finite being. It is not an event of the past; for it ontologically precedes everything that happens in time and space. It sets the conditions of spatial and temporal existence" (ST 2:36).

In order to grasp what sort of fact this is, we need to understand what Tillich means by the phrase, "the transition from essence to existence," his ontological translation of the mythological notion of the fall. This task, in turn, requires an examination of the meanings of the terms *essence* and *existence*. Tillich begins by observing that "essence" can have both

> an empirical and a valuating sense. Essence as the nature of a thing, or as the quality in which a thing participates, or as a universal, has one character. Essence as that from which being has "fallen," the true and undistorted nature of things, has another character. . . . [E]ssence as that which makes a thing *what* it is (*ousia*) has a purely logical character; essence as that which appears in an imperfect and distorted way in a thing carries the stamp of value. Essence empowers *and* judges that which exists. It gives it its power of being, and, at the same time, it stands against it as commanding law. Where essence and existence are united, there is neither law nor judgment. But existence is not united with essence; therefore, law stands against all things, and judgment is actual in self-destruction. (ST 1:202–03)

Both meanings of essence are important in Tillich's system, but the second valuative meaning is particularly relevant in any consideration of the human predicament. Essence represents for Tillich "the created nature" of a thing, what a thing is meant to be. Existence refers to a thing as it "stands out" of its essential nature and falls into ambiguous actuality. In the language of the ontological polarities, this "standing out" of essence is a matter of "universal destiny." The "transition" from essence to existence turns out not to be a transition at all, but a beginningless reality that requires not so much an explanation as a response, more specifically a divine response. The analogy with Sankara's *avidya* is striking indeed. Both reject a temporal fall.

The statement that both estrangement, Tillich's term for the transition from essence to existence, and ignorance (*avidya*) are "beginningless" realities should not obscure the truth that estrangement is for Tillich an *ontological* fact, albeit of a most peculiar sort. Christian theologians are compelled to strike a balance between maintaining the created goodness of all things and recognizing the brokenness of that created goodness. Imbalance inevitably leads to a fall into heresy. To ignore created goodness is to accept a Manichean vision of an originally distorted cosmos with an evil creator god from whom human beings must be redeemed. But care must be taken to see that the fall into brokenness is not made necessary for that would be to slip into a Gnostic vision in which the fall is a necessary precondition for human growth and eventual liberation. Tillich is aware of these risks and makes every effort to avoid them.

Despite clear awareness of the risks he faced in speaking of fallenness as a universal fact, Tillich felt compelled to assert that the Christian tradition "can never give up its knowledge of the tragic universality of existential estrangement" (ST 2:41). Tillich never shied away from the implications of this claim. He maintained consistently that "the transition from essence to existence is not an event in time and space but the transhistorical quality of *all* events in time and space" (ST 2:40; emphasis added). The implications of this statement are made starkly clear when Tillich goes on to add, "*This is equally true of man and of nature.* 'Adam before the Fall' and 'nature before the curse' are states of potentiality. They are not actual states. The actual state is that existence in which man finds himself along with the whole of universe, and there is no time in which this was otherwise" (ST 2:40–41; emphasis added).

But why should nature be included? Why not speak of humanity alone as fallen? These are questions that Tillich himself is first to pose. "Is it not more realistic to state that man alone is able to become guilty because he is able to make responsible decisions and that nature is innocent? Such a division is accepted by many people because it seems to solve a rather difficult problem in a simple way. But it is too simple to be true. It leaves out the tragic element, the element of man's destiny, in man's predicament. If estrangement were based only on the responsible decisions of the individual person, each individual could always either contradict or not contradict his essential nature. There would be no reason to deny that people could avoid and have avoided sin altogether" (ST 2:41). Tillich points out that Christian theology has found that notion deeply problematic; the church has consistently avoided such Pelagian ideas. Moreover, Tillich observes that human beings are part of nature; consequently, there is just no viable way to sustain the separation between "an innocent nature" and "guilty man" (ibid.).

Tillich's vision of the fallenness of both human beings and nature is not without parallel in Sankara's thought nor in Indic thought more generally. Some such notion seems at least implicit in the idea of transmigration. The notion that human beings are caught up in the continuous round of transmigration that includes everything from the creator god Brahma down to the blade of grass and the further notion that this entire cycle is fueled by the consequences of past action speaks to universal predicament. Indeed, Sankara's further contention that most pleasure-seeking and pain-avoiding human behavior is fundamentally akin to animal behavior also indicates that nature and humanity share basic traits. The difference, of course, is that such predicament, for Sankara, remains a cosmological rather than an ontological fact; there is never any ontological separation of human beings from Brahman.[12]

Tillich would insist that a separation between cosmology and ontology, between experience and being, is unsustainable. He would ask: What are the ontological grounds for such a cosmological condition? Why is it that everything is caught up in a predicament? As we have seen, Sankara would steadfastly refuse to answer. Any answer would acknowledge the validity of the question. There is no ontological reason for ignorance. Sankara would maintain only that creatures just are congenitally ignorant of their true identities. His most radical response is that because only Brahman is, there is in fact no ignorance and no one who is ignorant. To make ignorance real would amount to a dualism or it would somehow root ignorance in Brahman itself, something that Sankara refuses to do just as most Christian theologians refuse to root evil in God.

Whereas Sankara strives vigorously to avoid dualism, Tillich attempts to avoid Manichean corruption and Gnostic necessity. In the following critical passage, Tillich struggles mightily so to do.

> Creation and the Fall coincide in so far as there is no point in time and space in which created goodness was actualized and had existence. This is a necessary consequence of the rejection of the literal interpretation of the paradise story. . . . Actualized creation and estranged existence are identical. . . . He who excludes the idea of a historical stage of essential goodness should not try to escape the consequence. This is even more obvious if one applies the symbol of creation to the whole temporal process. If God creates here and now, everything he has created participates in the transition from essence to existence. He creates the newborn child; but, if created, it falls into the state of

---

12. By labeling the human predicament a "cosmological fact" I mean to say that the human predicament, as Sankara describes it, is a true description of human experience in the world, in the cosmos. It is an experienced, empirical, and existential reality. Nevertheless, that worldly experience of predicament is not rooted in being, in ontology, at least not for Sankara. Hence, the human predicament is cosmologically real but is not grounded in an ontological rupture or separation between beings and being-itself.

existential estrangement. This is the point of coincidence of creation and the Fall. But it is not a logical coincidence; for the child, upon growing into maturity, affirms the state of estrangement in acts of freedom which imply responsibility and guilt. Creation is good in its essential character. If actualized, it falls into universal estrangement through freedom and destiny. The hesitation of many critics to accept these obviously realistic statements is caused by their justified fear that sin may become a rational necessity, as in purely essentialist systems. Against them theology must insist that the leap from essence to existence is the original fact—that it has the character of a leap and not of structural necessity. In spite of its tragic universality, existence cannot be derived from essence. (ST 2:44)

Many aspects of Tillich's subtle ontological tightrope walk demand scrutiny. First, the sheer courage to accept the consequences of rejecting literalism must be noted. Tillich does not let God entirely off the hook. The created newborn child must participate in the transition from essence to existence and, if so, then God must be said to create the child who falls into estrangement. However, Tillich attempts to escape Manichaeism by insisting that created goodness still obtains and that estrangement remains a matter of human responsibility. Tillich makes this point with greater clarity in the third volume of his system wherein he makes plain that "life" is not just the brokenness of existence but the ambiguous combination of both essence and existence. "In all life processes an essential and an existential element, created goodness and estrangement, are merged in such a way that neither one nor the other is exclusively effective. Life always includes essential and existential elements; this is the root of its ambiguity" (ST 3:107).

Tillich also attempts to avoid the Gnostic doctrine of a necessary fall by arguing that freedom and choice are involved. The human being *chooses* the "pleasures of separated existence" and so actualizes estrangement. That choice, Tillich insists, is a matter of freedom even if it is also a matter of destiny. What Tillich seeks to avoid is a philosophical vision of the sort paradigmatically realized by G. W. F. Hegel. For Hegel, the fall is the logically necessary condition of the self-evolution of the Spirit (*Geist*). In making the fall necessary, Hegel can rightly be charged with making the grave consequences of the fall, the innumerable and ghastly cruelties of history, also utterly and absolutely necessary. By insisting that there is no *logically* necessary step from essence to existence, Tillich escapes Hegelian necessity but willingly accepts the *empirical* unavoidability of sin. The trouble with Tillich's solution is that it requires that life not only is but must always be an ambiguous mixture of essence and existence. The rupture between essence and existence may not be necessary, but it is inevitable. By declaring the transition a fact, Tillich comes close to Sankara's assessment that ignorance is a fact; the trouble is that, for Tillich, this empirical fact (the choice of creatures to actualize their natures in separation from God) actualizes an ontological rupture as well. When creatures embrace freedom, they are inevitably separated from the divine life.

Is it possible to acknowledge that the human predicament is universal and empirically inevitable without rooting that predicament in an ontological flaw? Put simply, can we acknowledge the gravity and reach of the human predicament but refuse to say that the predicament bespeaks a real separation between humanity and divinity? Sankara would answer decisively in the affirmative. For Sankara, creatures do not cease being Brahman even when ignorant. Nor is Brahman itself ignorant. For Sankara, when knowledge dawns nothing happens *ontologically speaking*. Human beings just get it; they realize what they already and always are. The merits of such an alternative approach cannot be explored at this point. However, it is worth suggesting that a stronger affirmation of the integrity of creation would go a long way toward overcoming Tillich's conviction that healing will always and only be fragmentary. It would also minimize the grave risk that Tillich runs: the near-identification of creation and fall.

Thus far, this investigation of Tillich's understanding of the human predicament has focused heavily on matters of destiny. However, Tillich's reference to guilt as a consequence of the transition from essence to existence indicates that, though this transition is a matter of universal destiny, human beings bear moral responsibility for estrangement. In Tillich's words estrangement is both "act and fact" (ST 2:55). He observes that the term *sin* brings out the sense in which estrangement is the result of an act whereas the term *estrangement* better testifies to the fact-like character of the universal transition from essence to existence. That said, the terms *estrangement* and *sin* ought to be understood generally as synonymous in Tillich's system. So Tillich can also say, "Sin is a universal fact before it becomes an individual act, or more precisely, sin as an individual act actualizes the universal fact of estrangement. As an individual act, sin is a matter of freedom, responsibility, and personal guilt" (ST 2:56).

Insofar as estrangement is also a matter of freedom, a causal explanation of sorts can be ventured. However, because "the state of essential being is not an actual stage of human development," Tillich notes that uncommon difficulties attend the task of describing the transition from essence to existence. In order to resolve these difficulties, Tillich proposes to treat the transition from essence to existence by way of the psychological metaphor of "dreaming innocence." Tillich compares the transition from essence to existence to the emergence in adolescents of their sexual potentialities and their conscious awareness of these potentialities (ST 2:34). At a certain point in their development, adolescents awaken from their "dreaming innocence" and face temptation. This temptation is rooted in the consciousness of freedom. The moment freedom comes to self-consciousness is central to Tillich's analysis of estrangement because it is at this moment that certain tensions emerge that eventually lead to a break from "uncontested innocence" (ibid.).

> Man is caught between the desire to actualize his freedom and the demand to preserve his dreaming innocence. . . . He experiences a double threat, which is rooted in his finite freedom and expressed in anxiety. Man experiences the anxiety of losing himself by not actualizing himself and his potentialities. He stands between the preservation of his dreaming innocence without experiencing the actuality of being and the loss of his innocence through knowledge, power, and guilt. The anxiety of this situation is the state of temptation. Man decides for self-actualization, thus producing the end of dreaming innocence. (ST 2:35–36)

Two features of this analysis demand special attention. First, it should be noted that the anxiety of which Tillich speaks is neither a sign of nor a product of estrangement in the way that guilt is. Anxiety precedes the transition from essence to existence. Because anxiety is not the product of estrangement but is instead intrinsic to finitude, Tillich believes that there is no escape from anxiety. Human beings are essentially finite and so inevitably anxious. What is needed is the courage to cope with anxiety.

Tillich and Sankara do not agree on the matter of anxiety, and this difference points to fundamental differences between the two. By redefining what the human being truly is, Sankara rejects the notion that human beings are essentially finite. It follows that he would also reject the idea that anxiety is an unavoidable feature of human situation. Because anxiety is due to ignorance, anxiety need last only so long as ignorance does. For Tillich, even in the state of ecstasy in which the finite is united with the infinite, anxiety is still present. Human beings are essentially finite despite their belonging to and participation in the infinite ground of being. Indeed, it is precisely because human beings are finite that the possibility of not realizing one's potentialities is a serious and anxiety-producing matter.

In the end, the transition from essence to existence is characterized as the inevitable decision to enter into ambiguous maturity. Though every particular exercise of freedom is subject to moral judgment, the very fact of actualizing freedom is not a moral error. What is problematic is that the step into maturity is also a step into what Tillich calls "separated existence." As Tillich's analysis of estrangement as "unbelief" demonstrates, the decision to realize one's potentialities ruptures essential unity with God.

With the notion of unbelief, we have arrived at the very heart of Tillich's etiology of the human predicament. He writes, "'Unbelief' for Protestant Christianity means the act or state in which man in the totality of his being turns away from God. In his existential self-realization he turns toward himself and his world and loses his essential unity with the ground of his being and his world. This happens both through individual responsibility and through tragic universality. It is freedom and destiny in one and the same act. Man, in actualizing himself, turns to himself and away from God in knowledge, will, and emotion" (ST 2:47). The act of turning away in freedom from God posits a real separation between humanity and divinity. Tillich calls that estrangement or separation "unbelief."

Tillich's analysis of estrangement as unbelief resonates with Sankara's analysis of the human predicament in one important respect. Although the language of turning away is foreign to Sankara's idiom, both thinkers share a common conviction that the human predicament is characterized by a mistaken sense of self-centered or self-enclosed finitude. By self-enclosed finitude, we mean that both thinkers recognize as problematic the human failure to be consciously related to an infinity to which it properly belongs. As Tillich puts it, "In estrangement, man is outside the divine center to which his own center essentially belongs. He is the center of himself and his world" (ST 2:49).

The very possibility of such separation presupposes freedom, and freedom in turn presupposes a distance between beings and being-itself. The reality of freedom is prior to moral error. Estrangement, as the actualization of such freedom, is not rebellion against God. "Unbelief is the separation of man's will from the will of God. It should not be called 'disobedience'; for command, obedience, and disobedience, already presuppose the separation of will from will. He who needs a law which tells him how to act or how not to act is already estranged from the source of the law which demands obedience" (ST 2:47–48). Separation from God makes both obedience and disobedience possible. For the one who is united with God, the question of obedience or disobedience does not arise.

For Sankara, *apparent* separation alone is a sufficient precondition for moral error. Arjuna's inability to do what he must is due to his ignorance of the infinite Self. Ignorance precedes moral error and gives rise to a self-centered finitude that causes him to fall prey to withering grief that obscures clarity regarding his deepest obligations. For Tillich, the separation is quite real and not merely apparent. The human predicament is caused by this separation, this distance between humanity and divinity, the distance of freedom, the distance that makes freedom possible.

One further clarification regarding Tillich's understanding of estrangement as unbelief is necessary. Unbelief is not a refusal to "believe in God." Tillich was allergic to forms of fundamentalism that reduced faith to an act of cognitive assent to dubious propositions. Instead, he maintains that "unbelief is the disruption of man's cognitive participation in God. It should not be called the 'denial' of God. Questions and answers, whether positive or negative, already presuppose the loss of a cognitive union with God. He who asks for God is already estranged from God, though not cut off from him" (ST 2:47). Estrangement must be understood as ontological separation and should not be reduced to a cognitive rejection of God's existence.

If estrangement is an ontological matter, then in what sense are human beings responsible for it? Tillich answers that human beings are responsible for the predicament in which they find themselves because they consciously choose to "leave the divine center," a choice despite the fact that it is also a matter of destiny. The role played by destiny complicates the question of causality. Nevertheless, insofar as human beings choose the "pleasures of a separated life," they are responsible for the predicament in which they find themselves.

Tillich's Diagnosis of the Human Predicament

Human responsibility for estrangement comes into clearer focus when one turns to Tillich's diagnostic analysis of the human predicament. For Tillich, there are three marks of estrangement of which unbelief is but the first. Unbelief appears to be functionally equivalent to Sankara's *avidya* in this regard. For Sankara, ignorance is in a sense the "cause" of the human predicament, but the human predicament cannot be understood apart from the defilements, such as desire and aversion, that issue from ignorance. Likewise, one must turn to an analysis of hubris and concupiscence in order to grasp fully what Tillich means by estrangement as unbelief.

An analysis of Tillich's notion of hubris poses a special problem for this comparative project. According to Tillich, "the main symptom" of hubris "is that man does not acknowledge his finitude" (ST 2:51). Because Sankara teaches that the true Self *is* the infinite Brahman, it is quite possible for Tillichians, and indeed Christians in general, to misconstrue nondualism as metaphysical hubris par excellence! If so, the conversation between East and West could be critically imperiled at this juncture. Is Sankara really guilty of hubris? Does Sankara recognize anything like hubris in his analysis of the human predicament?

In order to answer these questions, the meaning of hubris in Tillich's theology must be clarified. For Tillich, "*Hubris* is not one form of sin beside others. It is sin in its total form, namely, the other side of unbelief or man's turning away from the divine center to which he belongs. It is turning toward one's self as the center of one's self and one's world. This turning toward one's self is not an act done by a special part of man, such as his spirit. Man's whole life, including his sensual life, is spiritual. And it is in the totality of his personal being that man makes himself the center of his world. This is his *hubris*" (ST 2:50–51).

A somewhat glib though not entirely inaccurate response to the question, "Is there an analog to hubris in Sankara's thought?" might be that, for Sankara, the human predicament is not rooted in self-elevation but self-deprecation: Human beings do not recognize their true dignity. But that response does not penetrate deeply into the relevant issues and verges on polemics. In fact, Sankara does name *ahamkara*—a term that can be translated egotism—as a hindrance to liberation. One of Sankara's qualifications for the ideal teacher is that he should be entirely free of "egotism." (U 2.1.6, 212). Such egotism is evident in those moments in which some particular, finite feature of selfhood is overvalued and taken to be what one truly is. Advaitins regard caste pride as one such factor. The notion that being a Brahmin makes one superior to others is an example of *ahamkara*.

For Tillich, hubris is not pride exactly but rather "self-elevation" and such self-elevation is possible even in the moment of apparent humility. Nevertheless, *ahamkara* quite closely approximates Tillich's hubris; both name acts of self-elevation in which the finite self makes itself the center of the world. That Sankara also rejects such self-elevation demonstrates that it is a mistake to suggest that his theological anthropology is hubristic. Sankara is quite clear that the body-mind complex is not Brahman. Any and every conventional marker of identity is wholly finite and nothing more. True, every particular exists only because it has Brahman for its ground. One can even say that the being of every particular is Brahman, but the particular qua particular is not Brahman. The distinction is critical. To confuse finite particulars with the infinite Brahman is just as problematic for Sankara as it is for Tillich.

On the matter of hubris and *ahamkara*, Tillich and Sankara are in close proximity, but when analysis turns to the question of "concupiscence," we come to a moment in which important differences enliven comparison and provoke fundamental normative questions. At first, there appears to be a deep similarity between Sankara's analysis of desire (*raga*) and Tillich's understanding of concupiscence. Deeper probing, however, discloses fundamental differences. The following analysis of concupiscence will demonstrate that Tillich takes great care to distinguish between concupiscence, which is an *illegitimate* and distorted form of desire, and genuine desire or *eros* itself. For Tillich, salvation does not require the elimination of desire as such; desire is a good, natural, and essential part of the fully human life. For Sankara, on the other hand, liberated persons transcend desire entirely.

For Sankara, at the level of ultimate truth, there is no fundamental distinction between legitimate desire and illegitimate or destructive forms of desire. It is difficult to think of a Sanskrit term for desire within Sankara's work—*raga*, *kama*, and so forth—that does not carry a negative valence. There is only one locus in Sankara's thought in which desire plays an unambiguously positive role. This kind of desire is signified not by an independent term but rather by a desiderative grammatical form of the verb "to know." The relevant word is *jijnasa*, the desire to know, a term that is usually paired with *brahma* (Brahman). If there is an appropriate modality of desire, one that is non-possessive and non-addictive, then it is *brahmajijnasa*, the desire to know Brahman. But this form of desire is by nature provisional and penultimate. One desires to know Brahman only so long as one does not know that one already is Brahman. Once the seeker has *jnana* (knowledge), there is no longer any *jijnasa*. Desire is generated by lack, and liberating knowledge discloses that one does not lack Brahman.

The connection between the nature of desire and ontology is quite clear. For Sankara, desire is rooted in an error about one's ontological identity. Desire is caused by ignorance understood as superimposition. Superimposition gives rise to the mistaken notion that we are finite persons who stand over against objects desirable and undesirable. Knowledge liberates persons from desire by removing the notion that we are finite, limited creatures who can be enriched by objects of desire or threatened by undesirable objects. True knowledge of our ultimate identity, the nonduality of true self and the Absolute, extinguishes both the illegitimate desire for finite things and the legitimate desire for Brahman.

For Tillich, on the other hand, there is a sharp distinction between *eros* and concupiscence. As Alexander Irwin has convincingly shown, *eros* is a fundamental theme in Tillich's work.[13] That *eros* should play as commanding a role in Tillich's theology as it does may be a surprising matter for those aware only of Tillich's fundamental affirmation that God is not a being but being-itself. One might well wonder how longing for reunion with God is thinkable if God is not a being. What status can desire have in a theology in which God is not a being who can be the object of desire? The answer to this question hinges on Tillich's understanding of participation—our belonging to and our estrangement from the ground of being. This is the point at which desire and ontology meet in Tillich's thought. For Tillich, all talk of essential union between human beings and God must be understood with reference to a horizon in which separation and reunion are both at work. A proper understanding of the difference between legitimate desire and concupiscence can provide some help on the way to an understanding of the ontology of separation and reunion.

Unbelief and hubris lead human beings to leave the divine center and establish themselves as centers of their own world. Having done so, Tillich argues, they then attempt to draw the entirety of the world from which they are now separated into themselves (ST 2:52). "Every individual, since he is separated from the whole, desires reunion with the whole. His 'poverty' makes him seek for abundance. This is the root of love in all its forms" (ibid.). But love as such is not the problem. Human beings are in fact finite and separated from other beings and so legitimately yearn for that from which they are separated. The problem is unrestricted desire, namely concupiscence. "The possibility of reaching unlimited abundance is the temptation of man who is a self and has a world. The classical name for this desire is *concupiscentia*, 'concupiscence'— the unlimited desire to draw the whole of reality into one's self. . . . It refers to physical hunger as well as to sex, to knowledge as well as to power, to material wealth as well as to spiritual values" (ibid.).

---

13. Alexander C. Irwin. *Eros toward the World: Paul Tillich and the Theology of the Erotic* (Minneapolis: Fortress Press, 1991).

Tillich spells out the distinction between distorted desire and legitimate desire through a discussion of Freud. He argues that although Freud has much to contribute to an understanding of concupiscence and the active role played by desire in all arenas of human life, the psychoanalyst's work is flawed because of a crucial blind spot.

> Freud did not see that his description of human nature is adequate for man only in his existential predicament but not in his essential nature. The endlessness of libido is a mark of man's estrangement. . . . In man's essential relation to himself and to his world, libido is not concupiscence. It is not the infinite desire to draw the universe into one's particular existence, but it is an element of love united with the other qualities of love—*eros, philia,* and *agape.* Love does not exclude desire; it receives libido into itself. But the libido which is united with love is not infinite. It is directed, as all love is, toward a definite subject with whom it wants to unite the bearer of love. . . . Concupiscence, or distorted libido, wants one's own pleasure through the other being, but it does not want the other being. This is the contrast between libido as love and libido as concupiscence. (ST 2:54)

Tillich believes that the Christian who knows that the human being's essential nature is good achieves a more integrated, affirmative, and far less "puritanical attitude toward sex" than Freud can maintain. Tillich's verdict is striking: "In Freud's thought there is no creative *eros* which includes sex. In comparison with a man like Luther, Freud is ascetic in his basic assumption about the nature of man" (ibid.).

If Freud strikes Tillich as puritanical because he fails to affirm desire as a positive good, there is little doubt about how Tillich would regard Sankara's call to transcend desire as such. Sankara's understanding of desire is clearly formed by a monastic commitment to renunciation. Here again, one must bear in mind that for Sankara desire can and does have a legitimate role to play in matters of conventional life. There, desire can be channeled according to proper norms derived from scripture (*sruti*) and tradition. What is appropriate and legitimate in conventional matters is inappropriate only for those who pursue the ultimate goal of liberation. Such seekers must relinquish desire.

Feminists and postmoderns would no doubt see in Sankara's quest to transcend desire a fatal flaw whereas Tillich's affirmation of desire as both inevitable and essentially good would be celebrated. Sankara's emphasis on renunciation might even smack of repression rooted in a problematic rejection of the body. Such critiques are not wholly mistaken, but deeper questions linger here, questions that cannot be resolved without further interrogation.

These questions have to do with the ontological identity of the Self. Simply to dismiss Sankara as misguided and repressed would be a convenient way to bypass his fundamental ontological claims. Beginning with the long process of purifying the mind through the practice of *karmayoga* and appropriate meditative disciplines, Sankara believes that human beings can gradually free themselves from ordinary self-definitions. As persons become free from these conventional identities, the truth found in the Upanishads can have more than theoretical import. Now, freed from the bondage of habitual mental constructions, the Great Sayings such as "That thou art" and "I am Brahman" can elicit a radical cognitive transformation, which in turn leads to an elimination of desire. To engage Sankara adequately, one must struggle with such fundamental ontological and anthropological claims rather than appeal to ideas that have become *de rigueur* in contemporary philosophical and theological circles.

For now, it suffices to note that both Tillich and Sankara recognize the disfiguring power of compulsive desire. Tillich believes that such desire results from ontological disruption—separation from the divine life—whereas Sankara maintains that desire is due to an ignorance of ontological truth that one's true Self is divine. Both agree that limitless and uncontrolled desire emerges when finite selves attempt to erase that finitude by swallowing the world entire. Such distorted desire cannot be eliminated until the self comes to see and know itself otherwise.

What does life lived in the grip of unbelief, hubris, and concupiscence look like? What consequences follow from the power of these three components of estrangement? We have already stipulated that no comprehensive account of the consequences of the human predicament is possible. Because estrangement distorts every human activity and enterprise, the consequences of such distortions are many and profound. Substantial portions of each volume of Tillich's *Systematic Theology* are devoted to a detailed enumeration of the consequences of estrangement. Nevertheless, a rudimentary sketch of the consequences of the human predicament must be ventured to set the stage for an analysis of salvation as the healing of distortions generated by estrangement. Put simply, without an understanding of what needs healing, no understanding of healing is possible.

Tillich's understanding of the consequences of estrangement can be captured by the terms *self-contradiction* and *self-destruction*.

> Man finds himself, together with his world, in existential estrangement, unbelief, *hubris*, and concupiscence. Each expression of the estranged state contradicts man's essential being, his potency for goodness. It contradicts the created structure of himself and his world and their interdependence. And self-contradiction drives toward self-destruction. The elements of essential being which move against each other tend to annihilate each other and the whole to which they belong. Destruction under the conditions of existential estrangement is not caused by some external force. It is not the work of special divine or demonic interferences, but is the consequence of the structure of estrangement itself. (ST 2:59–60)

The structure of estrangement or "structure of destruction" are Tillich's ways of referring to the ontological structure described earlier. When the self-world structure, together with the ontological polarities that constitute that structure, are disrupted by estrangement, that life-giving structure becomes the "structure of destruction." When human beings are separated from the divine life, these poles—always in tension to begin with—now "tend to annihilate each other." The result is the violation of selfhood and the world to which it belongs; no punishing deity or malevolent evil force is needed to rupture human life.

For Tillich, "self-loss" and "world-loss" inevitably accompany each other. "Self-loss is the loss of one's determining center, the disintegration of the unity of the person. This is manifest in moral conflicts and in psychopathological disruptions, independently or interdependently. The horrifying experience of 'falling to pieces' gets hold of the person. To the degree in which this happens, one's world also falls to pieces. It ceases to be a world, in the sense of a meaningful whole" (ST 2:61).

There is little need to supplement this grim but insightful picture with a painstaking analysis of how this destruction comes about as each ontological polarity is disrupted. A brief summary of the third ontological polarity under the impact of estrangement will adequately illuminate Tillich's understanding of the process of disintegration. With respect to the pair of freedom and destiny, under estrangement, human action becomes increasingly alienated from the meaningful context in which it is properly situated, the context in which action has its own authentic content and purpose. The result is arbitrariness. Unconstrained by destiny and context, persons mistakenly take freedom to mean doing what one pleases. Tillich's analysis is poignant: "In the moment of aroused freedom a process starts in which freedom separates itself from the destiny to which it belongs. It becomes arbitrariness. Willful acts are acts in which freedom moves toward the separation from destiny. Under the control of *hubris* and concupiscence, freedom ceases to relate itself to the objects provided by destiny. It relates itself to an indefinite number of contents" (ST 2:62–63). The end result is that one's life is no longer one's own but rather the arbitrary production of choices that say little about who one truly is. What makes the situation all the more tragic is that such arbitrary action turns out to be all too predictable. "To the degree to which freedom is distorted into arbitrariness, destiny is distorted into mechanical necessity. If man's freedom is not directed by destiny or if it is a series of contingent acts of arbitrariness, it falls under the control of forces which move against one another without a deciding center. What seems to be free proves to be conditioned by internal compulsions and external causes. Parts of the self overtake the center and determine it without being united with the other parts" (ST 2:63). So goes the path from fragmentation to eventual disintegration.

Tillich's analysis of the "structure of destruction" sets the stage for a penetrating analysis of the relationship between finitude and estrangement. We bring this chapter to a close by highlighting a single theme present everywhere in discussions of the topics just enumerated—a theme that Tillich believes distinguishes Christian thought from its Eastern counterparts. Throughout Tillich's diagnosis of the human predicament, he takes great care to emphasize that *finitude as such* is not problematic. Finitude is experienced as problematic only when persons are separated from the power of being-itself:

> Participation in the eternal makes man eternal; separation from the eternal leaves man in his natural finitude. . . . In estrangement man is left to his finite nature of having to die. Sin does not produce death but gives to death the power which is conquered only in participation in the eternal. . . . If man is left to his "having to die," the essential anxiety about non-being is transformed into the horror of death. . . . Under the conditions of estrangement, anxiety has a different character, brought on by the element of guilt. The loss of one's potential eternity is experienced as something for which one

is responsible in spite of its universal tragic actuality. Sin is the sting
of death, not its physical cause. It transforms the anxious awareness
of one's having to die into the painful realization of a lost eternity.
(ST 2:67–68)

Tillich argues here that death and anxiety are not intrinsically evil. They
are but the inescapable warp and woof of finitude. They are felt as evil only by
those who stand separated from that power that helps human beings confront
death and meet anxiety with courage. This vital distinction between estrangement and finitude, Tillich believes, is inadequately formulated and sometimes
altogether neglected by Eastern religious traditions.

> Suffering, like death, is an element of finitude. . . . Under the conditions of
> existence, man is cut off from this blessedness [of dreaming innocence],
> and suffering lays hold of him in a destructive way. Suffering becomes
> a structure of destruction—an evil. It is decisive for the understanding
> of Christianity and the great religions of the East, especially Buddhism,
> that suffering as an element of essential finitude is distinguished from
> suffering as an element of existential estrangement. If, as in Buddhism,
> this distinction is not made, finitude and evil are identified. Salvation
> becomes salvation from finitude and the suffering it implies. But it is
> not—as it is in Christianity—salvation from the estrangement which
> transforms suffering into a structure of destruction. . . . In Christian-
> ity the demand is made to accept suffering as an element of finitude
> with an ultimate courage and thereby to overcome that suffering which
> is dependent on existential estrangement, which is mere destruction.
> Christianity knows that such a victory over destructive suffering is only
> partly possible in time and space. But whether this fragmentary vic-
> tory is fought for or not makes all the difference between Western and
> Eastern cultures. . . . It changes the valuation of the individual, of per-
> sonality, of community, and of history. It has, in fact, determined the
> historical destiny of mankind. (ST 2:70)

Tillich's overall point is clear: Whereas Christianity seeks to do battle only
against "destructive suffering" rather than suffering as such, the Eastern traditions, having equated suffering with finitude, seek to overleap death and
finitude itself. Tillich believes that this confusion has had world-historical

consequences inasmuch as the East has mistakenly come to see all forms of finite particularity as necessarily compromised.

Tillich's remarks brings us back full circle to the question with which this chapter began: Is Tillich right to maintain that what distinguishes Christian faith from the religions of the East is that Christianity accepts finitude whereas Eastern traditions do finitude a disservice by seeing it as intrinsically distorted? Sankara does often suggest that the finite world is problematic as such, particularly when he speaks about embodiment. The body, subject as it is to heat and cold, pleasure and pain, is itself the product of past karmic action and so bears the marks of its ambiguous heritage. It is not difficult to see how Tillich might have come to believe that liberation in the East is liberation from finitude as such rather than from its distortions.

However, for Sankara, finite experience is neither uniformly negative nor painful. The trouble with conventional experience—with life as it is ordinarily lived—is that it is a wholly relative matter of more or less: more or less pleasure, more or less pain. The longing for liberation is a longing for something qualitatively different from this quantitative round of more or less. To find the ultimate good (*paramapurusartha*) one must transcend finitude, this despite the fact that the finite world, including the body-mind complex, is necessary to discover that ultimate good.

The key question is this: In what sense does the Advaitin seek to transcend finitude? Sankara seeks to transcend finitude by demonstrating that the being of any finite thing whatsoever is the being of Brahman. Even though each and every particular qua particular is an evanescent affair, a thing without purchase on permanence, nonetheless insofar as we can say of that particular, "It is," the isness we find is the being of Brahman. This truth applies paradigmatically to the human soul, to the human being. Does this mean that we can pretend that our bodies and minds are not shot through and through with finitude and impermanence? Not in the least. Sankara is altogether aware that every contingent feature of human identity is finite. What Sankara aims to teach is that these finite particularities are *never* separated from Brahman. And that is why it simply will not do to suppose that human being is wholly defined by finitude. The person who is established in the knowledge of Brahman's presence is "endowed with understanding, memory, tranquility, self-control, compassion, favor and the like; he is versed in the traditional doctrine; not attached to any enjoyments, visible or invisible . . . a knower of Brahman, he is established in Brahman; he leads a blameless life, free from faults such as deceit, pride, trickery, wickedness, fraud, jealousy, falsehood, egotism, self-interest, and so forth;

with the only purpose of helping others he wishes to make use of knowledge" (U 2.1.6, 212). Far from being utterly removed from finitude, the knower of Brahman is superbly capable of engaging practical affairs with detachment and equanimity. In the end, all talk regarding the unreality of finitude and the absolute reality of the infinite Brahman must be understood as an attempt to show that the former cannot exist apart from the latter. This, after all, is the meaning of nondualism.

Nevertheless, we have argued that Sankara does not wholly succeed in being nondualistic (although he does on his own terms). There remains, in the end, a distinction between the real and unchanging Self and the unreal but changing world. The result of this dualism is that the exemplary Advaitin need not engage in the labor of mending the world and can instead opt for the transcendence of solitary renunciation. And that kind of detachment suggests that Tillich's critique is partially on the mark. At least some Eastern traditions in some modalities, Sankara's Advaita in particular, do not mandate active and transformative engagement with the broken world.

But is it not also possible to read Sankara otherwise? Ultimately, the finite world is indeed necessary for liberating knowledge. That knowledge is to be found, as we have shown, not by a mystical flight from conventional experience but by coming to know through revelation that the light of consciousness present in each moment is the true Self. When that knowledge is gained, then life under the compulsion of desire and aversion is overcome. The liberated self is the healed self now distinguished by the qualities listed above. Insofar as Advaitins aspire to embody self-control, compassion, and the like, and to be free of deceit and egoism, Tillich would have to concede that they hope to heal rather than to escape from ordinary life. Tillich's dichotomy between the East's quest for liberation from finitude and the Western struggle to transform finitude may be overdrawn.

Tillich is convinced that it is within finitude that one fulfills one's human potentialities. Furthermore, even in ecstatic union with the infinite, the finite person never ceases to be finite. Union with the ground and power of being heals finite beings, albeit in a fragmentary way under the conditions of existence. The task at hand is to examine in detail the dynamic nature of such healing in order to assess more accurately the differences at stake between Sankara and Tillich.

In this chapter, we have inaugurated an East-West conversation on the question of the human predicament. Special attention has been given to significant differences between Sankara and Tillich as these differences raise normative issues for theological anthropology. In each and every case of significant difference, a single ontological issue has loomed large. Whereas Sankara attributes the human predicament and its consequences to ignorance of one's identity with the Self of all, Tillich diagnoses a deeper ontological disruption. Human beings are separated from their essential natures and from each other because they are estranged from God who is the ground of being. Salvation is the healing of a real ontological rupture whereas liberation is the removal of the ignorant notion that there is any separation at all. For Tillich, salvation is the reunion of the estranged. Human beings can recover their essential nature and dignity and are restored to right relationship with each other only because they have been ecstatically grasped by the power of being-itself.

The "distance" of separation—which is also the space of reunion—therefore acquires a signal prominence in Tillich's system. This is a distance charged with longing and desire, right and inevitable. In the moment of reunion, desire is not eliminated; rather, desire becomes the desire *of* God *for* God manifested in and through love for finite beings. What remains to be determined is the precise nature of this ontological distance. How is a distance between creatures and the God who is being-itself possible? This fundamental question concerning the ontology of separation and reunion will provide an orienting focus for our analysis of Tillich's approach to the prognosis and treatment of the human predicament.

chapter five

Tillich on Salvation as Ecstatic Healing

Prognosis and Therapy

~~~

Ecstasy and Nonduality

The previous chapter demonstrated that for Tillich the human predicament is closely bound up with the question of freedom. If the creature is to be free from and for the divine, then the creature must be at some distance from the divine. Of course, this distance is not to be conceived spatially. God is not somewhere else than I am. Freedom just *is* the distance between divinity and humanity. My freedom is the distance that allows me to stand over against the divine, and it is also the distance that creates in me a longing for the divine. Human life in general and the process of healing in particular are caught up in this movement of separation and reunion. Separation or estrangement generates the human predicament, and union—or, more precisely, *reunion*—leads to healing.

For Tillich, reunion is ecstatic in character. Human beings standing in separation are grasped by the divine Spirit and reunited with their own divine depth, a depth to which they essentially and truly belong but from which they are actually estranged. In such reunion, the self is driven beyond itself but without being ruptured or fragmented because the power that grasps it is not alien. That would be the mark not of ecstasy but of possession. We are grasped by the power of being-itself in which we always already participate, a power to which we eternally belong. Ecstasy names both the event of reunion but also the structure of the God-human relationship, the structure that makes reunion possible.

This chapter will explore the nature of this movement of separation and reunion. Several critical questions will be in play. If I can only be free from and for God by standing in separation, standing on my own ground outside the divine life, does it not follow that human life is inevitably compromised? Given Tillich's definition of sin as separation and given the further conclusion that freedom is made possible precisely by separation, then freedom seems to come at an exorbitant price. Freedom appears to be both a blessing and a curse because the freedom that lets me choose God or choose against God puts me outside the divine life and thus in a situation where my life will inevitably and perhaps even necessarily be marred by brokenness.

How then is healing possible? If healing happens only when I am reunited with the divine life, how does that reunion take place? And what is the character of that reunion and the healing it brings? Is it fleeting and episodic or can it endure? To formulate the question in terms of the medical model, what is the expected prognosis? Can the human predicament and the disruptive consequences it generates for human communities and nature be healed, or is the condition more or less chronic, offering hope only for amelioration but nothing as definitive as a cure?

The great power of Sankara's account is the hope he offers for complete recovery. That hope is grounded in his deep conviction that human beings are, in actuality, *never* separated from Brahman. The presence of the immanent divine serves as the ground for radical hope. The human predicament, though grave and disfiguring, finally cannot endure for those who see that they are never removed from ultimate reality.

Tragically, even that profound hope comes at considerable cost. Human beings, by the grace of revelation and the grace of the guru, must learn to see that their ordinary identities and the entire world of flux are unreal. Only radical detachment from materiality makes healing possible.

Can Tillich's notion of ecstasy provide for a different kind of divine intimacy, one in which my action is also God's action? This possibility lies at the root and center of Tillich's thought. Tillich deliberately sought to reject conventional forms of Christian theistic dualism in which God is taken to be a being who stands over against self and world. As an alternative, Tillich developed a Pauline theology of ecstasy that attempts to think through and account for the experience of being prayed through by the Holy Spirit. In genuine prayer Tillich, with St. Paul, believed that the Spirit prays in and through persons. The result is a moment in which my prayer is also God's prayer, God's action my own. The conventional subject-object structure of reality is transcended when beings are grasped and ecstatically driven beyond themselves into reunion with the ground of being. Here we glimpse a kind of dynamic immanence, a Christian version of nonduality, impossible within Sankara's framework.

This kind of nonduality is most conspicuous in Tillich's central notion of ultimate concern, Tillich's term for faith.[1] In ultimate concern, Tillich argues, there is profound union between divinity and humanity. Tillich's own words are instructive:

> The ultimate of the act of faith and the ultimate that is meant in the act of faith are one and the same. This is symbolically expressed by the mystics when they say that their knowledge of God is the knowledge God has of himself. . . . Even a successful prayer is, according to Paul (Rom. 8), not possible without God as Spirit praying within us. The same experience expressed in abstract language is the disappearance of the ordinary subject-object scheme in the experience of the ultimate, the unconditional. In the act of faith that which is the source of this act is present beyond the cleavage of subject and object.[2]

Tillich defined unbelief as the separation of the total personality from the divine ground. Here, faith is defined as an act of the total personality in which the separation between human and divine is overcome. Faith cannot be produced by human initiative, but faith is most assuredly a total act of the human person. "The source of this act" is the ultimate itself "present beyond the cleavage of subject and object." Ultimate concern is at once the subject's concern *for* the ultimate and the work *of* the ultimate that refuses to remain merely an object.

Prayer and ultimate concern are moments of radical immanence in Tillich's vision. The question at hand is "What about Tillich's ontology makes such intimacy possible, and how nearly does this intimacy approach nonduality?" The basic challenge that stands in the way of reading Tillich as a nondualist is clear: His theology employs a language of separation and reunion and not the vocabulary of nondualism, a vocabulary in which no separation is posited. Tillich's rejection of theistic dualism does not rule out distance and separation between creature and creator. How can Tillich's ontology allow for the healing immanence experienced in faith and prayer and yet also allow for separation between God and creatures, the separation that makes possible the distortions

---

1. The following considerations on faith—the opposite of unbelief, which is the first mark of estrangement—anticipate a more extended discussion of the self-transcendent or ecstatic character of reality to follow.

2. Paul Tillich, *Dynamics of Faith* (New York: Harper & Row, 1957), 11. Hereafter DOF.

that mark the human predicament? Questions about separation and reunion can also be formulated in very traditional theological terms: What is the nature of transcendence and immanence in Tillich's theology?

Transcendence and Immanence in Tillich's Theology

Tillich believed that theologians must avoid two pervasive theological errors if they are to understand transcendence and immanence rightly: "supranaturalism" and "naturalism." Over against these two unsatisfactory possibilities, the first of which disfigures transcendence and the second of which distorts immanence, he presents a "self-transcendent" or "ecstatic" doctrine of God as being-itself (ST 2:5). A supranaturalist doctrine of God takes God to be a being, albeit a highest being who stands over against the universe. The supranaturalist's God "has brought the universe into being at a certain moment . . . governs it according to a plan, directs it toward an end, interferes with its ordinary processes in order to overcome resistance and to fulfill his purpose, and will bring it to consummation in a final catastrophe" (ST 2:6). Tillich finds this God-concept deeply problematic because it transforms ultimate reality into a being who stands over against finitude and is in fact limited by that very finitude. "This is done in respect to space by establishing a supranatural divine world alongside the natural human world; in respect to time by determining a beginning and end of God's creativity; in respect to causality by making God a cause alongside other causes; in respect to substance by attributing individual substance to him" (ibid.). Applying these categories to God, even in a superlative manner, only reduces the qualitative difference between God and the world by making God one entity among others. To correct for such deficiencies, Tillich believed that God must be understood instead as the ground and power of being.

But how does the notion that God is being-itself better secure transcendence? Tillich contends that the God who is being-itself is not merely one being among others but the source of being for all creatures. By adopting this revised conception, theologians can avoid the misguided task of paying God false compliments. As Tillich puts it, "When applied to God, superlatives become diminutives. They place him on the level of other beings while elevating him above all of them" (ST 1:235). The supranaturalist makes the mistake of reducing God to the level of other beings precisely when praising God as the best of them all.

Interestingly, safeguarding transcendence by dismissing spurious attributions of a special divine spatiality and temporality not only elevates the notion of God but also results in a richer conception of divine immanence. The God who is being-itself does not stand above or over against creatures. Rather, beings exist only by participating in the God who is being-itself. "The divine life participates in every life as its ground and aim. God participates in everything that is; he has community with it; he shares in its destiny. Certainly such statements are highly symbolic. They can have the unfortunate logical implication that there is something alongside God in which he participates from the outside. But the divine participation *creates* that in which it participates" (ST 1:245; emphasis added).

Tillich notes that even the term *participation* can be misconstrued if it is taken to name an external relation between two independent realities. However, because beings do not exist apart from their participation in God, the notion that God and creatures are external to each other is mistaken. God's participation in the creature creates and sustains the creature. For Tillich, "The doctrine of creation affirms that God is the creative ground of everything in every moment. In this sense there is no creaturely independence from which an external relation between God and the creature could be derived" (ST 1:271).

The significance of this vital claim for East-West conversation is hard to overstate. As noted in the first chapter, it has long been assumed that the doctrine of creation is the decisive stumbling block that separates Western theistic dualism from Eastern forms of nondualism. The chasm between the uncreated creator and the created world putatively cannot be bridged. Tillich's account of creation jettisons this dualism. The world derives its being by participating in being-itself and has no being apart from that participation. Thus, creation names the most intimate and radical presence of God to the world. By appealing to the notion of God as being-itself, Tillich effects a profound convergence between deep transcendence and radical immanence.

By rejecting the notion that God is *a* being and by rejecting the idea that the relation between being-itself and beings is external, Tillich departs from dualism and brings Christian theology into close proximity with Sankara's nondualism. Within Tillich's theology, there is no numerical relation between God and creature, between being-itself and beings. God is not a divine One over against a human one. Put simply, God plus creature does not equal two. Despite much talk of separation and distance in Tillich's system, this axiomatic commitment must not be overlooked.

If supranaturalists disfigure transcendence by reducing God to a divine being who inhabits a separate superworld of space and time, naturalists make a very different theological mistake, one that leads to a false account of divine immanence. A naturalist understanding of God "identifies God with the universe, with its essence or with special powers within it. God is the name for the power and meaning of reality. He is not identified with the totality of things. . . . But he is a symbol of the unity, harmony, and power of being; he is the dynamic and creative center of reality" (ST 2:6). Ideas of God as the "power of being" and as "creative ground" are integral to Tillich's own position; the naturalist position is patently closer to his own and less theologically flat-footed than the error of supranaturalism. But naturalism is problematic nonetheless despite its greater philosophical sophistication: "The main argument against naturalism . . . is that it denies the infinite distance between the whole of finite things and their infinite ground, with the consequence that the term 'God' becomes interchangeable with the term 'universe' and therefore is semantically superfluous. This semantic situation reveals the failure of naturalism to understand a decisive element in the experience of the holy, namely, the distance between finite man, on the one hand, and the holy in its numerous manifestations, on the other. For this, naturalism cannot account" (ST 2:7).

If supranaturalism is problematic because of an impoverished conception of transcendence, naturalism fails because it generates a mistaken immanence that leaves no distance between God and the world. But given Tillich's rejection of a distinctive divine spatiality, what can Tillich mean by speaking of the "infinite distance between the whole of finite things and their infinite ground"? The question is even more acute given Tillich's rejection of external relations between God and creatures. Clearly, this distance can neither be spatial in nature nor can it be distance of a sort that would result in supranatural dualism. Any such distance would violate Tillich's account of participation as a relation that creates the terms of the relation.

Tillich opens a "third way" beyond supranaturalism and naturalism. He acknowledges that this way is not far removed from naturalism. "It agrees with the naturalistic view by asserting that God would not be God if he were not the creative ground of everything that has being, that, in fact, he is the infinite and unconditional power of being or, in the most radical abstraction, that he is being-itself. In this respect God is neither alongside things nor even 'above' them; he is nearer to them than they are to themselves. He is their creative ground, here and now, always and everywhere" (ibid.).

Tillich distinguishes his position from naturalism by arguing for a "self-transcendent" or an "ecstatic" view of God and reality. The key to this vision of reality is a subtle definition of freedom as transcendence, a freedom that naturalism fails to recognize. For Tillich, God transcends the creature to the degree that the creature is able to stand against God. The term *transcendence* does not signify the unrelatedness of two distinct entities, one of which absolutely exceeds the other. The distance of transcendence is the space of freedom. "God as the ground of being infinitely transcends that of which he is the ground. He stands *against* the world, in so far as the world stands against him, and he stands *for* the world, thereby causing it to stand for him. . . . Only in this sense can we speak of 'transcendent' with respect to the relation of God and the world. To call God transcendent in this sense does not mean that one must establish a 'superworld' of divine objects. It does mean that, within itself, the finite world points beyond itself. In other words, it is self-transcendent" (ibid.; emphasis in original).

Having rejected the idea of a special divine realm with its own peculiar spatiality and temporality, Tillich is obligated to ascribe to immanence and transcendence nonspatial meanings (ST 1:263). Tillich's solution is to emphasize the *qualitative* meaning of these central terms. Immanence does not mean that God shares the same space as the world does. Immanence points to the fact that God is the world's "permanent creative ground" (ibid.). Transcendence, on the other hand, points both to the divine infinity and to the mutual freedom of finite and infinite. The point about freedom is more decisive than claims about God's infinity, however, because divine infinity as such does not separate God from the world. Rather, precisely God's infinity makes God immanent in and to everything.

> The religious interest in the divine transcendence is not satisfied where one rightly asserts the infinite transcendence of the infinite over the finite. This transcendence does not contradict but rather confirms the coincidence of opposites. The infinite is present in everything finite, in the stone as well as the genius. Transcendence demanded by religious experience is the freedom-to-freedom relationship which is actual in every personal encounter. (Ibid.)

To know what Tillich means here, one must unpack his passing reference to "the coincidence of opposites," a notion advanced most notably by Nicholas of Cusa, the fifteenth-century theologian and cardinal. Appealing to Nicholas, Tillich argues here and elsewhere (ST 1:81–82, 176, 277) that the relationship of the finite and the infinite must be reimagined otherwise than as a mere opposition in which the infinite stands over against the finite.

Nicholas invokes the notion of God as "Not-other" in order to advance a more satisfactory explanation of the relationship between finite and infinite. Briefly put, Nicholas argues that every finite reality is defined by its being *other* than every other finite reality. Finite identity consists, at least in part, in otherness. But God's otherness cannot be of the same kind. God cannot be different from me in just the same way that a table is different from a chair; that would amount to a merely relative otherness. God's otherness, Nicholas insists, must consist precisely in God's being "Not-other" than any finite reality. Only then is God's otherness wholly different in kind from relative otherness.

Whereas finite identity is constituted by exclusion, the sky being other than earth, the infinite is known otherwise, namely by the fact that God is Not-other than sky. Indeed, it is the very presence of Not-other in the sky that makes the sky be not-other than itself and also prevents it from simply not being. Nicholas writes, "all these things are *other* than their respective opposites. But because God is not *other* than [any] other, He is Not-other, although Not-Other and other seem to be opposed. But other is not opposed to that from which it has the fact that it is other. . . . You see now how it is that the theologians rightly affirmed that in all things God is all things, even though [He is] none of these things."[3]

Despite the obscurity of Nicholas's rhetoric, his basic thesis is comprehensible. God's infinity makes God radically present in and to everything as its source. Because Tillich accepts Nicholas's reading of the infinite as Not-Other, it follows that God's infinity, far from making God transcendent to finite realities, is the ground for divine immanence. Hence, transcendence must be understood otherwise than by appeal to God's infinity, and for Tillich, freedom is the key. The creature transcends God and God transcends the creature precisely because each is free for and from the other.

Another way to think transcendence other than by appeal to divine infinity comes from religious experience. More specifically, Tillich recommends a turn to experiences of God as "wholly other" of the sort described by Rudolf Otto. What is religiously significant is the experience of God as *mysterium tremendum*; in such experiences, transcendence signifies a *quality* of being that wholly exceeds the religious person. The human being is shaken by an encounter with

---

3. Nicolas of Cusa, *Nicholas of Cusa on God as Not-Other: A Translation and Appraisal of De Li Non Aliud* (Minneapolis: Arthur J. Banning Press, 1987), 57.

power, with an intensity of being and meaning of a wholly different order than is given in ordinary experience. Estranged human life is deeply diminished in vitality and intentionality. Human life is qualitatively impoverished because of its failure to be dynamically related to God. The ontological structure on which human life is based becomes distorted when human beings are estranged from the power and ground of being-itself.

In experiences of the transcendent, human beings meet something in which power and meaning are unlimited. God's otherness does not consist in God's being another being or even an infinite being, but rather in God's identity as the inexhaustible source of power and meaning, namely being-itself. The sense of the numinous given in religious experience does not indicate that God is another being but speaks instead to an encounter with the ground and abyss of being. God is no being who just happens to be more powerful that humans are; God is meaning and power-itself.

Human beings are incapable of living as vitally and meaningfully as they ought to—as their essential natures should allow—because they have turned away from this source of power and meaning. This capacity to turn away from God points back to the primary and critical meaning of transcendence in Tillich's theology. Transcendence consists in just this human freedom to be able to "turn away from the essential unity with the ground of its being." When human beings seek to realize, to actualize their own freedom, they stand outside the divine ground in the sense that they enter into "an existence which is no longer united with essence" (ST 1:255). Of course, this separation from the divine ground is never total. Freedom "presupposes two qualities of the created: first, that it is substantially independent of the divine ground; second, that it remains in substantial unity with it. Without the latter unity, the creature would be without the power of being. It is the quality of finite freedom within the created which makes pantheism impossible and not the notion of a highest being alongside the world . . ." (ST 2:8).

Tillich's reference to pantheism in this context is striking and somewhat unexpected. Clearly, he is aware that he is advancing a vision of divine intimacy that might be mistaken as pantheistic. Therefore, he contends quite carefully that what differentiates his own ecstatic naturalism from pantheism pure and simple is that on his account creatures are not mere modes of an underlying divine substance. Creatures stand in freedom over against God because they are "substantially independent" from God. As already noted, this freedom makes possible the distance required for relationship between God and creature even though this freedom is also tragically bound up with the diminished vitality and intentionality of creatures separated from their own home ground.

Tillich also rejects supranaturalism and naturalism because he finds the categories of causality and substance inadequate for thinking about the relationship between God and creation. He goes so far as to assert that "Both ways are impossible" (ST 1:237). Thinking of God as the world's substance "establishes a naturalistic pantheism . . . which denies finite freedom and in so doing denies the freedom of God. By necessity God is merged into finite beings, and their being is his being" (ST 1:237). Here, the problem with thinking of God as the world's substance is not God's radical presence in the world and creatures. Radical presence is fine so long as creaturely freedom is not annihilated. That negation of freedom is precisely the trouble with naturalistic pantheism.

Sankara also rejects the idea that Brahman is the substance of the world although he believes it is not a bad way to *begin* thinking about the Brahman-world relationship. At the level of conventional truth, the notion of Brahman as material cause can serve as a conceptual aid for leading beginners to nonduality. However, he ultimately rejects the idea that Brahman is the substance out of which the world is formed like jars and pots are formed out of clay. Such a notion draws Brahman down into the world and subjects Brahman to change.

Sankara wants Brahman to serve as world ground without having Brahman conditioned by this grounding relationship. Tillich finds substantialism problematic not because it compromises the immutability of divinity but because human beings would have no independence over against ultimate reality just as jars and pots have no freedom over against clay. Tillich is also concerned about protecting divine freedom, but the contrast with Sankara is more clearly evident when one observes that whereas Sankara focuses primarily on preserving Brahman's immutable transcendence, Tillich focuses on creaturely freedom.

Because substantialist accounts of the God-world relation threaten freedom, Tillich observes that Christian tradition has embraced causality as its preferred category. God is conceived not as the world's substance but rather as its cause. But causality is also inadequate from Tillich's perspective because, through causality, God is "drawn into" the series of cause and effects (ST 1:238). The inevitable result of such causal models is supranaturalism, which makes God just the first in a series of causes, albeit the most special.

Sankara also rejects causality as an adequate model for describing the relationship between Brahman and the world. If Brahman is the world's cause, then Brahman becomes really related to the world, but how can there be a real relation between two different orders of reality? The desert cannot be really related to the mirage. Brahman's radical transcendence is compromised by a real causal relation between Brahman and the world. In sum, both thinkers reject the adequacy of substance and causality models. Ultimate reality is neither material nor efficient cause.

Both are committed to searching for nonsubstantialist and noncausal ways to think about the relation between ultimate reality and the world but for different reasons. Sankara seeks to preserve the eternal, immutable independence of Brahman whereas Tillich seeks to preserve the "substantial independence" of the creature. Both succeed but at very high cost. Sankara maintains the independence of Brahman but at the expense of declaring the world to be unreal. Tillich preserves creaturely freedom but in so doing introduces a tragic and inevitable rupture between God and human beings. This rupture, as we shall see, is never wholly healed. Human life remains perpetually at risk and vulnerable to estrangement. No one is healed and reunited with the divine life in such a way that human life becomes even relatively invulnerable to estrangement and disintegration.

It is worth asking whether there may be some way of imagining the relation between being-itself and beings that neither compromises on the reality of the world nor seeks to preserve creaturely freedom at the expense of a tragic and universal separation between God and humanity. An adequate response to this question would require nothing short of a fully developed theological ontology, a task well beyond the scope of the present project. Nonetheless, a critical comparison of Sankara and Tillich can shed light on the way that leads toward this larger goal.

God as Living; God as Spirit

Here, according to Tillich, is where we stand: Opt for an account in which God is the substance of the world and creaturely freedom is lost, and the creature is reduced to a mode of the divine life. Choose instead an account of God as first cause, and God becomes the first being, just the first in a series of causes, and transcendence is compromised. Moreover, if God is a distinct albeit supranatural being, then again, human freedom is potentially if not actually threatened by that being's power and sovereignty. Neither account allows for ecstatic action in which my action is both genuinely my own and the action of God working in and through me. What is necessary is an ontology of ecstasy that can render plausible what Tillich calls "the mutual immanence" of the human spirit and the divine Spirit (ST 3:114), an immanence that does not negate freedom.

The work of formulating such an ontology is complicated because no concept can adequately describe the relation between being-itself and beings. In the final analysis, Tillich believes, only symbolic language will do. Even conceptual terms must function symbolically when applied to God, and that is most especially true when it comes to causality and substance (ST 1:238). Instead of these two terms, Tillich prefers "a more directly symbolic term, 'the creative and abysmal ground of being.' In this term both naturalistic pantheism, based on the category of substance, and rationalistic theism, based on the category of causality are overcome" (ibid.).

The term *ground* serves for Tillich as the symbol that best draws on the meanings of both causality and substance models while rejecting their literal adequacy. God can be *imagined* as substance inasmuch as beings cannot exist apart from God just as pots and jars cannot exist apart from clay; but God cannot *be* substance, metaphysically speaking, without denying creaturely freedom. Likewise, God can and must be imagined as cause because God makes creatures to be, but God cannot literally *be* a cause for reasons already enumerated.

The symbolic use of language takes its bearings from the observation that God grounds the structure of being. What one knows about God can be derived only from that very structure. By way of contrast, it should be noted that Sankara is unwilling to use Brahman's character as ground of the world as a reliable guide to Brahman's true nature. Ultimately, Brahman's function as world-ground is not intrinsic to the nature of Brahman as such. All assertions about Brahman derived by way of Brahman's function as world-ground must be affirmed as provisionally valid but ultimately inadequate. Tillich's talk about God as an abyss into which all forms disappear points to a similar insight regarding the utter transcendence of the divine. As the inexhaustible depth out of which all things emerge and into which all things disappear, God absolutely exceeds as mystery the structure of which God is ground.

But nonetheless, God really is the ground of being as well as its depth and abyss. God's character as ground of the structure of being is neither provisional nor contingent. Tillich definitively states, "There is no divine nature which could be abstracted from his eternal creativity" (ST 2:147). For Tillich,

"The ground is not only an abyss in which every form disappears; it also is the source from which every form emerges. The ground of being has the character of self-manifestation; it has *logos* character. This is not something added to the divine life; it is the divine life itself" (ST 1:157–58). Tillich's God is quite unlike Sankara's Brahman in this respect. Whereas Sankara's Brahman can be thought (though not known) apart from the world, Tillich's God cannot.

Having established that God's character as ground of the structure of being makes symbolic knowledge of God possible, two closely related notions central to Tillich's ecstatic doctrine of God can now be considered: God as living and God as Spirit. Here too, Tillich makes clear that God is not a living being but rather the ground of all life processes (ST 1:241). Tillich maintains that it is appropriate to conceive of God as living by appeal to biblical tradition, but his most basic contention is that God is *experienced* as living when human beings are healed. When persons experience healing transformation, the symbolic attribution of life to God is most appropriate because God makes new life possible. The one who grants new life must be symbolized as living.

The implications of such an assertion are extensive. A symbolic doctrine of God as living distinguishes Tillich's position from any conception in which ultimate reality is understood as unchanging. This is not to say that Tillich would speak of God as "becoming," a notion he firmly rejects (ST 1:247). Nevertheless, Tillich's understanding of God differs significantly from Sankara's eternally changeless Brahman. True, Brahman can be said to be the ground of life, but Sankara would not thereby conclude that Brahman ought to be characterized as living.

A fundamental point of contrast is evident. Sankara and Tillich can be shown to agree often when Sankara's statements regarding Brahman as world ground are compared with Tillich's symbolic doctrine of God. Sankara's Brahman as qualified by the world is very much like Tillich's God as ground of being: Both can be characterized as dynamic, living, and creative. However, Sankara ultimately rejects the notion that Brahman can really be characterized by its status as the world's ground. The world-grounding function of Brahman does not determine what Brahman is and so cannot provide valid knowledge about Brahman as it is in itself.

For Tillich, the key to knowledge of God rests on the ontological polarities that make up the structure of being. They constitute the rational structure of reality, and that structure is not arbitrary. The *logos* structure of reality discloses the *logos* structure of the divine life. So, the polarities of individualization and participation, dynamics and form, and freedom and destiny can be employed to symbolize the divine life, but with one critical difference. In the divine life, these polarities remain in harmony and do not fall into contradiction as they do in nature and in human life.

Throughout his corpus, Tillich frequently contrasts the harmonious character of divine life with the always imperiled and unbalanced quality of creaturely life. Such talk raises again the specter of dualism: Is God after all a supranatural being whose life is different from and stands over against the life of the world? Tillich is quick to reject such dualism. He insists that such discourse refers to the fact that the structure of being retains its integrity even when what that structure undergirds is distorted. The integrity of God's nature as ground and structure of reality endures even when human beings fall into estrangement and self-destruction. Far from being another reality, the divine life includes human life inasmuch as God is the creative ground of human life, but when creatures are estranged from God and their own essential natures, participation in divine life is experienced as the painful judgment of God's "burning fire" consuming that which stands opposed to God. God as structure resists that which violates structure. But whether resisting or supporting crea-turely life, the divine life is Not-other than the life of the world.

Having set forth the symbolic account of God as living, it is now possible to turn to the symbol that Tillich calls "the most embracing, direct, and unre-stricted symbol for the divine life," namely, God as Spirit. To understand what it means to symbolize God as Spirit, Tillich believes that theologians must begin with the proper, nonsymbolic, and conceptual use of the term as applied to human beings (ST 1:249). The concept *spirit* refers to the combination of power and meaning in the human being, to the character of human life as marked by both vitality and intentionality. Spirit refers neither to some non-bodily, ethereal component of human being nor to a particular function, like cognition, for example. Rather, spirit is the unity of power and meaning as expressed in the union of the ontological polarities. The human being, Tillich notes, is the only creature, so far as we are aware, in whom these polarities are fully realized. This is the meaning of the doctrine of *imago dei*. The image of God refers to the fact that the *logos* of being, the structure of reality, finds complete expression in human beings in whom that polar structure is fully actualized.

When the term is subsequently applied to the divine life, Spirit (always capitalized by Tillich when applied to God) names the way in which the divine life is experienced as that which drives the human being to greater vitality and intentionality. We call God Spirit because God as being-itself is experienced as the source of both power and meaning in human life. Divine power is manifest in the abyss-like character of being-itself whereas the element of meaning is present in the *logos* character of God.

> God's life is life as spirit. . . . Human intuition of the divine always has distinguished between the abyss of the divine (the element of power) and the fullness of its content (the element of meaning), between the divine depth and the divine *logos*. The first principle is the basis of the Godhead, that which makes God God. It is the root of his majesty, the unapproachable intensity of his being, the inexhaustible ground of being in which everything has its origin. It is the power of being infinitely resisting nonbeing, giving the power of being to everything that is. . . . The classical term *logos* is most adequate for the second principle, that of meaning and structure. . . . Without the second principle the first principle would be chaos, burning fire, but it would not be the creative ground. . . . As the actualization of the other two principles, the Spirit is the third principle. Both power and meaning are contained in it and united in it. It makes them creative. (ST 1:250–51)

This account of God as Spirit is the final ingredient we need to understand Tillich's account of ecstatic healing. It is now possible to see how it is that God can be said to grasp human beings in events of shaking and transforming power. The divine Spirit is not alien to human spirit; it is, rather, the depth of the human spirit, the depth to which the spirit belongs. God as Spirit does not stand over against human life. Tillich is quite explicit that "God is infinite because he has the finite . . . within himself united with his infinity" (ST 1:252). The living God, the God who is Spirit, is never separated from finite spirit. The infinite power of divine Spirit is present in beings driving them toward infinity.

Tillich argues that it is potentially misleading to speak of God as infinite, not least because human beings are themselves not merely finite. The human capacity to recognize finitude demonstrates that human beings are not exhausted by that finitude. There is in the human being an infinite drive toward self-transcendence. Human beings are never content to remain as they are, and this too testifies to the presence and power of the infinite within humanity.

Infinity is given in human experience, and it is given because human beings belong to being-itself. The presence of God as Spirit is experienced in the infinite drive toward self-transcendence negating and overcoming what is negative in human experience. The human spirit does not and cannot exist apart from the divine Spirit.

Tillich believes that human beings enjoy a double heritage, a conviction best expressed in his famous affirmation, "We belong to two orders of being."[4] In a sermon of the same title, Tillich asserts, "Man transcends everything in the historical order, all the heights and depths of his own existence. He passes, as no other being is able to pass, beyond the limits of his given world. He participates in something infinite, in an order which is not transitory, not self-destructive, not tragic, but eternal, holy, and blessed. Therefore . . . when he hears of the everlasting God and of the greatness of His power and the mystery of His acts, a response is awakened in the depth of his soul; the infinite within him is touched" (SOF, 22–23). The ecstatic reunion of the human and the divine is possible because the finite and the infinite, spirit and Spirit, belong to each other. The human being is essentially a part of the divine life. The very term *reunion* indicates that what is given in ecstasy is not a violation of the ordinary structure of human experience but rather its proper fulfillment.

Perhaps no term better speaks to this Tillichian approximation of nonduality than his constant reference to God as the "depth" of creaturely being. One's true depth cannot be a reality that stands over against oneself. If being-itself were other than the creature, then in the ecstatic situation, the self would cease to be itself in becoming another. The ecstatic situation would disrupt rather than fulfill the human being's membership in two orders of reality.

The other side of this picture must also be acknowledged: Tillich also speaks of the finite as pointing *beyond* itself. Tillich's view of reality is called self-transcendent precisely because the self must stand "outside" of itself in order to reach its proper depth. These distinctions speak to human separation and estrangement from divine life. The preceding account of finite-infinite unity is a picture of what is essentially true but not actually the case. Tillich maintains,

> since the finite is potentially or essentially an element of the divine life, everything finite is qualified by this essential relation. And since the existential situation in which the finite is actual implies both separation from and resistance to the essential unity of the finite and the

---

4. Paul Tillich, *The Shaking of the Foundations* (New York: Charles Scribner's Sons, 1948), 12–23. Hereafter, SOF.

infinite, the finite is no longer actually qualified by its essential unity with the infinite. It is only in the self-transcendence of life that the "memory" of the essential unity with the infinite is preserved. The dualistic element implied in such a terminology is, so to speak, preliminary and transitory; it simply serves to distinguish the actual from the potential and the existential from the essential. Thus it is neither a dualism of levels nor supranaturalistic. (ST 3:113–14)

In actuality, human beings are estranged from the depth to which they properly belong. That separation is not, Tillich notes, a separation of two levels of being let alone the separation between two beings, one finite and the other infinite. Tillich's system posits a *transitory dualism*, a dualism that persists only so long as beings are separated from Spirit (ST 3:114). In ecstatic healing, this dualism falls away because then finite beings are actually united with the infinite depths to which they belong.

How long does such reunion endure? Does this transitory dualism reassert itself after the ecstatic moment has elapsed? As we shall see, for Tillich, all healing is fragmentary under the conditions of existence. The healing power of ecstatic reunion can always be compromised by human freedom. Despite the essential unity of the finite and the infinite, that unity is never guaranteed to be actualized and remains threatened even when it is. These are some of the consequences of a vision that, despite its refusal of supranaturalistic dualism, nonetheless believes that human beings, in seeking to stand on their own ground, separate themselves from the ground to which they belong. Tillich's transitory dualism cannot offer the robust prognosis that Sankara's nondualism can.

Tillich on Therapy: Salvation as Ecstatic Healing

Having demonstrated that what makes ecstasy possible is the mutual immanence of the human spirit and the divine Spirit, the question now is, How is this potential human-divine relationship made actual? To answer the question of how human beings encounter God in salvation, one must explore Tillich's account of revelation. In the revelatory situation, God gives Godself when human beings are grasped by the power of being itself. Ecstasy is Tillich's name for the mind's experience of divine self-giving.

What does one know in the situation of ecstasy? How does ecstasy generate healing? How is ecstasy to be understood experientially? Does the term *ecstasy* designate some exceptional state of experience that must be distinguished from the flow of ordinary life? Or does ecstasy name a dimension of ordinary human life rather than an extraordinary interruption? If ecstasy is experienced in extraordinary moments, what is the relationship between those moments and the rest of life?

First, Tillich insists that revelation is not the supranatural disclosure of information. "Revelation is the manifestation of that which concerns us ultimately. The mystery which is revealed is of ultimate concern to us because it is the ground of our being" (ST 1:110). What God gives in revelation is Godself. The knowledge gained in the revelatory situation transcends the subject-object structure of reality within which ordinary knowing takes place. What is revealed is the God who is the ground of that structure and therefore the depth of reason itself. Far from being irrational, revelation discloses that which gives to reason its very capacities. This encounter with reason's depth heals reason of its own self-destructive ambiguities. Like every other dimension of reality, reason too suffers from the consequences of estrangement and stands in need of salvation. In the revelatory situation, such healing takes place.

> "Ecstasy" ("standing outside one's self") points to a state of mind which is extraordinary in the sense that the mind transcends its ordinary situation. Ecstasy is not a negation of reason; it is the state of mind in which reason is beyond itself, that is beyond the subject-object structure. In being beyond itself reason does not deny itself. "Ecstatic reason" remains reason; it does not receive anything irrational or antirational—which it could not do without self-destruction—but it transcends the basic condition of finite rationality, the subject-object structure. This is the state that mystics try to reach by ascetic and meditative activities. But mystics know that these activities are only preparations and that the experience of ecstasy is due exclusively to the manifestation of the mystery in a revelatory situation. Ecstasy occurs only if the mind is grasped by the mystery, namely, by the ground of being and meaning. (ST 1:111–12)

Many features of Tillich's description of ecstatic revelation demand consideration. First, ecstasy is said to be an extraordinary "state of mind." Its extraordinariness has to do with the fact that in ecstasy, the subject-object structure of reason is transcended. Tillich never makes transparent just what it means experientially to transcend this structure. Like any state of mind, ecstasy must presumably be temporary, all the more so since in the ecstatic situation the subject-object structure of reality is transcended. Given its exceptional epistemic status, the situation in which estrangement is overcome appears to be episodic. Unless the ecstatic state of mind turns out not to be a temporary state, there is no possibility of abiding in ecstasy over time. So, then, what is the relationship between such experiences and the rest of life as it is lived within the framework of subject-object experience?

Tillich clearly regards the ecstatic experience as exceptional. Consider his comparison of the ecstatic state with demonic possession:

> [W]hile demonic possession destroys the rational structure of the mind, divine ecstasy preserves and elevates it, although transcending it. Demonic possession destroys the ethical and logical principles of reason; the divine ecstasy affirms them. . . . In the state of demonic possession the mind is not really "beside itself," but rather it is in the power of elements of itself which aspire to be the whole mind which grasp the center of the rational self and destroy it. There is, however, a point of identity between ecstasy and possession. In both cases the ordinary subject-object structure of the mind is put out of action. But divine ecstasy does not violate the wholeness of the rational mind, while demonic possession weakens or destroys it. This indicates that, although ecstasy is not a product of reason, it does not destroy reason. (ST 1:114).

This comparison between demonic possession and ecstasy leaves little doubt that Tillich regards ecstasy as an exceptional state. And yet an important ambiguity remains. The consequences brought about by demonic possession are neither momentary nor episodic even if the experience of possession itself is. When the psychological center of a person is split and some element of the personality takes control over and dominates personal life, what happens is no isolated event or episode. Persons in the grip of addiction, for example, battle continuously with the strange power that the object of their addiction has acquired. What such persons have to face is an enduring condition rather than epistemologically exceptional episodes in which the "ordinary subject-object structure of the mind is put out of action." What about ecstasy? Is ecstasy likewise an enduring condition rather than an extraordinary moment or episode? Or put more precisely, does the ecstatic experience, even if it is exceptional, generate an enduring transformation of human experience?

The experiential meaning of ecstatic experience is clarified somewhat by close attention to a contrast that Tillich draws between ecstatic experience and the state of intoxication.

> Ecstasy, in its transcendence of the subject-object structure, is the great liberating power under the dimension of self-awareness. But this liberating power creates the possibility of confusing that which is "less" than the subject-object structure of the mind with that which is "more" than this structure. . . . Intoxication is an attempt to escape from the dimension of spirit with its burden of personal centeredness and responsibility and cultural rationality. . . . In the long run, however, it is destructive, heightening the tensions it wants to avoid. Its main distinguishing feature is that it lacks both spiritual productivity and Spiritual creativity. It returns to an empty subjectivity which extinguishes these contents coming from the objective world. It makes the self a vacuum. (ST 3:119)

Tillich's belief that ecstasy might be mistaken for intoxication calls to mind the Pentecost experience in which Peter and the apostles were taken to be drunk. In that instance, however, the apostles' ecstatic experience did not diminish their cognitive functions but rather enhanced them.

Careful consideration of Tillich's comparisons of ecstasy with demonic possession and intoxication suggests the following conclusion: Ecstasy appears to be an exceptional experiential state of unspecified duration (sometimes long, sometimes short) in which the capacities of reason are considerably enhanced. It would be more accurate to say that reason's capacities are fulfilled when reason is reconciled with its own true depth. Ecstasy, understood as the infusion of the Divine Spirit into the human spirit, is the healing and liberating power that makes it possible for human beings to transcend the essence-existence split and so to become what they truly are and ought to be.

The substantial language of infusion and the causal imagery of impact must be employed with care. A sure indication that Tillich wants to overcome dualism is his refusal to make of the divine Spirit a second reality over against the human spirit. In Tillich's words, "although the term 'impact' unavoidably uses causal imagery, it is not a cause in a categorical sense but a presence which participates in the object of its impact. Like the divine creativity in all its respects, it transcends the category of causality, although human language must make use of causality in a symbolic way" (ST 3:276). The divine presence is always given because God is the ground of being; however, in the ecstatic moment, that presence makes itself manifest unambiguously.

The power of the impact of the Spiritual Presence is felt in the work of the prophet, the mystic, and in every genuine prayer.

> He who pronounces the divine Word is, as is the keenest analyst of society, aware of the social situation of his time, but he sees it ecstatically under the impact of the Spiritual Presence in the light of eternity. He who contemplates is aware of the ontological structure of the universe, but he sees it ecstatically under the impact of the Spiritual Presence in the light of the ground and aim of all being. . . . In these experiences, nothing of the objective world is dissolved into mere subjectivity. Rather it is all preserved and even increased. But it is not preserved under the dimension of self-awareness and in the subject-object scheme. A union of subject and object has taken place in which the independent existence of each is overcome; new unity is created. (ST 3:119)

Tillich's examples of ecstasy clearly indicate that ordinary cognitive processes are not violated but are instead heightened and transcended when the subject-object character of existence is put out of commission. Ecstasy allows persons to experience reality beyond the subject-object split. The other is not experienced as separate from the self, and God is not experienced as one who stands over against me. The language of union dominates Tillich's reading of ecstasy.

However, Tillich displays a measure of skepticism about "those religious groups who claim to have special religious experiences, personal inspirations, extraordinary Spiritual gifts, individual revelations, knowledge of esoteric mysteries" (ST 1:112). He does not deny that such experiences can be genuine manifestations of spiritual ecstasy. He wishes instead to avoid a ready and simple identification of ecstasy with marginal and extraordinary phenomena. According to Tillich, "so-called ecstatic movements" that emphasize special religious experiences, "are in continuous danger—to which they succumb more often than not—of confusing overexcitement with the presence of the divine Spirit or with the occurrence of revelation. Something happens objectively as well as subjectively in every genuine manifestation of the mystery. Only something subjective happens in a state of religious overexcitement, often artificially produced" (ST 1:112–13). Given the dangers that accompany one-sided focus on the ecstatic experience, it is appropriate to attend to the objective side of ecstasy, namely, revelation.

Tillich's definition of revelation as "the manifestation of what concerns us ultimately" has already been introduced. Another feature of Tillich's account of revelation merits further analysis, however, especially as it is a matter on which Tillich and Sankara are in fundamental agreement. Tillich insists that the defining test of authentic revelation as opposed to the manifestation of unusual or marginal but nonrevelatory phenomena is that the object of genuine revelation remains a mystery. Revelation does not dissolve or remove the mysterious character of the reality experienced. As Tillich puts it, "Whatever is essentially mysterious cannot lose its mysteriousness even when it is revealed. Otherwise something which only seemed to be mysterious would be revealed, and not that which is essentially mysterious" (ST 1:109).

What ecstatic experience reveals is being-itself as the depth of reason. As the ground of the subject-object character of experience, the depth of reason transcends that subject-object structure. Consequently, what is given in ecstatic experience must necessarily remain mysterious. That the object of revelation remains mysterious does not mean that revelation generates no knowledge. On the contrary,

> revelation includes cognitive elements. Revelation of that which is essentially and necessarily mysterious means the manifestation of something within the context of ordinary experience which transcends the ordinary context of experience. Something more is known of the mystery after it has become manifest in revelation. First, its reality has become a matter of experience. Second, our relation to it has become a matter of experience. Both of these are cognitive elements. But revelation does not dissolve the mystery into knowledge. Nor does it add anything directly to the totality of our ordinary knowledge, namely, to our knowledge about the subject-object structure of reality. (Ibid.)

These statements about knowledge gained in ecstatic experience demonstrate well the inseparability of revelation and salvation, of epistemology and soteriology. In revelation, one is not informed but transformed. In revelation, we learn that we are never totally separated from the God from whom we are estranged. To be grasped by the power of being is to be reconciled to the depth to which we belong and so to be healed. The split between one's essential self and one's existential self is repaired and human beings are able to be what they ought to be. As Tillich puts it, "In terms of classical theology one could say that no one can receive revelation except through the divine Spirit and that, if someone is grasped by the divine Spirit the center of his personality is transformed; he has received saving power" (ST 1:146).

The soteriological character of ecstasy is experienced in and through successful self-transcendence. Tillich argues, "If the divine Spirit breaks into the human spirit, this does not mean that it rests there, but that it drives the human spirit out of itself. The 'in' of the divine Spirit is an 'out' for the human spirit. The spirit, a dimension of finite life, is driven into successful self-transcendence; it is grasped by something ultimate and unconditional. It is still the human spirit; it remains what it is, but at the same time goes out of itself under the impact of the divine Spirit. 'Ecstasy' is the classical term for this state of being grasped by the Spiritual Presence" (ST 3:111-12).

In this highly symbolic use of spatial language, Tillich maintains that the human spirit by its very nature, that is, because of its very belonging to the ultimate, longs for ultimate meaning and purpose. This drive for meaning and purpose, under the impact of the power of the Spiritual Presence, moves human beings out of captivity to self-enclosed finitude and into communion with God, other human beings, and nature. The inherently vital dynamism of life is restored rather than short-circuited by sin and estrangement. "[L]ife drives beyond itself as finite life. It is *self*-transcendence because life is not transcended by something that is not life. Life, by its very nature as life, is both *in* itself and *above* itself, and this situation is manifest in the function of self-transcendence" (ST 3:31; emphasis in original).

Despite the human being's essential belonging to the infinite, it cannot attain to union with Spirit under its own steam. The Spiritual Presence "does something the human spirit could not do by itself. When it grasps man, it creates unambiguous life. Man in his self-transcendence can reach for it, but man cannot grasp it, unless he is first grasped by it. Man remains in himself. By the very nature of his self-transcendence, man is driven to ask the question of unambiguous life, but the answer must come to him through the creative power of the Spiritual Presence" (ST 3:112). No human work can reach the infinite, and that is why Tillich argues that the divine Spirit must invade the human spirit. However, such inbreaking does not violate "the structure of the centered self" precisely because of the essential not-otherness of beings and being-itself sketched above. The mutual immanence of the human spirit and the Divine Spirit makes successful self-transcendence possible.

The subtle resonance here between Tillich's thought and Sankara's theology is evident and intriguing. Both theologians reject any and all self-help conceptions of spiritual life. Only revelation that comes from without can heal and liberate. But what comes from without is not alien. In Sankara's case, revelatory knowledge offered by scripture and interpreted by the guru teaches the truth of the Self's innate divinity. In Tillich's case, revelation heals and fulfils the human being's essential union with God, a union that is disrupted by estrangement.

For Tillich, "The two terms 'inspiration' and 'infusion' express the way in which man's spirit receives the impact of the Spiritual Presence" (ST 3:115). These terms aptly capture and name the human experience of Spiritual Presence as "a meaning-bearing power which grasps the human spirit in an ecstatic experience. After the experience, the teacher can analyse and formulate the element of meaning in the ecstasy of inspiration (as the systematic theologian does), but when the analysis of the teacher begins, the inspirational experience has already passed" (ibid.).

Here perhaps we have the clearest indication that Tillich conceives of ecstasy as a distinct, exceptional, and transient experience that infuses meaning-bearing power into human life. What has yet to be determined is the relationship between such experiences and the whole of life. Tillich's answer to this question is that such experiences draw persons into the "transcendent union of unambiguous life." Human life is marked by a rupture between what we essentially are and so are meant to be and what we actually are in estrangement. Life as ordinarily lived and experienced is the ambiguous combination of both of these elements. In revelation, the divine Spirit creates unambiguous life by bringing "about the reunion of these elements in life processes in which actual being is the true expression of potential being. . . . In the reunion of essential and existential being, ambiguous life is raised above itself to a transcendence that it could not achieve by its own power" (ST 3:120). In unambiguous life, the Spiritual Presence enables us actually to be what we are meant to be.

If estranged life is marked by unbelief, hubris, and concupiscence, the transcendent union of unambiguous life is marked by faith, surrender, and love (ST 2:177). Ecstatic experiences draw persons into a life of faith and love by moving us out of captivity to self-enclosed finitude. "The 'transcendent union' answers the general question implied in all ambiguities of life. It appears within the human spirit as the ecstatic movement which from one point of view is called 'faith,' from another, 'love.' These two states manifest the transcendent union which is created by the Spiritual Presence in the human spirit" (ST 3:129).

But what precisely is the relationship between passing ecstatic experiences and the ecstatic movement that generates faith and love? Do faith and love endure beyond the ecstatic experience in which the subject-object character of existence is transcended and, if so, how? Clearer definitions of faith and love are necessary in order to answer this question. Tillich writes, "faith is the state of being *grasped* by the transcendent unity of unambiguous life—it embodies love as the state of being *taken into* that transcendent unity" (ibid.; emphasis in original). Tragically, for Tillich, unambiguous life is always experienced in human life only fragmentarily: "Revelation as it is received by man living under the conditions of existence is always fragmentary; so is salvation. Revelation and salvation are final, complete, and unchangeable with respect to the revealing and saving event; they are preliminary, fragmentary, and changeable with respect to the persons who receive revelatory truth and saving power" (ST 1:146).

Here, readers receive a clear intimation of Tillich's guarded prognosis for the human condition. In the saving event, in ecstatic experience, human beings meet and are claimed by the unqualified power of divine life as "final, complete, and unchangeable," but we who receive that saving power continue to live ambiguous lives. We are healed, but never wholly; we become part of the divine life, but we do not abide there. For us, revelation and salvation remain "preliminary, fragmentary, and changeable." The work of receiving and incorporating what is received in ecstatic experience is altogether fraught with ambiguity.

What is the relationship between ecstatic experience and the life of faith and love as it is lived after ecstatic experiences have elapsed? A hint at an answer can be found in Tillich's claim that "Faith is the state of being grasped by the Spiritual Presence and *opened* to the transcendent unity of unambiguous life" (ST 3:131; emphasis added). Revelatory ecstatic experience makes the presence of God known to human beings. The power of being-itself disrupts finite self-sufficiency manifest in unbelief, hubris, and concupiscence. Human beings are unable under their own power to become transparent to the power of being-itself until they are "opened up" by ecstatic experience. After ecstatic experience, the challenge is "obedience in faith."

Tillich understands such obedience as the "act of keeping ourselves open to the Spiritual Presence which has grasped us and opened us" (ST 3:132). There is no question of human response without divine initiative because "faith cannot be created by the procedures of the intellect, or by endeavors of the will, or by emotional movements" (ST 3:133). Nevertheless, after the initial moment of faith characterized by sheer passivity, faith takes on the character of response, of accepting acceptance. Faith then is "the human reaction to the Spiritual Presence's breaking into the human spirit; it is the ecstatic acceptance of the divine Spirit's breaking-up of the finite mind's tendency to rest in its own self-sufficiency" (ST 3:135).

Faith understood as human response to divine initiative cannot merely be one exceptional cognitive state among others. It is instead a fundamental orientation or disposition of the entire person toward responsiveness to the power of being-itself. Such faith "is actual in all life processes—in religion, in the other functions of the spirit" (ST 3:134). Likewise, "love is actual in all functions of the mind and . . . has roots in the innermost core of life itself. Love is the drive toward the reunion of the separated; this is ontologically and therefore universally true" (ibid.).

In faith and love, human beings encounter realities that cannot be confined within the narrow boundaries of ecstatic experience. If faith as ultimate concern is what "gives depth, direction and unity to all other concerns and, with them, to the whole personality," then faith cannot just be one concern among many or one state of mind among others (DOF, 105). Faith understood as the vital center of human personality is the integrating and healing power active in every state of mind and in the entirety of human life. Therefore, ecstatic experiences must be understood as singular moments of transformation in which the constant struggle between the forces of health and the forces of disease is interrupted by a wholly unambiguous experience of the power of being-itself. Faith, however, is not confined to such moments although it is created, renewed, and sustained by them.

Unfortunately, faith inevitably comes up against "the forces of disintegration and disease which prevent faith from creating a fully integrated personal life, even in those who represent the power of faith most conspicuously, the saints, the great mystics, the prophetic personalities. Man is integrated only fragmentarily and has elements of disintegration or disease in all dimensions of his being" (DOF, 108). Tillich is convinced that no one is exempt from ambiguity.

When it comes to the relationship between human beings and ultimate reality, do ecstatic experiences serve to disclose something that is always already the case, or do ecstatic experiences create something new? For Tillich, the answer must be the latter. Revelation creates New Being over and above disclosing the reality of being itself as always already active in human life. This distinction must be borne in mind lest ecstatic revelation is understood to be nearly identical in function to liberating knowledge (*jnana*) in Sankara's thought. Liberating knowledge reveals that one just is and has always been Brahman. Ecstatic revelation in Tillich's theology creates reunion beyond the essence-existence split. It heals and annuls a genuine breach between God and humanity. Simply put, ecstatic revelation *makes* and shows whereas *jnana* only *shows*. Because Sankara understands the true Self to be unchanging Brahman, the moment of revelation only discloses what is always already the case. On the other hand, Tillich understands the moment of revelation to be one in which self-enclosed persons are brought into unambiguous union with the Spiritual Presence. Every such experience is new because the human being is always "outside" the divine life as well as within it.

Despite this critical point of difference, Tillich and Sankara are in basic agreement on many other fronts when it comes to revelation. Sankara wholly agrees that the reality revealed in liberating knowledge is beyond the subject-object experience; consequently, no ordinary means of knowledge can make Brahman known. Sankara would also agree with Tillich that knowledge of ultimate reality does not add to our knowledge about anything else within the subject-object realm. Sankara would agree also that what is given in revelation is the depth of reason, or, in Sankara's idiom, consciousness (*cit*) understood as the condition for the possibility of knowledge in general. Sankara is absolutely clear that the term *consciousness* does not refer to a cognitive state but rather to a light that transcends the mind even though it is present in every mental state. Furthermore, consciousness itself cannot be known nor does it need to be known. Though it is the condition for the possibility of all knowledge, *cit* transcends knowledge. What revelation shows is that the Self is Brahman. Revelation discloses the nonduality of Self and Brahman. It does not make Brahman known because Brahman is unknowable. In Sankara's apophatic theology, Brahman remains essentially mysterious. Finally, Sankara would also maintain that revelation does not merely inform but instead transforms. When knowledge dawns in the minds of properly prepared students who hear scripture, they come to know their true identity and are set free. Here, too, epistemology and soteriology are inseparable.

The vital difference is ontological. Whereas for Sankara knowledge generated by scriptural revelation discloses what the Self already is, the revelatory event in Tillich creates unambiguous reunion between God and humanity beyond the essence-existence split. As already noted, this reunion is always fragmentary under the conditions of existence. There is no once-and-for-all moment in which revelation discloses a truth about the Self that leads to a decisive break from life as it had thus far been lived.

It is true that Sankara allows for meditative practice after liberating knowledge has arisen. The goal of such meditation appears to be to secure knowledge already gained. Sankara is not particular that the noetic event must happen in an instantaneous moment of insight. What matters is that one must be established in knowledge regardless of how that knowledge comes about. These qualifications seem to suggest that even liberated persons can make spiritual progress. Sankara appears in some slight measure to allow for the truth of fragmentariness so pervasive in Tillich's thought. Nevertheless, the difference between Sankara and Tillich on this point is more striking than the similarity. Whereas Tillich insists that even the saint remains a sinner, Sankara merely acknowledges the practical point that continued practice may be a contingent part of spiritual life. There is no sense in which Sankara's liberated person is ignorant and no sense in which the liberated person remains perpetually threatened by ambiguity.

The reason for this fundamental difference between Tillich and Sankara rests in Tillich's conviction regarding the "universal transition from essence to existence." Human beings ex-ist, they stand out from the ground of being to which they belong. Such standing out means that human beings are really separated from their essential being. Because Tillich believes that "actualized creation and estranged existence are identical," human-divine reunion is always only fragmentary and given in ecstasy. Human beings must be driven beyond separated existence in order for union to obtain. Life in space and time is always a mixture of the essential and the existential, of the created and the fallen. Consequently, there is no way that a person can wholly be healed and so attain to their essential selves without ambiguity. The disintegrating forces of separation always remain active so long as life and history shall last.

Tillich believes, of course, that it is precisely such separated existence that makes human freedom possible. He cannot conceive of the possibility of freedom apart from some kind of "substantial independence" over against the ground and power of being. Consequently, existence is both the source of freedom as well as the reason for divine-human alienation. For Tillich, freedom always remains a potential source of disruption whereby persons can act against the powers of integration and healing. No temporal line of demarcation can be used to divide a person's life so as to separate a period of Old Being and New Being. Both are given in life and in all moments of life. Consequently, no one is completely healed and no one is completely diseased. For human beings, "there is always the state of being grasped by the Spiritual Presence, followed by profanization and demonization in the process of reception and actualization" (ST 3:148). Tillich's prognosis is sobering indeed.

The sole and paradoxical exception to this rule is Jesus the Christ. Unlike other human beings, Jesus' life is not marked by profanization or demonization because "The Spirit never leaves him; the power of the transcendent union of unambiguous life always bears him up." (ST 3:146). Tillich never makes it clear just how or why "his human spirit was entirely grasped by the Spiritual Presence," and just why our spirits cannot likewise grasped (ST 3:144). No adequate answer to this question presents itself in Tillich's theology.

Despite Tillich's deep sense of the fragmentariness of all healing, he does argue for the possibility of sanctification. Tillich observes that Christian traditions differ internally regarding the possibility of sanctification. His comments on Lutheranism are particularly revealing: "In Lutheranism the emphasis on the paradoxical element in the experience of the New Being was so predominant that sanctification could not be interpreted in terms of a line moving up toward perfection. It was seen instead as an up-and-down of ecstasy and anxiety, of being grasped by *agape* and being thrown back into estrangement and ambiguity. This oscillation between up and down was experienced radically by Luther himself, in the change between moments of courage and joy and moments of demonic attacks, as he interpreted his states of doubt and profound despair" (ST 3:230).

No reader of Tillich can miss his deep sympathy for the Lutheran position. His sense of the ambiguous and fragmentary character of life gives profound witness to his Lutheran sensibility. Nevertheless, Tillich does advance a picture of "life under the Spiritual Presence," a life that is marked by growth in four areas. The process of sanctification according to Tillich is marked by "first, increasing awareness; second, increasing freedom; third, increasing relatedness; fourth, increasing transcendence" (ST 3:231).

Tillich's description of increasing awareness is particularly intriguing. He writes, "man in the process of sanctification becomes increasingly aware of his actual situation and of the forces struggling around him and his humanity but also becomes aware of the answers to the questions implied in this situation. Sanctification includes awareness of the demonic as well as of the divine. Such awareness, which increases in the process of sanctification, does not lead to the Stoic 'wise man,' who is superior to the ambiguities of life because he has conquered his passions and his desires, but rather to an awareness of these ambiguities in himself, as in everyone, and to the power of affirming life and its vital dynamics in spite of its ambiguities" (ibid.). Of course, what Tillich says of the Stoic can also be said of liberated Advaitins. Such persons do understand themselves to have conquered their passions and desires. They have seen through the passions because the liberated know that they are not their passions. For Tillich, such a vision of sanctification is entirely unrealistic and untrue to life. The process of sanctification does not free persons from the ambiguities of life; it only gives them material insight into the power of those ambiguities.

Increased freedom is also part of the process of sanctification. Tillich writes, "The more one is reunited with his true being under the impact of the Spirit, the more one is free from the commandments of the law. This process is most difficult, and maturity in it is very rare. The fact that reunion is fragmentary implies that freedom from the law is always fragmentary. In so far as we are estranged, prohibitions and commandments appear and produce an uneasy conscience. In so far as we are reunited, we actualize what we essentially are in freedom, without command" (ST 3:232). A great deal of weight rests on three little words, namely, "in so far." The life of faith, if it can be characterized as a progressive movement at all, is incremental at best. Ecstatic experiences are unambiguous, but life as such most assuredly is not. Life as it is lived in the wake of these experiences is always marked by more or less. Nevertheless, a life marked by increasing freedom is characterized by increasing openness to the demands of any concrete situation. Moral decision making, for example, becomes less and less a matter of casuistry. Rather than apply preexistent codes to particular situations, the person who is under the impact of the divine Spirit can respond beyond the law to what is called for by the situation at hand.

The process of sanctification also results in "increasing relatedness." Tillich indicates that "The New Being as process drives toward a mature relatedness. The divine Spirit has rightly been described as the power of breaking through the walls of self-seclusion. There is no way of overcoming self-seclusion lastingly other than the impact of the power which elevates the individual person above himself ecstatically and enables him to find the other person—if the other person is also ready to be elevated above himself" (ST 3:234). Whereas hubris and concupiscence are failed attempts to escape the trap of "self-seclusion" by drawing the world into oneself, the process of sanctification makes relatedness possible by freeing persons from their narrow and constricted selves.

The final mark of sanctification is "increasing self-transcendence." Tillich understands increasing self-transcendence to mean growth in devotion toward the holy. Increasing awareness, freedom, and relatedness, Tillich informs us, is impossible apart from such progress in devotion. He also takes care to clarify that by devotion, he does not refer only to narrowly religious acts such as prayer and formal worship. In fact, Tillich notes that "maturity in self-transcendence" may lead away from formal or institutional religious life (ST 3:235–36). The more persons move into a deeper awareness of Spiritual Presence, the more likely it is that conventional forms of religiosity will fail to be adequate or even threaten movement into self-transcendence.

> The self-transcendence which belongs to the principles of sanctification is actual in every act in which the impact of the Spiritual Presence is experienced. This can be in prayer or meditation in total privacy, in the exchange of Spiritual experiences with others, in communications on a secular basis, in the experience of creative works of man's spirit, in the midst of labor or at rest, in private counseling, in church services. It is like the breathing-in of another air, an elevation above average existence. It is the most important thing in the process of spiritual maturity. (Ibid.)

Tillich's Prognosis:
Sanctification, Doubt, and the Ineradicable Fact of Estrangement

The cumulative effect of Tillich's treatment of sanctification suggests that he does not wish to characterize life under the impact of the Spiritual Presence as mere oscillation between courage and anxiety. Tillich presents a vision of spiritual life as transformed by the impact of exceptional experiences but not restricted to them. So strong is Tillich's language regarding increasing transcendence that it even calls to mind Sankara's characterization of fully liberated persons. They too transcend the conventional religious life of ritual and moral duties. Freed from private egocentric interests and motivations, liberated sages act spontaneously for the welfare of the world. They too are beyond the law. They too breathe in another air.

In Tillich's system, however, persons who move toward increasing self-transcendence do not give up the idea that they are agents. Nevertheless, because they continue to remain open to the power of Spiritual Presence that has opened them up (in ecstatic experience), their actions are less and less the product of estrangement, and more and more an expression of their growth in reconciliation to divine depth. Such reconciliation does mean that the actions of such persons are increasingly also the actions of the divine Spirit. Just as liberated persons are free from egoism (*ahamkara*) and desire (*kama*), having been set free of ignorance, so too persons under the impact of the Spiritual Presence are increasingly free from hubris and concupiscence having been brought into faith and out of unbelief.

Despite Tillich's sincere attempt to give a credible account of sanctification, his ontological commitments lead to a qualitatively different vision of theological anthropology than that of Sankara. For Tillich, no one, regardless of the degree of his or her transparency toward the divine, escapes estrangement. Speaking of the saints of the Christian tradition, Tillich writes, "they are also, in every moment of their lives, both estranged and reunited, and it may be that in their inner selves not only the divine but also the demonic forces are extraordinarily strong" (ST 3:238). Indeed, the movement into self-transcendence appears to bring with it the risk of greater vulnerability to the demonic! Notwithstanding Tillich's vision of sanctification as a process of increasing awareness, increasing freedom, increasing relatedness, and increasing self-transcendence, the threat remains that all this might be undercut at any moment by human freedom.

Tillich's talk about the heightened presence of the demonic in the lives of the saints demonstrates just how precarious and even dangerous spiritual life remains on his account. This pessimism goes well beyond Sankara's acknowledgment that the liberated must still contend with the ambiguous reality of embodiment and the force of karma already set in motion (*prarabdhakarma*). Sankara knows that even the liberated person may need to engage in spiritual discipline to prevent confusion, but he believes that once knowledge has dawned, it cannot be undercut. The metaphor of the person whose faulty vision generates the appearance of a double-moon is quite apt. Sankara observes that once a person afflicted by double vision knows that there is only one moon, that knowledge cannot be lost. He may be fooled momentarily by force of habit, but his insight remains sure.

Tillich disagrees. To the question, "Does the religious experience of a man in an advanced stage of sanctification remove the possibility of doubt?" Tillich says no.

> Doubt is unavoidable as long as there is separation of subject and object, and even the most immediate and intimate feeling of union with the divine, as in the bride-mysticism describing the union of the Christ and the soul, cannot bridge the infinite distance between the finite self and the infinite by which it is grasped. In the oscillations of feeling, this distance is perceived and often throws him who is advanced in sanctification into a profounder doubt than people with less intensity in their religious experience. . . . theology must state the necessity of doubt which follows from man's finitude under the conditions of existential estrangement. (ST 3:239–40)

Tillich does not mince words. Unlike Sankara who recognizes only the psychological possibility of doubt, Tillich characterizes doubt as a necessity required by the ontological distance between finite and infinite under the conditions of existence. We are left with a sharp tension between a vision of the life of faith as gradual growth in divine-human union and a vision of spiritual life as marked by inevitable oscillation between union and separation. On balance, oscillation seems to have the upper hand although Tillich seems to want to have it both ways. Ontologically speaking, this ambivalence in Tillich's theological anthropology is caused by his conscious and deliberate affirmation of the not-otherness of beings and being-itself *and* his postulation of a real distance between beings and their ground.

Tillich's theological anthropology is powerful, sober, and consoling. It serves to assure Christians that doubt and oscillation are unavoidable and so need not be the object of moralistic condemnation. But do the benefits of Tillichian realism require an ontology that makes doubt *theologically* necessary and estrangement inevitable? Tillich *may* have succeeded technically in avoiding Hegelian commitment to a necessary fall, but his position, practically speaking, comes too close for comfort. Tillich believes that he has avoided the Gnostic heresy of making sin necessary. I have my doubts. At any rate, sin remains inevitable and ultimately ineradicable. If creatures are to be free, they must be separated from the divine life, and such separation leaves human life perpetually imperiled by ambiguity and threatened by the demonic. Freedom and fallenness seem inseparable. Tillich's vision is not only sobering but also offers little hope for sustained transformation. Tillich's account of sanctification, despite its considerable merits, remains fairly minimal and constrained. Persons moving into sanctification do not overcome estrangement; they only become ever more keenly aware of life's ambiguities. The fundamental problem with Tillich's system seems to be that he is incapable of imagining human freedom otherwise than by postulating a substantial independence between creature and creator, and he does not know how to affirm substantial independence without separation; and with separation comes estrangement. The end result is a deeply ambiguous vision of spiritual life as always insecure and inevitably imperiled.[5]

Sankara's theology, on the other hand, offers the deepest hope for sanctified life. These possibilities are the fruit of a nondualistic ontology in which human beings are never separated from Brahman. The problem with Sankara's vision is that robust hope for radical transformation is secured only for those who maintain that mind, body, activity, and desire are all extrinsic to the true Self. He too ends up offering an account that erects a deep divide between ultimate reality and the world of change and flux.

Despite the very different problems that plague the genuine accomplishments of each thinker, a common underlying problem threatens both theological systems: a substantialist conception of ultimate reality. Sankara cannot reconcile the world of change with Brahman because he is constrained by a vision of Brahman as unchanging ground for a changing world, this despite the fact that Sankara explicitly denies that Brahman is a substance. Tillich, on the other hand, wants very much to construe ultimate reality as dynamic and living, but he remains convinced that creatures must be substantially independent from God in order to keep creatures from being reduced to the status of mere modes of a divine substance. This worry demonstrates that he continues, at least in part, to imagine God in substantialist ways despite his explicit disavowal of such a position. Tillich finds it impossible to imagine that beings might be wholly internal to the divine life and yet also free.

---

5. Tillich's tragic reading of human possibilities is surely the product of his traumatic experiences in the trenches of WW I and his experience of the rise of Nazi fascism. He has good reasons for painting a grim picture of the human predicament. The question here is whether Tillich is right to insist that human possibilities are limited because of an ontological rupture between human beings and divinity. That argument not only leads to a sober diagnosis of the human predicament but imperils any genuine hope for radical sanctification. On Tillich's experiences in WW I and in Germany before his exile, see Wilhelm and Marion Pauck, *Paul Tillich: His Life and Thought* (New York: Harper & Row, 1976).

What both thinkers need is a truly dynamic conception of ultimate reality as that which gives rise to all determinate realities but is inseparable from those realities.[6] On such a conception, God is best understood as ontological creativity, a creativity that gives rise to free creatures whose very freedom is ever sustained by that creativity. Far from imagining immanence as a threat to freedom—as one would have to if God is taken to be akin to an underlying substance of which creatures are mere modes—it is possible to imagine divine creativity as a radically immanent source of free creatures. Such a theology would amount to a genuine nondualism in which nature and human beings are free occasions within the divine life. Such a position would be quite similar to Sankara's nondualism save for the fact that ultimate reality is imagined as dynamic rather than static. As dynamic creativity, God would be the source of both my being and my doing. Such a dynamic nondualism could, like Tillich's ontology, generate a vision in which my acting could also be God's acting, a vision in which God is all in all. Our concluding chapter will summarize the results of this comparative enterprise and then sketch the possibilities for a theological anthropology that flows from such a conception of ultimate reality, one that combines elements from Eastern and Western accounts of the immanent divine.

---

6. Such a theology is proposed by both Joseph Bracken and Robert Neville; their positions will be considered in the conclusion.

chapter six

Reimagining Immanence

Toward a Christian Nondualism

~~~~

Moving from Comparison to Construction

The comparative work undertaken in this book has ruptured the all-too-familiar, even stereotypical, dichotomy between a Christian West enamored of transcendence and a Hindu East entranced with immanence. At stake instead are two different visions of the immanent divine. Christian immanence of Tillich's variety can be characterized as ecstatic whereas Hindu immanence of Sankara's variety is nondual. The searching question for this particular comparative venture is, What is the relationship between ecstasy and nonduality, between the Spirit who prays in me and Brahman that just is my truest self?

Whereas Sankara argued that the true Self is Brahman, Tillich argued that the human being belongs to two orders of reality. Human beings are finite, but they belong to infinity as well. Tillich recognized that beings have no being apart from participation in being-itself. In this sense, one is kept in being by the being of God. But this basic truth does not yet point to the kind of union that Tillich finds most important. Because of the split between essence and existence, between what we are meant to be and what we are in our fallenness, human participation in the divine is compromised. Just as being Brahman does not help persons so long as they believe that they are drowning in the ocean of transmigration, participation in being-itself is no solace for those estranged from God even as they abide in God. What is religiously significant is the experienced reunion of humanity and divinity given in ecstasy, a reunion that heals the split between what we have become and what we were created to be. Faith is the name for this healing reunion. In faith, human beings are reunited with their true depth when grasped by the Spirit and taken into the divine life.

In sum, both Sankara and Tillich believe that simply being Brahman or being part of the divine life is not healing. Transformation must take place. For Sankara, spiritual exercises like *karmayoga* and meditation prepare the mind for knowledge by bringing about detachment. The properly prepared mind can then receive the truth of nonduality as more than mere information. Then and only then does the truth that one is Brahman lead to liberation. Tillich does not speak about spiritual exercises. Protestant qualms about works-righteousness and self-salvation prevent Tillich from considering this possibility. In this respect, he remains Lutheran through and through. Human beings are transformed only when they are grasped by the Spirit and driven into reunion with the divine life. Only such reunion brings New Being. Participation in the divine life by way of creation alone does not.

The religiously vital kind of human-divine union *happens* in Tillich's theology. It has the character of an event whereas in Sankara's thought nonduality obtains eternally. One just is Brahman; one does not have to be reunited with Brahman by Brahman's activity. The seeker needs only to realize what is always already the case. It is possible that such transformative realization may occur in a single dramatic event. A single hearing of scripture can engender in ideally prepared persons the conviction that they are Brahman. But how such transformative knowledge comes about is largely immaterial to Sankara because the moment of insight only discloses what has always been true. Human beings experience life as radically new in the light of liberation, but nothing transpires in Brahman. In Tillich's case, however, the experience of reunion with God is both an event in human life *and* in the divine life.

In the end, despite moments of rich agreement, Sankara and Tillich present two different visions of divine immanence. Both theologians maintain that nothing can exist apart from being-itself. Both believe that human action cannot by itself heal the human predicament. Both contend that human identity is misconstrued if it is considered apart from its relation to the infinite. The significance of these deep resonances should not be underestimated. Nevertheless, the comparative theologian must recognize and contend with the different ways in which these truths find ontological expression in Sankara and Tillich. That will be the task of this concluding chapter.

Comparative theology becomes properly theological when it takes up the constructive task of assessing the meaning, importance, and truth-value of the similarities and differences discovered through comparison. The comparativist discovers those similarities and differences only by using comparative categories formulated with care and tested in practice. Because these categories give rise to the common vocabulary for interreligious conversation, the normative work of comparative theology depends heavily on what comparativists learn by employing them. Given their importance, comparativists are obliged to be self-critical about the adequacy and applicability of even the most treasured comparative categories.

Constructive proposals, however, do not just follow logically from comparison. Theological conclusions have to be argued out. No similarity or dissimilarity discovered during comparison can compel theologians to adopt a particular conclusion about what to make of that similarity or difference. Antecedent commitments, creative readings of figures and traditions, the traditions chosen for comparison, and personal transformations inaugurated by interreligious encounter will influence constructive theological proposals. Because of these independent variables, constructive proposals will not yield broad consensus of the sort that can emerge from careful comparison. We are more likely to agree about the similarities and differences discovered during comparison than we are about what to make of them.

Much will depend on what transpires in the life of the theologian who takes up comparison. Comparative theologians who return unchanged after travels to other religious worlds may justifiably face the charge of trafficking in mere theological tourism, but theologians whose journeys have become pilgrimages shoulder other burdens and risks.[1] Are such theologians still Christian? How should their theological proposals be received by their home communities? And how are theological proposals to be judged if the very criteria for theological construction may be transformed by interreligious encounter? In what sense is a theology that has been deeply shaped by another religious tradition still Christian? Does it even matter whether a position is recognizably Christian, or does it matter only that a given position appears to be reasonable, attractive, compelling, and true?

These far-reaching questions cannot be answered with prefabricated formulae that seek to bypass the cumulative work of comparative theologians

---

1. No one has articulated the intrapsychic dimension of interreligious dialogue better than Raimon Panikkar. Panikkar contends that encounter with another religious tradition remains incomplete unless it leads to a radical internal dialogue within the mind and heart of the theologian. Interreligious dialogue must inaugurate within the theologian a deep "intrareligious dialogue." His argument suggests that comparative theology cannot do without the prayerful work of personal struggle and transformation. See Raimon Panikkar, *The Intrareligious Dialogue*, rev. ed. (New York: Paulist Press, 1999).

produced over the historical long haul. Formulating criteria for assessing the fruits of comparative theology prior to comparison risks domesticating the process itself. Voyages to uncharted territories cannot be made with map in hand. Moreover, the historicist sensibility of contemporary theology has largely disabused theologians of the idea that it is possible to isolate criteria that have remained constant everywhere and at all times for determining whether a given position can be judged to be Christian.[2]

But acknowledging the internal pluralism of Christian theology does not mean that comparative theologians can go it alone, unmoored from tradition and free of accountability. Ultimately only sustained conversation between theologians and their home communities will determine whether the fruit of any particular venture in comparative theology will be received by those communities as contributing to their collective flourishing. Comparative theologians cannot afford to be solo operators.[3] They are obliged to articulate why their proposals ought to be received by their home communities even if globally valid *a priori* criteria are unavailable.

I entertain both modest and immodest hopes for my constructive proposals. My modest hope is that these proposals will be appealing because they resolve critical aporia in the theologies of Sankara and Tillich. The conversation created between these two theologians is promising because each has resources for resolving problems internal to the other's theological program. A more ambitious hope is that Christian thinkers who follow in Tillich's wake will learn from Sankara that we need not posit a tragic ontological separation between human beings and divinity, as Tillich does, to make room for freedom and to explain the gravity of the human predicament. Sankara can teach Christian theologians that a realistic and sober account of the human predicament need not curtail robust hope for sanctification so long as Christians recognize that human identity is not exhausted by finitude. Sankara can also teach Christians that the radical immanence of nonduality need not eliminate transcendence. The Advaitin can help Christians to discover how an apophatic anthropology that recognizes human beings as infinite mystery can preserve a form of transcendence that does not compete with immanence. Conversely,

---

2. Sheila Davaney has offered the most compelling argument against theological essentialism of this sort; see Sheila Greeve Davaney, *Pragmatic Historicism: A Theology for the Twenty-First Century* (Albany: State University of New York Press, 2000).

3. Indeed, I have argued elsewhere that academic comparative theologians are obliged to at least four different constituencies: their home communities, the new tradition under investigation, the community of scholars, and the theologians' students. John J. Thatamanil, "Managing Multiple Religious and Scholarly Identities: An Argument for a Theological Study of Hinduism," *Journal of the American Academy of Religion* 68, no. 4 (December 2000): 791–803.

Tillich's dynamic theology of ecstatic union is compelling because it attempts to overcome dualism without defining away the world of experience as Sankara is tempted to do. A creative synthesis of elements from both theologians will lead to a more adequate vision of divine immanence.

The criteria behind these theological decisions remain to be articulated, but what should be evident is that these decisions arise from within the parameters of this particular conversation. Moreover, I make no one-sided claims on behalf of the wholesale superiority of one thinker or theological tradition over another. What is offered here is a theology of nondualism that emerges out of the conversation between Sankara and Tillich. Is the resulting theology Hindu or Christian? That question is not easily answered. The commitment to a dynamic theology of ecstasy places this venture securely within a Christian theological framework. However, the commitment to an apophatic anthropology drawn from Sankara complicates the picture and gives rise to a hybrid Hindu-Christian theology that might appeal to both communities. What matters more than labels is whether theologians from both communities find the results compelling. As comparative theology continues to flourish in the coming decades, theology will increasingly become an interreligious activity that renders obsolete monoreligious labels of all kinds.[4]

Our examination of Sankara and Tillich has also surfaced internal difficulties in each that cannot be resolved by appeal to the other. Specifically, a residual substantialism compromises both visions by perpetuating forms of dualism that both theologians hope to avoid. The solution lies in adopting a wholly nonsubstantialist theological ontology of the sort proposed by Joseph Bracken and Robert Neville, in which ultimate reality is understood entirely as activity rather than as substance. Such an account can provide a skeleton for integrating apophatic theological anthropology (what Sankara gives us) with an ecstatic account of human activity as at once also divine activity (what Tillich gives us). Sankara and Tillich together teach the importance of overcoming dualism and embracing the immanent divine, but the final step toward that destination requires additional resources that neither can deliver. Before moving ahead to that constructive work, I summarize the results of the comparative process and briefly assess the relative merits of the categories employed to derive those results.

---

4. That, of course, is Frank Clooney's central contention. Clooney hopes that comparative theology will "promote a new, more integral theological conversation wherein traditions can remain distinct although their theologies are no longer separable." See Francis X. Clooney, *Hindu God, Christian God: How Reason Helps Break Down the Boundaries between Religions* (New York: Oxford University Press, 2001), 8.

Diagnosis: The Human Predicament as Self-Enclosed Finitude

Our investigation has demonstrated that Sankara and Tillich are in broad agreement that the human predicament may be diagnosed as self-enclosed finitude. Both thinkers believe that human beings suffer and act in misguided ways because they are turned in upon themselves and see the world through the lens of egoistic desire. Sankara and Tillich believe that human beings have never been otherwise; both understand that there is no moment in time when human beings fell into predicament out of a primordial plenitude.

Within the parameters of this general agreement, subtle but important differences emerge. Tillich alluded to some when he admonished Eastern traditions for taking finitude as such to be problematic. He argued that finitude itself is not problematic, but the distortions introduced by estrangement most certainly are. Finite life is compromised when lived in separation from its infinite ground. In Sankara's theology, the trouble with human life cannot be traced to separation; the trouble is that persons take themselves to be exhaustively defined as finite. Sankara's goal is to teach the Upanishadic truth that *ontologically* one is nothing other than Brahman. Finite realities have no being apart from Brahman. His pedagogical goal is to evoke in readers a shift in perspective so that the eternally present comes into view. This shift does not amount to a rejection of finitude. That Sankara leaves open the possibility of action after the dawn of liberating knowledge suggests otherwise. After all, Arjuna returns to the battlefield after understanding the truth of nonduality. If liberated persons continue to act for the world's well-being, they are plainly not jettisoning the finite realm for immersion in infinite mystical bliss. Enlightened persons just recognize that the everyday world of experience is merely conventional whereas ordinary actors mistake the conventional for all there is. A contemporary Advaitin can plead not guilty to Tillich's charge that Advaita *necessarily* regards finitude and not estrangement as problematic.

Nevertheless, differences persist and are best disclosed in each theologian's approach to desire. For Sankara, the human predicament, understood as transmigration, is perpetuated by desire and aversion. Although Sankara distinguishes between legitimate and illegitimate desire at the level of conventional truth, nondual knowledge extinguishes all desire. Desire depends on the mistaken belief that one is a finite individual who suffers lack. The infinite reality of Brahman suffers no such lack and so does not desire. Once seekers realize that they are that infinite reality, desire is dissolved.

Even the desire for Brahman (*brahmajijnasa*) is provisional whereas Tillich's ultimate concern is not. When one understands that one *is* Brahman, desire *for* Brahman comes to an end. On Tillich's side, desire for the ultimate never ends. Ultimate concern refers at once to human desire for the ultimate and, paradoxically, the desire of the ultimate for itself. In Sankara's theology, desire cannot be postulated of Brahman even symbolically. From the point of view of ultimate truth, desire is problematic because it is a psychological manifestation of an error regarding one's true nature. One is tempted to ask Sankara whether he can imagine a desire that is not itself a product of lack or deficiency but of the kind of plenitude enjoyed by the liberated person, but that appears to be an extrinsic possibility inconceivable from within the parameters of Sankara's worldview. Although the Advaita tradition does speak of the compassion of the liberated person, that compassion is never understood as a form of desire.

For Tillich the real error is to suppose that finite beings can exist apart from the infinite. Human beings really are finite, but Tillich would add that the infinite is Not-other than the finite. Tillich affirms the reality of the finite and the infinite, what is grounded and the ground, even as he affirms the radical dependence of the finite on the infinite. For the Advaitin, the ultimate truth of Brahman, self-existent and immutable, trumps conventional identity. Persons surrender the idea that they are ephemeral, finite beings when they realize that they are the immutable infinite. Such a move is inconceivable within Tillich's ontology.

This disagreement about finitude explains their differences on etiological matters. For Tillich, the predicament is caused by the propensity of human beings to separate themselves from the divine depth to which they belong. Human beings are estranged from God when they opt for a shallow autonomy over against the infinite ground and power of being-itself. Such estrangement fragments the self because it is separated from the power that holds the self together. This quest for autonomy also gives rise to estrangement between self and others.

Whereas Tillich stipulates that beings can be estranged from divinity, Sankara insists that persons are never other than divinity. Human beings only mistakenly believe that they are separated from Brahman. This error is a matter of ignorant wrong-headedness and not ontological alienation. To assert that ignorance has no ontological standing is not to minimize its devastating consequences. To claim that the afflictions are ultimately unreal is not to assert that they are incapable of making life miserable. The karmic consequences of action generated by these poisons and the transmigratory cycle are not imagined either. The claim that the afflictions are unreal is intended to teach persons that there is nothing *ontologically* awry with the human condition. Ignorance is a deep existential problem, but it is neither inevitable nor permanent. It simply does not have to be this way. The pains of the human predicament are produced by a deeply flawed understanding of the way things are and so can be corrected when human beings comprehend their true dignity.

To maintain that ignorance is the root cause of the human predicament does not imply that persons can just snap out of it and spontaneously come to their senses. Persons need the grace of the guru who mediates the meaning of scripture if they are to escape the human predicament. Bondage cannot be wished away. Robert Neville's contention that "Although we enjoy the fullness and the freedom of the divine, if we think we are bound to sin, if we act in accordance with that bondage, and if we teach others that this is the way of the world, then we are in fact estranged" resonates well with central elements of Sankara's position.[5] The felt pain of the human predicament is the same regardless of whether that predicament is rooted in a real or imagined separation from God.

Even at the level of ontology, the differences between Tillich and Sankara should not be overstated. After all, Tillich rejects the idea that the relation between beings and being-itself is external and for that reason explicitly states that his theology amounts to a rejection of dualism. Given that Tillich refuses to characterize the human predicament in the language of traditional theism, it is not surprising that his description of hubris is remarkably similar to Sankara's notion of egoism (*ahamkara*). Hubris can also be described, in a fusion of Tillichian and Advaita terminology, as the act of raising a purely conventional reality to ultimate status. Sankara undercuts egoism by calling persons to see that the true Self is the self-effulgent light of consciousness and not the finite ego. Tillich believes that hubris can be overcome only when the power of being grasps the finite self and brings about an ecstatic union between beings and being-itself.

For Tillich, desire becomes distorted and problematic only apart from such union. Finite beings legitimately desire their own fulfillment, desire each other, and desire God. Such longing is never eliminated nor transcended. These desires are right and good. *Eros* is a legitimate and even healing part of human experience, and *eros* is not concupiscence. Only the latter

---

5. Robert C. Neville, *Eternity and Time's Flow* (Albany: State University of New York Press, 1993), 213.

is problematic. Concupiscence is desire distorted because it is desire unlimited. When finite beings are estranged from essential unity to the power of being-itself, legitimate desire becomes uncontrolled, self-serving desire. A true and genuine longing for the infinite is exchanged for unlimited longing. Sankara, on the contrary, maintains that because human beings are not ultimately finite (though conventionally they most certainly are), desire can be entirely overcome. If one knows oneself to be Brahman, what can one possibly need or want? Despite this noteworthy point of difference, both Sankara and Tillich concur that the human predicament can be characterized as self-enclosed finitude.

Comparing Etiologies

What is the cause of the self-enclosed finitude that marks the human predicament? How is it that beings who are so intimately related to ultimate reality fail to realize the nature of this relation? As we have seen, neither Sankara nor Tillich offer simple answers to such etiological questions.

Both can offer relatively straightforward answers to the proximate question regarding the source of self-seeking desire. Sankara argued that ignorance (*avidya*) is the cause of the human predicament as marked by desire, aversion, and delusion. Ignorance regarding the true nature of the Self generates the mistaken notion that one is a finite self and this, in turn, gives rise to desire and the rest to which human beings are habitually bound. Likewise, Tillich argued that unbelief is the cause of hubris and concupiscence. He describes "unbelief" as "the act or state in which man in the totality of his being turns away from God" (ST 2:47). Tillich first describes unbelief as a kind of premoral separation. Unbelief is not the willed refusal to believe in God. Rather, the term names the truth that human beings ask about and after God, and such asking already evinces separation from that for which one seeks.

Both ignorance and unbelief name a congenital transtemporal fact, something antedating those actions for which we are morally culpable. The difference between unbelief and ignorance emerges in Tillich's volitional emphasis and the consequent stress on the psychological reality of guilt. Human beings embrace separation and do what they know they ought not to and so fall prey to guilt. Unbelief, enacted as hubris and concupiscence, leads to an awareness of missing the mark, of failing to be what one ought to be and essentially is.

Sankara's analysis of the human predicament, emphasizing as it does cognitive factors, has no treatment of guilt and forgiveness as Tillich's volitional analysis does.

There may be more to this difference than a question of relative emphasis on cognitive as opposed to volitional factors. In this difference, comparison appears to confront seismic differences in civilizational structures and cultural habits of identity formation. There are reasons for believing that guilt just may not plague Sankara and his cultural milieu in the way that guilt seems to trouble Tillich and the West, broadly speaking. Here, comparative theology, especially in its anthropological dimension, needs data from cross-cultural psychology before venturing a guess about the relative importance of guilt as a factor in the human predicament. Clearly there is a complicated dialectic between culturally determined ways of being human and conceptions of ultimate reality. At any rate, it would be a grave error to accuse Sankara of providing an inadequate analysis of the human predicament for failing to take guilt seriously if guilt turns out not to be an anthropological universal. It would be even more absurd to maintain that Sankara's theology is inadequate because his Brahman cannot forgive sins.

For comparative theology, the most significant difference between unbelief and ignorance is Tillich's claim that unbelief bespeaks a real ontological distance between beings and being-itself. Tillich's qualitative conception of being-itself as that which gives power and meaning to human life implies that the human incapacity to live with genuine vitality and intentionality points to a rupture between beings and being-itself. Creatures are free and so capable of self-contradiction because they are not "kept within the divine ground." The cost of freedom is estrangement or separation from the divine life.

As we have seen, Tillich believed that any theology that did not posit an ontological distance between beings and being-itself would be indistinguishable from naturalism or pantheism; in any such account, creatures would be reduced to mere modes of the divine substance. Tillich also maintained that one must not attempt to avoid the Scylla of naturalism by recourse to the Charybdis of supranaturalism. That theological move would compromise divine infinity by rendering God a mere being among beings and not the power and ground of being-itself. For Tillich, the only viable alternative—and this is the crucial failure of imagination on Tillich's part—is a theological vision in which creaturely freedom is understood as an *ontological* substantial independence.

In such a vision, creatures must stand outside the divine life if they are to live autonomously.

Tillich's insistence that freedom requires ontological independence leads to a tragic vision of human life in which creatures *inevitably* violate their own essential natures. To ex-ist is to be estranged, to stand outside the divine depth. Creatures who are estranged from the divine life lack the power to become what they most truly are.

Tillich believed that he avoided making the fall *logically* necessary. As noted in the previous two chapters, the idea of a necessary fall amounts to heresy. If the fall is in any sense necessary, then how could one distinguish between God's good creation and fallen nature? By what criteria could we insist that some actions amount to a violation of God's intention for humanity and for the world? An identification of creation and fall brings with it countless theological dangers, including the deeply troublesome possibility that God's own evolution requires fallenness and all the evil that fallenness brings with it.

Tillich believed he escaped these perils by insisting that no logical reason can be given for the transition from essence to existence; no reason can explain the brokenness of the fallen world. How can there be a rational explanation for the irrational? Beings just fail to be what they are created to be. Nevertheless, Tillich did make the fall ontologically inevitable by making the following argument: If I am to be free from and for God, I must stand at some distance from God. There can no freedom without distance. That distance leads ineluctably to estrangement. Tillich freely admits the upshot of his position: "Creation and the Fall coincide in so far as there is no point in time and space in which created goodness was actualized and had existence. . . . Actualized creation and estranged existence are identical" (ST 2:44). Tillich may have managed to avoid making the fall logically necessary, but he does make fallenness absolutely inevitable. The distinction between logical necessity and ontological inevitability seems perilously slim.

How does Tillich get himself into the bind of making the fall inevitable if not necessary? The trouble is that Tillich's theological imagination is compromised by the very substantialism he was so keen to avoid. To stipulate that creatures can enjoy substantial independence if and only if they are separated from the divine is to continue to imagine ultimate reality in substantial terms. On this account, two realities can be free for and from each other only if they are separate and stand over against each other. Feminist theologians have argued that such intuitions are ultimately rooted in and disclosive of a compromised and patriarchal account of maturation in which freedom, especially for men, mandates separation from the fluid and enveloping mother. Freedom, on this account, is the mark of self-possessed, self-enclosed, and autonomous egos.[6] I can be free only to the extent that I am at a remove from you.

To suppose that creaturely freedom requires substantial independence generates a precarious theological vision in which unbelief is inevitable. Of course, Sankara also believed that ignorance is a pervasive feature of experience; that is just the way the world is. Human experience is compromised by egoism. But Sankara offers no *ontological* reason why it has to be or remain so. Sankara rejects the idea that human freedom requires separation from divinity. After knowledge dawns, human beings are no longer compelled to live lives marked by oscillation between knowledge and ignorance because human life is not marked by one foot in and one foot outside the divine life. Human beings just are Brahman.

Comparing Prognoses: Liberation and Salvation

Among some philosophers of religion and comparativists, it has become customary to employ salvation as a general term for characterizing the ultimate goals or aims sought by religious traditions. The thinker who best exemplifies this approach is John Hick. Hick argues that Axial Age religions are soteriological traditions whereas pre-Axial Age or archaic traditions sought instead to ensure harmony or unity between human beings and their world. Hick claims that Axial Age traditions seek to move persons from "self-centeredness" to "reality-centeredness." All such religions are "soteriological vehicles" that make ultimate transformation possible. This same pattern, Hick argues, is manifestly evident in both Hinduism and Christianity. Indeed, he often uses the expression "salvation/liberation" to suggest that the meaning of the two terms is essentially equivalent inasmuch as both name materially identical processes of transformation.[7]

---

6. A now-classic work that well articulates these themes with power and elegance is Catherine Keller's *From a Broken Web: Separation, Sexism, and Self* (Boston: Beacon Press, 1986). Many of these themes resound again in her more recent *The Face of the Deep: A Theology of Becoming* (New York: Routledge, 2003).

7. John Hick, *An Interpretation of Religion: Human Responses to the Transcendent* (New Haven: Yale University Press, 1989), 36–55. Hick continues to speak in this way even in his most recent work; see "The Next Step beyond Dialogue," in *The Myth of Religious Superiority: A Multi-Faith Exploration*, ed. Paul F. Knitter (Maryknoll, N.Y.: Orbis Books, 2005), 3.

Others have contested the notion that there is a single generic process of salvation that all traditions share. Most notably, S. Mark Heim claims that religious traditions pursue radically different ends. The very title of Heim's book, *Salvations: Truth and Difference in Religion* directly introduces his claim that there may be many different and legitimate religious goals.[8] Heim's claim that religions seek different ends raises questions about whether the use of the term *salvations*, even in the plural, is justified. Put in terms of Neville's theory of comparison, it remains to be seen whether salvation can really function as an abstract or vague category with wide applicability and adequacy. Reasons to be cautious are manifold. The Latinate term *salvation* refers in its root meaning to the notion of healing. Comparativists must ask if the world's many religions do in fact share a common quest for healing.

If liberation (*moksa*) is understood as escape from the cycle of transmigration, then the prognosis for the human predicament in Advaita is not healing. In fact, the medical model as such seems inappropriate. Escaping bondage is not in truth a prognosis because bondage is not an illness. While talk about human predicament continues to be appropriate, it seems misleading to understand liberation by way of the medical model. On a narrow reading of liberation in Sankara's Advaita, Tillich and Sankara appear to have different ideas about how to address the human predicament, and so there are good reasons to avoid using the term *salvation* as a vague comparative category.

These differences notwithstanding, the appearance of radical contrast diminishes upon further analysis. Sankara insists that liberation is just another term for Brahman. The deepest meaning of *moksa* turns out not to be escape. The true religious goal is realizing that liberation is one's true nature.

The religious problem, therefore, cannot be understood merely as bondage to transmigration. The predicament can also be described as a disease in which desire, aversion, grief, and delusion disfigure experience and blind us to our true nature. When knowledge arises, human beings are set free from these ignorance-born afflictions. The movement into freedom from afflictions can be characterized fairly and faithfully as a process of healing. Those who are healed can then live with equanimity, wisdom, and compassion.

Despite the possibility that the knowledge of the liberated person can be partially obstructed by the operation of karma already in motion, Sankara is

8. S. Mark Heim, *Salvations: Truth and Difference in Religion* (Maryknoll, N.Y.: Orbis Books, 1995).

far more optimistic than Tillich is. Sankara understands liberation as complete recovery from the disease of ignorance. There remains, in Sankara, the possibility that persons can grow and become more firmly rooted in wisdom, but liberated persons can no longer be derailed.

For Tillich, on the other hand, complete recovery from the diseases that mark the human predicament is impossible. Indeed, despite his affirmation of sanctification, or New Being as process, he largely regards human life as a process of oscillation; human life is a battleground between the forces of Old Being (disease) and the power of New Being (health). The power of New Being, though always at work in human life, episodically breaks into human consciousness in ecstatic moments in which human beings are made transparent or permeable to the power of being-itself. These are transformative occasions in which the split between essence and existence is healed and human beings unambiguously become what they ought to be, but what is disclosed and accomplished in ecstasy remains perpetually vulnerable to disruption and profanization. Tillich's prognosis for the human predicament is guarded at best. Even the deepest experience of healing can be threatened and undone. That threat is not rooted in human recalcitrance alone. The reason for life's precariousness is fundamentally ontological. Human beings stand outside the divine ground and so are and will always remain prone to fragmentation. Human freedom can always undo and even negate what is accomplished by the Spirit in and through ecstasy.

In the ecstatic moment, by the power of the Spirit, human activity is made simultaneously divine. In mystical experience, in genuine prayer, in prophetic utterance, human beings become more than they are ordinarily but not other than themselves. The transitory dualism between God and creature is annulled, albeit temporarily, when creatures are infused by the meaning-bearing power of the Spirit that brings them into their true ontological dignity. These ecstatic events open up human beings to their divine depths and drive persons toward sanctification but such sanctification is always vulnerable to dissolution.

Evaluating the Medical Model

Because religious interpretations of the human predicament differ, religious visions of the human telos will likewise differ. Any category that might be used to compare ultimate aspirations must be capacious enough to account for the possibility of important differences. The medical model appears to be, on balance, a fruitful category for comparative work, one that does not disfigure Sankara or Tillich. This category, or rather network of categories, has made possible comparison that does not distort the work of either theologian. For example, using the subcategory "prognosis for the human predicament" has made it possible to identify how salvation and liberation can be fruitfully compared and distinguished. We have noted the important sense in which liberation is not a prognosis—not a projected cure for the human predicament but rather than an escape from that predicament. We have also been able to show how liberation can in fact be characterized as a process of healing that leads to the robust prognosis of living liberation.

What, if anything, does this particular exercise in comparison suggest about the debates between Hick and Heim? This particular venture in comparison has yielded complex and cross-cutting patterns of similarities within difference and differences within similarity. The differences registered are so significant as to problematize talk of a single identical process of transformation happening in both traditions. Sankara would find Tillich's prognosis limited and inadequate and Tillich would contend that Sankara's prognosis is unrealistically optimistic. Both identify healing as the religious quest, but their assessments about how much and what kind of healing is possible differ markedly. Hick's language of transformation from self-centeredness to reality-centeredness can work, but only if it is taken as a vague comparative category. It cannot be taken to describe an identical cross-cultural invariant.

Heim's claim that the world's religious traditions offer fundamentally different religious ends also seems premature. While there are significant differences between Sankara's liberation and Tillich's salvation, the presence of important analogies between these two notions hardly justify claims that each has in mind an utterly different religious goal. We can imagine Heim objecting that it takes no great sophistication to see that bringing an end to the cycle of rebirth is not the same thing as being healed by the power of being-itself. However, careful and patient comparison demonstrates that summary judgments of incommensurability are off the mark. Neither Hick's identity claim—all religious traditions aim for the same ultimate religious end—nor Heim's claim of stark difference—the world's religious traditions propose radically different religious goods—seem warranted. At least in this particular case, a complex and overlapping pattern of similarities and differences is evident.

Toward a Dynamic Apophatic Nondualism

Despite several important differences between Sankara and Tillich, the possibilities for Christian conversation with nondualist traditions are far richer after Tillich's theological labor than before. His argument that the relationship between being-itself and beings is internal, his appeal to a Pauline theology of the Holy Spirit, and his turn to neglected strands within the Christian tradition (Eckhart, Nicholas of Cusa) demonstrate that interreligious engagement need not be derailed by the presumably unbridgeable chasm between East and West.

Many have assumed that a dualistic theism is an essential and nonnegotiable feature of Christian tradition. Tillich, on the other hand, persuasively argued that the created world can have no being apart from God who is being-itself. Without denying the distinction between the finite and the infinite, he argued that the infinite cannot be other than the finite and still be infinite. The infinite is precisely what is Not-other than the finite. Clarifying the logic of infinity through a doctrine of God as being-itself provides a foundation for fruitful conversation with Hindu nondualism.

That Tillich's theology holds great promise for constructive dialogue with other traditions has long been appreciated. What has not been sufficiently appreciated is the argument made here: Tillich's ecstatic ontology and his theology of transitory dualism contain the seeds for a distinctively Christian nondualism.

The impression of irreconcilable difference between Christianity and Hinduism has been sustained in part by the false impression that nondualist traditions do not recognize the severity of the human predicament. However, as I have shown here, such a caricature is manifestly false. Sankara recognizes the gravity of the human predicament without denying the truth of nonduality. Ignorance of our true nature is sufficient to precipitate the human predicament; human beings can be Brahman and yet suffer miserably.

To insist on nondualism while affirming the experiential reality of ignorance is to raise the perennial question that plagues Advaita: "Whose is *avidya*?" If one is never other than Brahman, then how is it possible to avoid positing Brahman as the locus of ignorance? As we have seen, Sankara refuses to answer the question and prefers instead to deconstruct it by arguing that ignorance has no ontological status and so need not need be located anywhere.

Sankara's trouble with ignorance is analogous to the question of evil in Christian theology. Since Augustine, the claim that evil has no independent ontological status has been and continues to be a respectable option in Christian theology. Any nondualist theology must deal with the problem of evil either by locating evil in God (as there is nothing other than God within a nondualist frame) or by denying to evil any ontological status. Sankara adopts the latter strategy without wishing away the misery of the human predicament. Understanding these features of Sankara's theology makes it difficult to dismiss his theology as nothing more than naïve optimism.

Furthermore, Sankara's theology does not prescribe a quasi-Stoic resolve rooted in a confidence that human beings can save themselves by solitary effort. This misleading picture of Advaita as a tradition that urges persons to struggle through to liberation under their own steam has been taken by Christian theologians to render Advaita entirely incompatible with Christian convictions about human fallenness and the need for grace. However, Sankara clearly maintains that liberating knowledge requires revelation as given in scripture and embodied in the guru. Sankara nowhere suggests that mere introspection suffices for knowledge of the Self.

Finally, the picture of Advaita as a tradition of mystical knowledge in which ultimate reality is entirely known has been presented as a violation of Christian convictions regarding divine transcendence. As it happens, Sankara vigorously argues that the Self cannot be cognized. The scripture provides knowledge *that* one is Brahman. *What* Brahman is transcends cognition. Sankara would agree with Tillich's claim that genuine mystery remains mysterious even after revelation. In revelation, mystery is encountered as mystery. Liberated persons know best that the Self cannot be known. Sankara maintains a deep commitment to the unknowability of the true Self. What liberates is knowledge that I am no merely finite creature perishing in the sea of samsara. What liberates is the truth of nonduality and not comprehensive knowledge of Brahman, which is impossible. Sankara's nondualism culminates in a true apophatic anthropology.

After dismissing apparent points of irreconcilable difference, rich possibilities emerge for a robust conversation between traditions. The richest of these possibilities is a Christian nondualism in which God is understood to be all in all, a vision that maintains that a God who is anything less is no god at all. Christian nondualism promises and achieves a deep coincidence between immanence and transcendence. Tillich contributed to the possibility of Christian nondualism by showing that traditional theism yields impoverished notions of transcendence and immanence. Instead, Tillich offered a theological vision in which God is at once qualitatively transcendent in power and meaning and yet also the radically immanent ground of being. Sankara, in like fashion, affirmed the radical cognitive transcendence of Brahman while insisting on the radical immanence of Brahman as being (*sat*) and consciousness (*cit*).

Unfortunately, both Sankara and Tillich failed to surmount dualism altogether. Sankara left in place a split between an unreal world of change and a real and changeless Brahman. Tillich, for his part, cannot imagine that human beings can be free without standing in some ontological sense outside the divine life. A residual substantialism persists in Tillich's theological imagination. The result is a relatively diminished view of human possibilities in which human beings only experience unambiguous life fragmentarily.

Is it possible to absorb the virtues of Sankara and Tillich and also overcome what is inadequate in both by playing each against the other? I believe so. But neither Sankara nor Tillich, alone or together, provides all the resources necessary for an adequate Christian nondualism. In order to overcome the substantialist deficiencies in both thinkers, the insights of Sankara and Tillich need to be brought into conversation with the work of Joseph Bracken and Robert Neville, two contemporary theologians whose engagement with process theology has enabled them to discard substantialist notions of divinity altogether. Bracken explicitly characterizes his project as nondualistic. Neville does not. Nevertheless, Neville can also be read as advancing a Christian nondualism, one that is, moreover, in clear continuity with possibilities envisioned for the future of Christian reflection by Tillich himself. Both thinkers demonstrate how we might extricate ourselves from dilemmas that Sankara and Tillich could not avoid.

Joseph Bracken's Proposal for a Dynamic Nondualism

Joseph Bracken, in a remarkably concise article entitled "Infinity and the Logic of Nondualism," argues that certain logical and metaphysical problems inevitably arise whenever any entity is characterized as infinite.[9] If one claims that some entity (Brahman in Sankara's case) is infinite, then it must follow that nothing other than that entity can truly exist. The reason is clear. If there truly is something other than Brahman, then Brahman would not really be infinite as it would be limited by what is other to it. Strictly speaking, nothing, not even a second entity that is wholly dependent for its being

---

9. Joseph Bracken, "Infinity and the Logic of Non-Dualism," *Hindu-Christian Studies Bulletin* 11 (1998): 39–44. The article is a highly condensed and lucid summary of his philosophically rigorous and impressive book, *The Divine Matrix: Creativity as the Link between East and West* (Maryknoll, N.Y.: Orbis Books, 1995).

on the first, can exist without limiting and thereby violating the infinity of the first entity.

Of course that is why Tillich insisted that God is not an infinite or absolute being. Tillich's claim, that it would be truer to say that God does not exist than to say that God does, recognizes that unfortunate conclusions follow from supposing God to be *an* infinite being. Such an infinite being would necessarily be limited by finite beings and so be finite itself. Sankara also recognized the dangers of supposing Brahman to be a being or entity. To deny as he explicitly did that Brahman is a substance, quality, activity, or relation is a rigorous attempt to avoid likening Brahman to any conventional reality whatsoever. Sankara's further claim that Brahman transcends both ideas of being and nonbeing also indicates that he wanted to avoid any entitative conception of Brahman. Put simply, both seek to think theologically in ways that anticipate Bracken's concerns.

The trouble is that despite their stated intentions, both failed to abide by their deepest commitments. As we have shown, Sankara clearly thought of Brahman as an unchanging reality, one without a second. Brahman is, in Sankara's imagination, finally an unchanging and eternal Absolute. Sankara so rigorously affirms the transcendent immutability and absoluteness of Brahman that even Brahman's character as the world's substratum is ultimately denied lest Brahman be qualified by that relation. The consequence of so rigorous a stance is an irresoluble dualism between Brahman and the world of flux. The only way Sankara can avoid dualism is to deny to that world any reality, and that denial gives to his theology the appearance of acosmic monism. A monism that denies the reality of the world is utterly contrary to his more complex commitments and purposes.

Likewise, Tillich falls over into substantialist thinking when he maintains that without "substantial independence" creatures would be reduced to mere finite modes of an infinite substance. The implicit premise is that God must be in some way substantial such that creatures could not be free if they were not in some sense other than God. Tillich's appeal to a qualitative conception of God as the depth dimension of reality and his commitment to think beyond notions of substance and causality represent a bold attempt to reimagine divinity beyond dualism. Nevertheless, Tillich's attempt falls short. This lack is most clearly disclosed in his incapacity to think of freedom otherwise than by way of substantial independence.

The way out of these residual substantialisms is to take up Bracken's pro-posal that the infinite reality must be construed as *activity* rather than as *sub-stance*. Bracken recommends that we hold that all beings exist "by virtue of an underlying activity which serves as the ontological ground for their exis-tence and activity." Without that grounding activity, creatures could not exist, but that grounding activity is not itself something separate from what it cre-ates. The relation between that activity and the beings to which it gives rise is nondual. As Bracken puts it, "the grounding activity is not an entity, and the entity is other than the grounding activity. At the same time they are not-two since only together, namely, as grounding activity and that which exists in virtue of the grounding activity, are they one concrete reality. This grounding activity, moreover, is infinite because it serves as the ontological ground for literally everything that exists. . . . it transcends them all since it is their com-mon ground or source of existence and activity. Whereas entities are inevitably limited or defined by their relations to one another, this grounding activity is strictly unlimited and therefore infinite."[10]

This kind of nondualism can honor many of Sankara's deepest commit-ments and resolve the worst of his conundrums. Dynamic nondualism has no trouble affirming the reality of the empirical world, but it can do so without positing something that stands over against Brahman. The empirical world is created by this underlying activity, but that world is never separate from that activity. It has no self-existence apart from that activity. We have noted that Sankara is deeply committed to affirming the reality of the experienced world as opposed to Buddhist idealists who deny to the world extramental reality. This distinguishes the waking world from the world of dreams; the dream world is no more when the dreamer wakes. In a dynamic nondualism, the world is most definitely real but *not real apart* from Brahman. Brahman is all there is. Sankara's root commitment to the principle that the world has no independent ontological reality over against Brahman is honored but with the added benefit that the world is not defined out of existence.

Bracken's conception of Brahman as an underlying infinite activity that gives rise to the world of flux goes a long way to resolving Sankara's awkward problem about what to do with the world. Under Bracken's scheme, the being of beings is, shall we say, *becoming-itself.* No determinate reality has any being apart from the infinite all-encompassing activity that grounds every entity. However, beings are also defined in all the ordinary ways that any determi-nate reality would be. In Bracken's vision, I do not have to deny my particular

---

10. Bracken, "Infinity and the Logic of Non-Dualism," 41.

determinate identity in order to assert that I am Brahman. Because Brahman is the creative ontological ground for all determinate entities, I can be both a determinate reality and Brahman without having to posit the reality of two or more substances. The reason is clear: Brahman is not a substance but rather the eternal ontological activity that gives rise to determinate realities.

Suppose that Bracken's proposal does in fact resolve critical problems in Sankara's theological ontology. We would still need to ask, Can this proposal from an alien philosophical tradition just be grafted into Sankara's Advaita Vedanta? As our extensive discussion of Sankara has shown, Advaita soteriology hinges on the idea that Brahman is unchanging. The way to escape from action and its karmic consequences is to insist that the true Self, namely Brahman, is utterly inactive. If the Self is intrinsically active, then there can be no escape from karma. Hence, Brahman's immutability must be preserved. When seen in this light, Bracken's dynamic Brahman appears to threaten the entire soterio-logic of Sankara's thought. Bracken, focused as he is on ontological matters, does not consider the consequences of his proposal for Advaita soteriology, but comparative theologians who do their work in conversation with another tradition cannot be unmindful of the soteriological and anthropological consequences of their revisionist proposals.

A possible indigenous resource for resolving problems created by positing an active Brahman can be found in Sankara's contention that the liberated person can act without accruing karma. Readers will recall that Sankara maintained that liberated persons act for the welfare of the world but incur no karma from such action so long as they know that activity is a function of the body and not the doing of immutable Brahman. Because they no longer believe themselves to be agents, they acquire neither merit nor demerit. They remain wholly detached from those actions. It seems possible that even within the framework of a dynamic nondualism, persons can still act with deep detachment even if it is no longer possible to assert that Brahman is inactive. One can imagine that liberated persons who are deeply rooted in a conviction of their identity with Brahman can be entirely beyond action driven by narrowly egoistic motivations. In that sense, they can also leave behind the idea that they are merely private agents advancing private purposes. What would such conviction look like were it given verbal expression? Perhaps it would take the following form: "I do not act but Brahman acts in me." Of course, that result would likely sound too Christian for Advaita theologians. Moreover, this purported solution brings with it other dangers, not least of which is that an active Brahman might be implicated in karma. The solution to that problem might well be that Brahman's activity is, like the activity of the liberated person, wholly beyond egoism and so also beyond karmic constraints.

At any rate, the compassionate comportment of liberated persons is the same regardless of the underlying ontology to which they subscribe. Sankara is, after all, a two-truth thinker interested in having persons relativize conventional self-conceptions in order to awaken his listeners to the truth of their ontological status as Brahman. Bracken's conception of ultimate reality as the dynamic ontological creating of worldly entities is compatible with the structure of two-truth theory. Persons can affirm their conventional finite identities and yet relativize them in order to let the truth of their ontological infinity come into focus. Brahman, though now imagined as infinite activity rather than infinite substance, would remain an absolute mystery beyond speech and beyond cognition.

The foregoing analysis has demonstrated that Advaitins have strong internal reasons to be sympathetic to Bracken's version of nondualism. Likewise, Tillichians must also abandon the residual substantialism that lingers in Tillich's theology by adopting this dynamic vision of being-itself as ontological creativity. The greatest benefit would be that such an account can undergird a far more robust prognosis for the human predicament than Tillich was able or willing to provide. A theory of God as ontological creativity can provide a framework in which human beings need not stand on their own ground outside the divine life in order to be free. If being-itself is construed as the ontological creativity that brings free entities into being, then it is possible to conceive of human beings as wholly internal to the divine life and yet also free.

The potential advantages for theological anthropology as reconstituted along these lines are many. If human freedom does not require substantial independence over against the divine life, then there need be "no point of identification" between creation and fall. There would be no reason to affirm that creatures stand outside the divine life just by virtue of their existence, and hence existence need not become synonymous with estrangement. We can refuse Tillich's contention that there must be a point at which actualized creation and estrangement must coincide.

Freed from this deeply problematic and dualistic feature of Tillich's thought, we can reconstruct his theology in ways that fulfill the profound promise of his account of ecstatic action. We can imagine that promise fulfilled in a performative account of human-divine nonduality in which human beings enjoy stable and enduring union with divinity and not merely fleeting episodes of fragmentary ecstasy. Because human beings are *always* within the divine life, one need not imagine ecstasy as inevitably momentary, an exceptional moment in which human beings are taken into the divine life, only subsequently to fall back into the ambiguity of separated existence. One can even entertain a strong vision of sanctification that transcends perpetual oscillation and conflict and understands human becoming as a process of divinization in which human beings are rendered ever more permeable or transparent to their ontological depth, to their eternal belonging to the eternal. Such a reconstructed Tillichianism that does not, at any point, identify actualized creation and fall would be far closer in spirit and substance to Sankara's Advaita. In both visions, there would be no ontological gap between finite beings and their infinite depth. Life can still be messy, violent, and even tragic but only because we fail to realize and become what we truly are, and not because of a fundamental ontological chasm between human beings and divinity.

Robert Neville's Dynamic and Nondual Theory of Creation *Ex Nihilo*

The way forward to this vision lies through the work of Robert Neville. Neville, like Bracken, advocates a vision of being-itself as ontological creativity. Neville has also thought through the matter of freedom that is absolutely critical to Tillich's reflections. We now turn to a brief sketch of Neville's theory of creation *ex nihilo* in search of an ontology of creation that does not suppose that creaturely freedom requires ontological distance between beings and being-itself.

Neville's metaphysics describes all determinate entities as harmonies of essential and conditional features. Conditional features are those features of a thing that relate it to other entities whereas essential features are those features of a thing that give to it its own being, its own place and time. Without conditional features, a thing would be a contentless, atomistic monad unrelated to other things. Without essential features, a thing could not be anything such that it could harmonize conditional features and thereby assume its own time and place. Essential features make it possible for beings to be related to each other through their conditional features. But what accounts for the togetherness of essential features? There needs to be a ground that makes it possible for the essential features of determinate things to be together. The togetherness of essential features must be ontological such that the conditional features can have a context for relating.[11] For Neville, that context is that they are created to be together. God is the eternal creating that allows the world its together-ness. For present purposes, what is crucial is Neville's claim that God must be construed as the dynamic act that gives rise to the world of related beings. The determinate entities of the world are together because they have God's eternal activity as an "ontological context of mutual relevance." Ontological creativity is responsible for the being and being-together of things. More radically, onto-logical creativity *is* the being of things.

Neville also goes on to propose a trinitarian conception of God as source, act, and product. He maintains that the world as product of the divine act of creating has no being of its own apart from the act of creation. Consequently, the world as product is divine. Furthermore, in the act of creating, God becomes the source of the world. That is to say that God's character as source of the world is one of the things God creates. God becomes God in and through the act of creating. Apart from creating, God is wholly indeterminate. In sum, Neville argues that God must be understood as source, act, and product. This rough-and-ready sketch of Neville's ontology leaves much unsaid, but our present task does not require a comprehensive explication of Neville's massive and intricate system. Our focus remains squarely on the human predicament.

Among the most important consequences of Neville's ontology for theo-logical anthropology is the idea that the world has no own-being apart from God. The world as product is not and cannot be outside the divine life, because there is no outside. Here, we can identify elements of Neville's theology that may clearly be identified as nondualistic. Because the singular act of divine creativity is the being of things, there is no other place for creatures to be. Consequently, human life, whatever it may be empirically, is not ontologically other than the being of God. Moreover, and this is the point that is central for theological anthropology, Neville's strong emphasis on divine immanence in no way compromises creaturely freedom. Contrary to Tillich, who had to posit a kind of substantial independence in order for creatures to be free, Neville believes that freedom does not require ontological independence. On the contrary, Neville argues that a person's free act is not hers alone but is also a divine action. Neville offers a "two authors theory" in which every activity is ontologically divine and cosmologically human. *That* I can act at all is God's doing and is due to divine creativity. *What* I do and what I make of myself is my doing. That God is the source of my being, that God creates my freedom, does not determine what I do with that freedom. Moreover, I would have no freedom whatsoever, indeed I would not be, save for God's creative activity.

---

11. Neville, *Eternity and Time's Flow*, 156–57.

In a sense, there are two authors of every decisive moment, God and the creature in the moment itself. The spontaneous creativity in the moment is part of the larger singular creative act by which God creates the whole world; it is part of the act of creation *ex nihilo*. At the same time . . . that spontaneity is the event's own self-definition. Where the event is part of a person's life, it is part of the person's own self-definition. . . . the creativity by which we define ourselves and by means of which we take responsibility for what we do and are is the same creativity that is part of the larger divine creative act of which the whole world is a product. . . . There is no conflict between divine creation and human freedom unless the creator is seen as an external agent who might force certain options upon a person.[12]

Of course, with Tillich, Neville rejects the idea that God is a being. God is, therefore, in no sense an external agent. Hence, even Neville's talk about a two-author theory of creation must not be taken literally. God, after all, is not *an* agent.

The vital implication of this line of reasoning is that one does not have to suppose that the exercise of creaturely freedom requires an ontological distance between creature and creator. God understood as ontological creativity is neither a coercive super-agent nor a substance of which persons are mere modes, and so at no point does creaturely existence have to be placed outside the divine life. It follows that there is no ontological reason why human beings have to fall into sin by virtue of any necessary separation from the divine life. Neville puts the point rather strongly.

It should be understood that there is no necessity in creation that people sin. Rather, the fact of sin is simply empirical. Look around, and you see that the world is sinful. Look within, and you see the same thing. . . . We grow up learning that the normal world is the sinful one of our parents. That we follow it is our responsibility after a while, and not theirs. There is no metaphysical necessity that our choices or responses are sinful, but there is a practical inevitability that comes from becoming individuated through membership in a human community.[13]

The differences between Neville's account of sin and Tillich's account are important and instructive. Tillich argued that the transition from essence to existence is something that happens; there is no necessary reason for sin. We

---

12. Ibid., 166–67.

13. Robert Neville, *A Theology Primer* (Albany: State University of New York Press, 1991), 87–88.

have also seen that Tillich maintained that human beings choose to actualize their own freedom and in so doing turn away from God. But Tillich would strongly reject the idea that sin is *simply* empirical. He would also reject the idea that human beings sin because they are predisposed to do so solely by way of birth and socialization. For Tillich, sin may not be *necessary* but it is *ontologically inevitable*. Creatures who stand outside the divine life will inevitably fall into sin and not just because of contingent factors like socialization. Neville's analysis leaves open the possibility that a given person may not sin; it just happens empirically to be the case that freedom from sin is unlikely given the sinful structures and societies into which human beings are born. Tillich contends instead that estrangement is a matter of both fact and act, of both destiny and freedom. Because all finite creatures stand outside the divine ground (as well as within), sin is the ontological destiny of all creatures even if it also a choice they willingly embrace. Sin is just not a matter of ontological destiny for Neville.

This basic ontological difference between Neville and Tillich about what freedom entails is of vital significance for theological anthropology and soteriology. The possibility of and limits to sanctification are shaped by the ways in which ontological factors contribute to or impede human possibilities. Neville rejects the idea that sin is inevitable for ontological reasons; in this respect, his analysis of the human predicament brings him far closer to Sankara than to Tillich. Ignorance and sin are the way of the world, but there is no ontological reason why it has to be so. For Tillich, freedom requires that creatures stand outside the divine ground, a ground that is conceived in substantialist fashion. That is why sin is a part of creaturely destiny.

Because Neville believes that human beings are not external to the divine life, even when they are in bondage to ignorance and sin, his ontology imposes no necessary limit on human transformation. This does not mean that Sankara and Neville believe that human beings are capable of overcoming the human predicament by their own power. Both maintain that grace is necessary for human beings to be rightly related to their ontological depths. Nevertheless, both Sankara and Neville also believe that once human beings are reoriented to their true ontological dignity, human beings can enjoy deep capacities for sanctification that are unimpeded by the sheer fact of creatureliness. For Tillich, on the other hand, sanctification is always imperiled by the fact that creatures in their freedom stand outside the divine life. Freedom always poses a threat to what has heretofore been accomplished. The key difference between

Neville and Tillich is that Neville conceives of divinity as ontological creativity that gives rise to free beings. Even when persons act in ways that display ignorance of their divine nature, such action does not presuppose ontological separation.

The Religious Possibilities Offered by Dynamic Nondualism

The preceding appeal to Bracken and Neville was intended to advance several objectives. First, I have argued that both Sankara and Tillich are plagued by substantialist conceptions of being-itself that generate dualisms that obstruct and interfere with their deepest goals. So long as Brahman is taken to be a substantial reality, the world either stands as a second entity over against Brahman, or the reality of that world is denied. The solution is to repudiate the notion that Brahman is an unchanging substance and embrace the alternative idea that Brahman is infinite ontological creativity apart from which nothing would be. In such an account, the world of name and form is real but, ontologically speaking, has no existence apart from divine creativity. Rejecting the idea that divinity ought to be imagined in substantialist terms means that there is no need to posit an ontological distance between beings and being-itself, as Tillich does, in order to secure creaturely freedom.

Second, Bracken and Neville provide an ontological foundation for a vision of human life that is more than an oscillation between courage and despair, between ecstatic union and estranged separation. Both Bracken and Neville believe that it is possible to recognize that human identity is not exhausted by one's finite particularities. Knowledge of one's eternal and divine identity deconstructs unduly narrow conceptions of personhood and leads, especially in Neville, to a strong affirmation of the possibility for personal and social sanctification that considerably exceeds what Tillich offered.[14] Bracken and Neville provide invaluable resources for Christians who wish to affirm, along with Advaitins, that the being of creatures is the being of God. Their conception of God as dynamic ontological creativity honors traditional Christian convictions while opening up the Christian tradition to Sankara's Hinduism.

In so doing, they have moved further along a path that Tillich traveled. Tillich was prevented from proceeding further because he believed that the Spiritual Presence is experienced largely in fits and starts, in moments of dramatic healing followed all too quickly by periods of profanization.

14. Ibid., 115–26.

Despite Tillich's radical rejection of dualism and his strong sense of divine immanence, he maintained that all healing, under the conditions of existence, remains fragmentary.

Bracken and Neville rightly argue that a logically adequate account of infinity requires that the infinite must not be conceived as an entity, an argument that Tillich had already anticipated. Bracken extends Tillich's basic insight further by contending that any conception of God that makes God out to be an infinite entity logically implies either that nothing other than the infinite entity exists or that the infinite turns out to be limited by what is other than itself. The cumulative force of the arguments made by Tillich, Bracken, and Neville indicates that infinity must be conceived nonentitatively as the infinite creative activity apart from which beings cannot be. A truly nonsubstantialist conception of the infinite leads also to a nondualism in which beings are not other than the grounding activity that gives rise to them.

These arguments suggest that Tillich erred in rooting the problems that mark the human predicament in ontology. No ontological break is required for or entailed by human freedom. Both Sankara and Neville suggest that it is possible to generate a grave and realistic account of human ignorance and sin without rooting these problems in an ontological rupture between divinity and humanity. Neville, in particular, demonstrates that a nonsubstantialist account of God as ontological creativity can provide a strong account of created goodness and divine immanence without trivializing the human predicament.

How would the theological anthropologies of Sankara and Tillich differ if they conceived of ultimate reality as ontological creativity? If this way of understanding the divine delivers a stronger account of immanence, then how might their soteriologies be transformed? How might we rethink what it means to be human if God is reimagined as becoming-itself rather than as being-itself?

Sankara believed that a nearly total solution to the human predicament is possible. He understood religious life as a long process of preparation for knowledge. This preparatory process purifies the mind by gradually setting it free from unreflective attachment generated by ignorance. This process is accomplished by a series of disciplines, including meditation and *karmayoga*, defined as action without attachment to the fruits of action. Sankara believed that these preliminary processes would gradually give rise to detachment; such detachment would enable persons to hear and understand the truth that they are not merely finite transmigrating selves. When properly prepared persons hear and understand scriptural truth, conventional understandings of the self are relativized. When such persons realize that they are Brahman, desire and aversion are extinguished because error about one's supposed finitude is undercut.

If, however, Brahman is reinterpreted as the dynamic ontological act of creating, then persons need not deny their finite identities in order to posit another, deeper identity that lies behind the scenes. If ultimate reality is understood instead as the dynamic letting be of finite realities and if that creativity is not given apart from finite realities that this creating generates, then it makes no sense to speak of negating one's false finite identity in order to understand one's true infinite identity. Both modalities of identity are utterly inseparable.

What then are we to make of the traditional affirmation that hearing scripture deconstructs conventional identity and generates a new conviction regarding one's true Self as the infinite and eternal Brahman? Can this *sine qua non* of Advaita be preserved? How can we be sure that we have not eviscerated the essence of Advaita teaching by introducing the idea that Brahman is ontological creativity?

One can quite plausibly maintain that properly prepared aspirants, upon hearing the truth of this modified Advaita, can relativize the truth of particularity in order to see that, ontologically speaking, they are Brahman. After all, Sankara does not deny empirical truth but instead demotes its relative importance so that a more basic saving insight can come into view. His aim is to introduce persons to the truth that they are the infinite Brahman. A revisionist reading in which Brahman is understood as ontological creativity preserves the essential truth of nondualism. Human beings can still come to understand that their being is Brahman even if Brahman is no longer understood to be an immutable and absolute entity.

Purging substantialist elements from Tillich's conception of God also introduces significant changes to Tillich's soteriology. For those who would follow in Tillich's wake, the major soteriological reward generated by eliminating his residual substantialism is the possibility of a nontrivial and qualitatively deep sense in which human action can at once also be divine action, not just now and then in moments of ecstasy but in more stable and enduring ways. Recall the implications of Neville's two author theory of creation: My capacity to act freely is a product of divine creativity. God creates in me my freedom; hence all my activity is also divine activity. As important as this truth is at the ontological level, because any and every action can qualify also as divine action, there is nothing religiously special about Neville's two author theory. But Neville's approach can also provide a foundation for a religiously important sense in which human action can also be said to be divine. Our reading of Tillich, particularly our analysis of his notion of ecstasy, has indicated that central to his religious imagination was a special kind of performative nonduality, in which human beings become transparent or permeable to their divine depths under the impact of the Spiritual Presence. Tillich's familiar examples are mystical experience, prophetic inspiration, and, most especially, prayer. In these activities, the transitory dualism between beings and being-itself is annulled. These religiously distinctive and ecstatic events point to a qualitatively special sense in which my action is also God acting in and through me.

Tillich was never altogether clear about the nature of ecstasy, but the following observations seem to hold. First, despite his occasional use of the term *possession*, he insists that in ecstasy, human faculties are not incapacitated. On the contrary, Tillich's language about the infusion of meaning-bearing power or the impact of the Spiritual Presence suggests that these are the only moments in which human beings are in full command of their powers, albeit not self-consciously so. Human beings become more themselves, not less, but in a way that decenters conventional notions of agency. The experience of divine power leads us to affirm, as St. Paul did, that the Spirit prays in us and that the narrow self of everyday experience is healed and opened up into divinity.

As central as these transformative experiences are in Tillich's religious imagination, he understood them to be episodic and impermanent. Indeed, their very status as ec-static, as experiences in which the self is driven *outside itself* in order to attain to a union with the divine depths, indicate that these experiences must necessarily be fragmentary. When human beings are grasped by the Spirit, understood as the union of power and meaning, they are driven out of separated existence and into union with their divine depths. In these moments, the essential Not-otherness of the infinite becomes actualized but actualized—and we must always add this tragic Tillichian refrain—fragmentarily.

Despite his customary characterization of ecstasy as impermanent, Tillich also spoke of ecstasy as an ontological category and as a mode of being. This broader account suggests that ecstatic experiences offered, for Tillich, a window into a mode of being in which the human being could, like Jesus the Christ, be wholly and enduringly claimed by the Spiritual Presence. Indeed, Tillich's central notion of faith as ultimate concern speaks of human life as it is lived under the continuous impact of the infinite and so constantly driven toward self-transcendence. This important possibility remains largely undeveloped in Tillich's thought. Jesus' experience of spiritual union remains the paradoxical exception, an exception that proves the rule; life for the rest of us is marked by episodes of healing reunion followed by periods of distortion and estrangement.

Can a dynamic nondualism provide the ontological framework needed for a less fragmentary account of ecstatic life? I believe so. Within a dynamic nondualism, one does not have to be driven *outside* oneself in order to move *into* the divine life. One is always already within the divine life. Dynamic nondualism thus provides the ontological hardware for an enduring kind of performative nonduality that Tillich hinted at but could never explain. Tillich's system, left to its own devices, can only yield a transitory dualism that can, at best, provide an episodic account of ecstasy.

If Tillich's unreconstructed theology imagines spiritual life largely on the model of ecstatic prayer, theologies of dynamic nondualism open Christian life to the possibility of the indwelling Christ. Galatians 2:20 may prove to be more fundamental than Romans 8:24 for spiritual life when that life is imagined otherwise than as a series of episodic ecstasies. This other Pauline proclamation, to wit, "no longer I who live but it is Christ who lives in me," names an aspiration for sanctification understood as deep, enduring, and abiding rather than episodic. Here, sanctification opens up into *theosis*, into deification, and the distance that separates Christian accounts of sanctification from the experience of the Hindu *jivanmukta* is drastically diminished.

What such a life might look like must largely be the object of future investigations. Sankara's description of the *jivanmukta*, of the liberated being, who acts for the sake of the well-being of the world, provides a helpful account of some features of this perfected life. Sankara understands the liberated person to be someone who is established in the knowledge of his infinite identity. This knowledge of one's true nature relativizes and finally eliminates the egoistic attachments and aversions of conventional life; liberated persons enjoy a plenitude that negates the penury that inevitably follows from a narrow and impoverished sense of self. Sankara presents us with an Upanishadic vision in which persons who come to know that they are not-other than the divine conquer ravaging grief and crippling delusion. But against Sankara's vision, I see no reason to suppose that salvation requires relinquishing desire as such. After all, finite and contingent identities are not negated within a dynamic nondualism. With Tillich, we can hold open the possibility of a desire that is not self-seeking, a desire that longs for communion with and motivates work for the good of others.

What becomes of agency within a dynamic nondualism? Tillich's theology takes its bearings from the experiences of persons who, when grasped by the Spirit, declare that the Spirit is at work in them. They experience and speak of a kind of passivity, of a being grasped that undoes autonomous agency, but nonetheless makes persons more, rather than less, themselves. Of course, all this is necessarily evanescent within the framework of Tillich's theology. Within the framework of a dynamic nondualism, it is possible to imagine that agency might be altered in a deeper and more abiding fashion. Paul's proclamation to the Galatians affirms the possibility of dying to the self, and such a death is plainly not episodic. The one in whom Christ lives is perpetually grasped and claimed by divine creativity such that human activity and divine activity become co-extensive. Having died to the egoistic self, the human being is now wholly transparent to the divine life and so becomes an expression of that life.

No one has considered these dimensions of the spiritual life more keenly than the medieval Christian theologian Meister Eckhart. The meaning of Christian nondualism for spiritual life cannot be appreciated apart from a thoroughgoing encounter with Eckhart's theology. Such an encounter is obviously impossible in the concluding pages of this book. For now, it must suffice to say that Eckhart's theology is critical because it calls human beings to *become* what they already truly *are*. Human being and divine being are not-two. Spiritual life is the process of making this nonduality real. Reiner Schürmann aptly and succinctly characterizes the meaning of spiritual life in Eckhart as follows: "What we are, void and divine in our innermost being, we have yet to become. In detachment, what is given becomes ordered; identity by nature becomes the process of identification."[15] In other words, "we are identical with God, but still on the way to union."[16]

Bracken and Neville provide in contemporary idiom an ontological framework that shows how the kind of spiritual transformation that Eck-

15. Reiner Schürmann, *Wandering Joy: Meister Eckhart's Mystical Philosophy* (Great Barrington, Mass.: Lindisfarne Books, 2001), 164–65.

16. Ibid., 166.

hart calls for might be possible. Taking seriously the truth of such nonduality in spiritual life requires moving into union with the divine life, a union in which I no longer live but Christ lives in me. My own sense of myself as a directing, controlling agent of the affairs of my own life is superceded. Here, all talk of two authors seems to fall apart. That framework seems inadequate to the intimacy of spiritual life read in an Eckhartian key. The human being is no longer an agent in a traditional sense nor is the divine. The only adequate expression of such nonduality is Eckhart's affirmation, "Acting and becoming are one, God and I are one in operation: he acts and I become."[17] The meaning of spiritual life within Christian nondualism will require a deep excavation of the riches contained in this dense Eckhartian dictum.

Can this vision of spiritual life be characterized as ecstatic? That is not at all clear. Strictly speaking, the term does not apply if one does not have to be driven *outside* oneself to be reunited with the divine. Nor is the union that Eckhart describes temporary. Hence, the term *ecstasy* can be employed only so long as these Tillichian implications are bracketed. Nonetheless, the term can serve usefully to name the kind of dynamic union possible within a Christian nondualism.

Sankara's unreconstructed Advaita also leads to a qualification of ordinary agency, but of a very different sort. Here, the liberated person is said to dwell securely in the knowledge that he does not act. Because he is convinced that he is the unchanging Brahman, when he acts, the liberated person knows that only the strands of material nature are active. This is a very different picture of how a transformed relation to the infinite reconfigures conventional agential life. However, once Sankara's Advaita has been modified so that Brahman is understood to be the divine creativity that both creates and is not other than the finite self, it no longer makes sense to characterize the body as other than one's true self. This dualistic feature of Sankara's system cannot hold. What can and must be preserved from Sankara's theological anthropology is his rich portrait of liberated persons as established in the knowledge of Brahman, a knowledge that liberates persons from the self-serving compulsions of conventional life. Typically such persons embrace a life of renunciation, but it is also possible that such persons can engage in spontaneous and compassionate action on behalf of the world's well-being.

17. Ibid., 183.

Apophasis, Ecstasy, and Divine Immutability

Essential to this comparison of models of ultimate reality has been the contrast between Tillich's dynamic conception of the divine life and Sankara's insistence on Brahman as unchanging. I have clearly endorsed a dynamic conception of nonduality that does not require the liberated person to dismiss the activity of mind and body as alien to his or her true nature. But is there any sense in which an affirmation of divine immutability might still be meaningful? Can this feature of Sankara's theology find meaningful articulation within the framework of this reconstructed nondualism?

I contend that Sankara's insight can be preserved within an apophatic reading of Neville's theory of divine creativity. Borrowing language from Pseudo-Dionysius, it is possible to show that Neville's vision of divine creativity suggests that ultimate reality is "not immovable, moving, or at rest."[18] As already indicated, Neville's theory of creation *ex nihilo* regards the divine act of creativity as the ontological context of mutual relevance; things are together because they are created together. Neville also argues that all determinate things are created *including* temporality. He maintains that each of the three modes of time is real and irreducible to the others. Like all determinate things, the modes of time also have essential and conditional features. Because the essential features of each of the modes of time have to be together to make temporal flow possible, the togetherness of each of the modes of time cannot itself be temporal. That is to say, there is no *time* in which the past, present, and future are together. Rather, they are together in eternity, in the eternal divine act. In order for each mode of time to be at all, they need a transtemporal ground in order to be related. The transtemporal ground for the togetherness of the three modes of time is the eternal creative divine act.

For Neville, God is source, act, and terminus of the creative process. The world as product of divine creativity has no ontological independence over against God as source and act. Because the created product is not other than God as source and God as act, and because the created product is characterized by temporal flow, the divine life is in one sense dynamic.

However, Neville also specifies that the eternal creative act that gives rise to temporal flow is itself *not* temporal. The creative act is not in time although it creates time. Because the eternal creative act is nontemporal, it has no duration, and what has no temporal duration does not change. Neville is quite clear on this point: "*The eternal act does not change, because it does not endure from*

---

18. Pseudo-Dionysius, "The Divine Names," in *Pseudo-Dionysius: The Complete Works*, 141.

one moment to the next. The temporal things within it change, however, actualizing efforts that add to the past and shift the future's possibilities."[19]

The divine act of creativity that creates time does not change. Only an entity that endures in two or more times and undergoes some modification of state can be said to change. The eternal divine act is not in time; it does not endure. Consequently, the divine creativity is transtemporal. It follows, therefore, that Sankara's claim that ultimate reality is beyond change can be incorporated within a dynamic nondualism. Sankara's error lies in attributing changelessness to an absolute reality taken to be immutable in *every* respect.

For Neville, the eternal act of ontological creativity is inclusive of temporality. When so considered, temporality is in the divine life, and consequently it would be inaccurate to say either that the divine reality is "immovable" or "at rest." Both these ways of characterizing eternity fail to appreciate that eternity is both changeless and dynamic depending upon the perspective in question. Neville's ontology of divine creation clearly demonstrates why apophatic reserve must be exercised with respect to the divine life. Although Neville's theory makes it possible to specify how and in what way God can be said to be both unchanging and dynamic, metaphysical models do not capture the divine life. Neville's God is both dynamic (as inclusive of the life of creation), unchanging (as the unified, partless eternal act of creating), as well as beyond both change and changelessness. It is a great virtue of a theory to show how each of these statements can be true, but it is an even greater virtue to appreciate that the divine reality necessarily exceeds any metaphysical model.

As noted earlier, apophatic theology denies the adequacy of both affirmative and negative language. Apophatic theology negates affirmations, and then negates the negations, not in order to return once again to affirmation, but to indicate that the divine reality exceeds both affirmation and negation. Sankara is, without doubt, a paradigmatically apophatic theologian. His rigorous insistence that Brahman cannot finally be known as either being or nonbeing and is indeed beyond all language clearly instantiates an apophatic logic. However, he violates the logic of genuinely apophatic discourse in just one instance: Unlike Dionysius, Sankara never qualifies his claim that Brahman is unchanging. This negative descriptor is left in place as entirely adequate to the reality of Brahman.

The intriguing implication of Sankara's authentic apophaticism is that because Brahman is our being, it follows that the human being is also ultimately beyond knowing. Although every particular feature of my identity

---

19. Neville, *Eternity and Time's Flow,* 173; emphasis added.

can in principle be known, my being is not exhausted by the knowable particulars that constitute who I am. Because I am not other than the divine creativity, my identity is not exhausted by the places and dates and the accidents of my biography. Sankara is right. We are not merely our conventional identities nor are we exhausted by our mortal passing away.

Ours is a time in which the mystery of human being is under considerable assault. The human genome has been mapped and categorized. The capacity for genetic engineering will for the first time enable a species to direct its own evolution. Even the irreducible particularity of the individual is threatened by the technological capacity for cloning. There are very good reasons to believe that human beings will soon, if they have not already, come to believe that they are entirely comprehensible. We will soon come to believe, twisting a Pauline phrase, that we know ourselves even as we are known. Within the context of these aspirations to totalizing knowledge, Tillich and Sankara make the compelling and invaluable argument that human beings are irreducible to the sum total of their finite particularities because they belong to and, indeed, are incomprehensible mystery. Without denying our thrownness into our particular times, places, and bodies, Tillich and Sankara remind us that we are not merely in time but also in eternity, not only finite and perishing but also infinite and imperishable. Ours is a time in which forgetting this truth will exact an incalculable cost. Sankara and Tillich are important teachers because they can help us remember that we shall and must necessarily remain a mystery to ourselves and to each other.

On the Coincidence between Immanence and Transcendence

What are we to make of this affirmation of mystery? How has our search for an ever more robust conception of divine immanence brought us around to unknowablity? Here perhaps is Sankara's deepest lesson. The search for the immanent divine is driven by our knowledge that human beings are saved, that is to say healed, not from absolution from on high but by divine self-giving. I am made whole only when I am taken into the divine life. The knowledge that only God's self-disclosure can lead to wholeness is the compelling motivation that drives the quest for deeper immanence.

In theologies of nonduality, immanence reaches its absolute limit. No more robust conception of immanence can be imagined than one that asserts that the human being is, at bottom, divine mystery. And yet, it is precisely at this juncture that a non-negotiable transcendence presents itself. To say as Sankara does, "I am Brahman," is not to declare that ultimate reality can be comprehensively known. On the contrary, the affirmation of nonduality culminates in the wisdom that I cannot know what it is that I truly am. Nonduality deprives human beings not only of a graspable God but also of the delusion that the Socratic quest for self-knowledge is attainable. I can neither know God nor can I know myself because these two are not-two.

This noetic transcendence is different in kind from spatial accounts of transcendence that depict God as unknowable because God dwells in another divine realm of time and space. Rather, the transcendent divine is absolutely near, so near as to be the very being of all that is. The result is an absolute coincidence of immanence and transcendence. To speak either word is to say the other in the same breath.

God's transcendence on this account is rooted neither in God's immutability or unrelated inaccessibility. The history of theology, East and West, is littered with accounts in which God is said to be transcendent because God is different in kind from the world. The world is wholly mutable, relative, and relational; ultimate reality, on the other hand, is said to be immutable, absolute, and unrelated. Those who seek after such versions of transcendence will likely find dynamic nondualism unsatisfactory. For dynamic nondualism, God is neither immutable, absolute, nor unrelated. The world cannot be apart from divine creativity; divine creativity is inseparable from what it creates. Dynamic nondualism is deeply and irrevocably relational, even if peculiarly so, because creation is a relation that creates the terms of the relation. It follows that transcendence cannot and must not be thought as separation.

How then are we to think of transcendence otherwise than by appeal to the idiom of separation? Tillich provides the requisite vocabulary: Transcendence must be thought as qualitative depth. God is an infinite depth and abyss, the inexhaustible source of all meaning and value and sheer creative power. Because of God's qualitative depth, God can be experienced as the Holy Other even though God most assuredly is not "Wholly Other."[20] Nondualism allows

---

20. I am influenced here by relational philosopher Harold H. Oliver, who argues that God is portrayed in biblical narrative as the "Eminent Other." Oliver maintains that God, who is depicted as a "character-in-relation," must not be made into a nonrelational object. In this context, Oliver states that the Eminent Other is the Holy Other. Nevertheless, "'Eminent Other' does not mean 'Wholly Other,' for 'other'—from a relational perspective necessarily entails 'mutuality.'" See Oliver, *Relatedness: Essays in Metaphysics and Theology* (Macon, Ga.: Mercer University Press, 1984), 163–64.

for divine holiness even as it rules out ontological depictions of God as a remote and infinite being. Holiness is not incompatible with nondual immanence. Immanence does not rule out divine transcendence.

Having distinguished between two senses of transcendence, one salutary and one problematic, a question remains: What are we to make of the two very different kinds of immanence discovered during the course of this conversation, namely ecstatic immanence and nondual immanence, between immanence as enacted and immanence as ontologically given? In ecstasy, immanence is an event, in the latter a fact. Nondualistic moments in Christian tradition have always been dominantly performative in character. Here, Reiner Schürmann's account of Meister Eckhart's theology puts the point rightly. The identity between self and God is not that of "a substantial 'suppositum' but of event. . . ."[21]

Quite likely ecstasy and nonduality have their origins in variant forms of practice and religious experience. Families of religious experience can neither be parceled out by geography nor tradition. Ecstatic experiences can be found within Hindu traditions and nondual convictions in the West. This book has sought to compare and learn from *theologies* of immanence derived from traditions of ecstasy and traditions of nonduality. Religious practices and experiences will surely remain multifarious within and across religious boundaries, but comparative theologians are interested in asking whether there can be a cross-pollination of theological ideas derived from diverse sources. I have demonstrated that such cross-pollination and mutual transformation is both possible and necessary. It seems altogether possible to integrate both varieties of immanence in a conception of God as eternal divine creativity.

Sankara and Tillich share a deep commitment to rejecting theological dualism. Both believe that ultimate reality is not a being among beings. Both believe that human beings find healing when human beings understand their belonging to the divine life. We have also discovered that both traditions are plagued by residual dualisms that are rooted in substantialist ways of imagining divinity. Sankara relapses into dualism by distinguishing sharply between a changeless Brahman and a changing world, and Tillich falls prey to a sharp and tragic dualism when he insists that creatures can only be free if they stand outside the divine life. Adopting a dynamic ontology enables us to overcome these flaws while preserving the deepest intuitions of both traditions.

21. Reiner Schürmann, *Wandering Joy: Meister Eckhart's Mystical Philosophy* (Great Barrington, Mass.: Lindisfarne Books, 2001), 183.

Within this overarching framework, Christian reflection and experience can hope for profound transformation in which human beings are grasped by and rendered transparent to a God to whom and in whom they belong and from whom they are never separated. Human beings become what they truly already are when they are liberated from imprisonment to self-enclosed finitude and are drawn into the fullness of the divine life, a fullness in which they already dwell unawares.

Glossary

꼬시꼬

adharma | vice, injustice, or wickedness; actions that run contrary to moral obligations.

adhikara | a special prerogative, eligibility, or qualification and hence responsibility for a particular set of duties or obligations; for example, persons of lower castes do not have *adhikara* to read the scriptures as Brahmins do.

adhyasa | superimposition; the act of confusing the true Self that is pure consciousness with the qualities of mind and body. More generally, *adhyasa* is superimposing the qualities of the objective and material world onto the purely subjective and immaterial Self or Brahman and vice versa.

Advaita | nonduality; the name of the school of Vedanta that affirms that the true Self is the infinite Brahman. In this school, the relationship between Self and Brahman is thus nondual.

ahamkara | a term used neutrally to name the cognitive function of self-awareness. More negatively, the term means self-centeredness, egoism, or pride.

anatman	whatever is other than the eternal Self; in principle, this can refer to the entirety of the material world.
anitya	impermanent; the capacity to distinguish between what is impermanent and thus ultimately unreal and what is eternal (*nitya*) is a basic prerequisite for would-be seekers of liberating wisdom. The entirety of the experienced world—whatever is other than Atman/Brahman is impermanent.
anta	end, conclusion, or summation; the Upanishads are regarded as the end or summation of the Vedas. Hence, they are called the Veda-anta or Vedanta.
anugraha	grace or favor; the term can refer both to the grace of Brahman when Brahman is encountered as personal Lord or to the grace of the guru who teaches liberating knowledge.
apophatic theology	sometimes characterized as negative theology but better understood as theology that knows God or ultimate reality to be language-transcending mystery beyond either positive or negative description.
aranyakas	forest treatises; one of the four categories into which the Hindu scriptures are divided, namely, the Vedas, Brahmanas, Aranyakas, and Upanishads. The *aranyakas* mark the transition from ritual concerns central to the Vedas and Brahmanas to concerns about spiritual knowledge central to the Upanishads.
asariratva	the state or condition of being disembodied. Atman, the eternal Self, is in truth disembodied. The term is the antonym of *sariratva*, the state or condition of being embodied.
asat	whatever is unreal, nonexistent, or false.

atmajyoti	the light of the Self; a way of speaking of consciousness (*cit*) as the true eternal light that illumines the mind.
Atman	Self; one of Sankara's two basic terms for naming ultimate reality. Atman refers to ultimate reality understood as the true, infinite, and eternal Self. Sankara teaches that the Atman is Brahman, the infinite world ground.
avidya	ignorance; the root cause of the human predicament. *Avidya* is the failure to realize that one's true Self is not the finite mind-body complex but the eternal Self, namely Atman.
avidyakamakarma	ignorance, desire, and action; three basic factors that perpetuate the cycle of transmigration. Ignorance (*avidya*) gives rise to desire (*kama*), which leads persons to action and its consequences (*karma*).
bhasya	commentary or commentarial text; all save one of Sankara's authentic writings are commentaries on sacred texts such as the Upanishads and the *Bhagavad Gita*.
brahmajijnasa	the desire to know Brahman; investigation into the reality of Brahman.
Brahman	the transpersonal ultimate reality at the heart of non-dualistic Hinduism; Brahman is being-itself, the ultimate world-ground. Advaita teaches that this ultimate reality is one's true Self, namely Atman.
Brahmanas	ritual treatises that seek to explain the meaning and significance of Brahmanic rituals; one of the four categories into which the Hindu scriptures are divided, namely, the Vedas, Brahmanas, Aranyakas, and Upanishads.

cit	consciousness; in Sankara's thought, consciousness is not a function of the mind but rather an eternal reality that shines in the mind thereby giving rise to the impression that the mind is intrinsically conscious. Consciousness is ultimately just the eternal Self, namely Atman.
comparative category	a formal description of the respect in which two or more things are to be compared.
deharanyam	forest of the body; a vivid metaphor employed by Sankara to speak of reincarnation as the state of being lost in the forest of the body.
dharma	duty; one's moral obligations as defined by scripture, ethical treatises, and the teachings of those who are wise. The term can also refer to the moral order that sustains the universe.
dosa	fault; one of Sankara's terms along with *klesa* (affliction) for naming those fundamental motivating factors such as ignorance, delusion, grief, craving, and aversion that perpetuate self-seeking action and so keep persons bound to samsara.
duhkha	suffering; a vital term central in both Buddhism and Hinduism. In Buddhism, *duhkha* is the First Noble Truth, the basic diagnosis of the human predicament.
dvesa	aversion or hatred; one of the faults or afflictions that drives persons to self-seeking action that perpetuates rebirth.
gunas	strands of material nature; in Sankara's cosmology, one he shares with a number of other Hindu traditions, material reality is understood to be made up of three

material strands, one light and clear (*sattva*), the other active and fiery (*rajas*), and the third dark and heavy (*tamas*). A person's temperament, dietary preferences, and even relative spiritual capacity is determined, in part, by the relative balance of these three factors in his or her body-mind complex.

isvara   Lord; Brahman experienced as personal Lord and world creator; a penultimate but nonetheless valid way of experiencing Brahman who is in truth a transpersonal absolute.

jijnasa   the desire to know; see also *brahmajijnasa*.

jiva   the individual soul or self, to be distinguished from the cosmic Self, namely Atman. Sankara teaches that, ultimately, there is only Atman, who appears to be pluralized into individual body-mind complexes thereby giving rise to the appearance that there really are individual souls.

jivanmukta   a person who is liberated while living.

jivanmukti   the state of living liberation in which one transcends karmic bondage to samsara while remaining embodied. Not all Hindu traditions agree that living liberation is possible. Some contend that liberation is attained only after the body falls. Those who affirm that *jivanmukti* is possible contend that liberation is not just a postmortem condition. One who has attained *jivanmukti* is a *jivanmukta*, one who is liberated while living.

jnana   knowledge, usually liberating knowledge that is the cure for the disease of ignorance (*avidya*), the fundamental cause of the cycle of reincarnation.

jnanakanda	that portion of the scriptures, namely the Upanishads, that have as their primary aim the teaching of liberating knowledge.
kama	desire, longing; one of the faults or afflictions that perpetuate rebirth.
karma	act, action, or performance; performance of ritual activities; karma generates merit and demerit, which leads to rebirth.
karmakanda	that portion of the scriptures that have as their primary aim teaching about ritual obligation.
karmayoga	action performed without attachment to the fruits of action or action performed free from self-interest and motivated by devotion to God alone. Such action purifies the mind and prepares it for liberating knowledge.
kartr	the soul seen as an agent or actor; Sankara teaches that the true Self is not an agent but rather actionless Atman.
kasmalam	timidity or faintheartedness.
klaibyam	cowardice, unmanliness, impotence.
klesa	affliction; see also *dosa*.
kshatriya	warriors or soldiers; those with responsibility for governance. Arjuna, in the *Bhagavad Gita*, is a member of the *kshatriya* class.
Madhva	thirteenth-century Hindu theologian and founding teacher of Dvaita Vedanta, which teaches a thoroughgoing dualism; against Sankara, Madhva teaches that the soul and God are really and eternally different and will never be or become one. Madhva insists that

individual selves are really different from God, really different from each other, and really different from matter.

manas mind; the organ of cognition.

moha delusion or bewilderment; the fault that prevents clear-minded discrimination of the truth of nonduality and so perpetuates transmigration.

moksa liberation from the cycle of rebirth; for Sankara, liberation is not a thing to be accomplished because the true Self is eternally liberated.

New Being Tillich's term for healing power experienced by human beings grasped unambiguously by the Spiritual Presence. The new state of affairs for those living under the power of the Spirit.

nitya eternal and unchanging; for Sankara, only Brahman is, strictly speaking, *nitya*.

Old Being Tillich's term for life as lived in estrangement and alienation; life in its diseased state apart from an experience of the healing power of New Being.

panentheism any theological position that affirms that the world is a part of God's life although God's life is more than or greater than the life of the world. In panentheistic theologies, the world is not merely an extrinsic product of the divine will but is instead a part of God's very being.

papa demerit, evil, or misfortune accrued by the performance of wicked or unrighteous deeds.

paradharma the duties of others; see also *svadharma*.

paramapurusartha	the supreme or highest of human goals, namely liberation. In Tillich's terminology, the term can be defined as one's ultimate concern.
paramarthikasatya	ultimate truth; truth about ultimate reality or Brahman and hence liberating truth.
pramatr	the soul as knowing agent or knower; the true Self is not a knowing agent but is instead pure consciousness.
prarabdhakarma	karma that has already begun to bear fruit; every embodiment is the result of past karma; this particular embodiment is the result of past karma that is now in operation. Sankara believes that karma that is not yet germinating can be destroyed by liberating knowledge, but nothing can done about karma that is now bearing fruit.
pratyagatman	the innermost Self; a way of speaking of the absolute interiority of the eternal Atman who is the eye of the eye, the ear of the ear, etc.
punya	merit; the positive consequences accruing to those whose actions are in conformity with duty or dharma. *Punya* is proximately desirable, but as it too perpetuates rebirth, from the point of view of ultimate truth, it is undesirable for those who aspire for liberation.
purusartha	any one of four legitimate aims, purposes, or objectives of human life, namely pleasure, wealth, moral duty (dharma), or liberation (*moksa*). Liberation is the supreme goal.
raga	desire or craving; one of the faults or afflictions that perpetuate rebirth.
Ramanuja	(c. 1017–1137); founding teacher of Visistadvaita Vedanta, a school of Vedanta that teaches qualified

nondualism and rejects the absolute nondualism of Sankara. Ramanuja maintains that the world is God's body. There is still only one reality, but that one reality is an internally differentiated or qualified (*visista*) whole.

sadhana	spiritual disciplines that prepare persons for liberating knowledge.
samsara	reincarnation or transmigration; the beginningless round of birth and death perpetuated by karma.
samsarabija	seed (*bija*) of samsara; a way of naming ignorance (*avidya*), which is the fundamental cause of the cycle of transmigration.
sariratva	the state or condition of being embodied and so subject to reincarnation.
sarvagata	all-pervasive or omnipresent; Brahman is all-pervasive.
sat	being or being-itself; one provisional way of referring to Brahman as the world's ground and source of being.
satkaryavada	a theory of causality that maintains that effects are preexistent in their material causes as clay pots and jars are contained in clay.
satya	real or true; ultimately, only Brahman is real in the most rigorous sense.
soka	grief; one of the faults or afflictions caused by ignorance and that perpetuates action that binds human beings to transmigration.
sruti	"that which is heard," namely revelation or scripture; the term refers to the Hindu scriptures, namely the Vedas, Brahmanas, Aranyakas, and Upanishads.

superimposition	see *adhyasa*
svadharma	one's own proper duty or dharma; the notion is to be contrasted with *paradharma*, which is the misguided attempt to take up the duties and responsibilities of others. At the beginning of the *Bhagavad Gita*, Krishna almost forsakes his *svadharma* and contemplates embracing a life of renunciation, which is not his *svadharma*.
tat tvam asi	"You are That"; one of the concise and memorable Great Sayings of the Upanishads, which, according to Sankara, teach the truth of nonduality—the identity between one's true Self and ultimate reality, Brahman.
transtheism	any theological position that rejects the notion that God is a distinct being who stands over against the world and opts instead for a vision of God as the ground of being or being-itself. Transtheists seek to transcend theism; they are neither atheists nor do they reject the possibility that God can be experienced as personal even though they reject the notion that God is a being among beings.
upadhi	limiting adjuncts; anything that gives the appearance of limiting or conditioning ultimate reality. The mind and body, for example, are limiting adjuncts of the Infinite Self, limiting adjuncts that give rise to the impression that the Infinite Self is embodied.
upaya	skillful means; provisional and instrumental teachings and strategies employed by a teacher to lead students onto ultimate truth, often by way of indirection. Partial truths that prepare students for ultimate truth can be an *upaya*, a skillful means.

varnasramadharma   the duties of class and stage of life; Hindu traditions have a richly contextualized understanding of duty as it is determined by one's class or caste and stage of life. For example, the duties of a Brahmin student are not the same as the duties of adult *kshatriya*.

vyavaharikasatya   conventional, worldly, or empirical truth; right knowledge about the world of empirical experience. The contrast term is *paramarthikasatya*, or ultimate truth, which is the truth about Brahman that alone leads to liberation.

Index

჻჻჻